EVOLVING LEADERSHIP FOR COLLECTIVE WELLBEING

EVOLVING LEADERSHIP FOR COLLECTIVE WELLBEING

Lessons for Implementing the United Nations Sustainable Development Goals

Edited by

SEANA LOWE STEFFEN
Restorative Leadership Institute, USA

JAMIE REZMOVITS
*Restorative Leadership Institute and
Scheitler & Rezmovits, USA*

SHANAH TREVENNA
Conscious Leadership Institute, USA

SHANA RAPPAPORT
GreenBiz Group, USA

United Kingdom — North America — Japan — India — Malaysia — China

Emerald Publishing Limited
Howard House, Wagon Lane, Bingley BD16 1WA, UK

First edition 2019

Reprints and permissions service
Contact: permissions@emeraldinsight.com

British Library Cataloguing in Publication Data
A catalogue record for this book is available from the British Library

ISBN: 978-1-78743-879-8 (Print)
ISBN: 978-1-78743-878-1 (Online)
ISBN: 978-1-78743-998-6 (Epub)

ISSN: 2058-8801 (Series)

ISOQAR certified
Management System,
awarded to Emerald
for adherence to
Environmental
standard
ISO 14001:2004.

Certificate Number 1985
ISO 14001

INVESTOR IN PEOPLE

In loving memory of Seana Lowe Steffen who is still lighting the way.

ACKNOWLEDGMENTS

Many thanks to all those whose support helped me to edit this book. As with most things in life, the people walking the path beside me on this journey have made all the difference (and there were many, without whom, this book would not exist).

I am grateful to my co-editors Shanah Trevenna and Shana Rappaport for birthing the possibility of this book into existence alongside Seana Lowe Steffen. It is a true delight to know you in such a deeply meaningful way. Thank you for creating the opportunity for me to carry the torch.

I am grateful for the contributions and extraordinary time and effort given by the authors in this volume. I learned from every one of you.

Thank you to Sierra Brashear, Mary Adams, and Juliet Biagi for your love, support, and willingness to step in to support this project at all hours of the night and day.

Thank you to Debra DeRuyver, at the International Leadership Association, for your invaluable and patient guidance and enthusiastic encouragement. Without you, this book would have never seen the light of day. I am also grateful to Emerald Publishing for seeing the potential in this book.

A special thank you to Martha Lang for your brilliant assistance and expertise with editing, and for walking me through this process in such a kind and compassionate way.

To Mom, Dad, and Matt for taking such good care of me when it was down to the wire!

And most importantly, thank you to Seana Lowe Steffen for inviting me on this journey with you. Working on this project has helped me to heal my broken heart from losing my best friend.

Jamie Rezmovits
Co-Editor

CONTENTS

PART V: GROWING OUR FUTURE LEADERS

ABOUT THE EDITORS

Seana Lowe Steffen, PhD, deceased, was the founder and CEO of the Restorative Leadership Institute (RLI), which cultivates leadership and enterprise that fulfills humanity's potential to thrive in balance with all life. As a certified B Corp, RLI received "Best for the World" recognition among all certified B Corps globally in 2017, 2016, and 2013. Seana brought nearly 25 years of experience in strategic consulting, capacity building, and leadership and organizational development. Her client community spanned sectors and continents including Tostan, The Sustainability Consortium, National Civilian Community Corps, Hewlett Packard, Denver Water, and the Carter Center. For her positive impact, Seana was invited to be a delegate at the prestigious Skoll World Forum.

Jamie Rezmovits, JD, as the Chair of the Restorative Leadership Institute, supports purpose-driven organizations and planet-minded leadership to increase their positive impact. With specialties in environmental conflict transformation, education, and community development, her heart-centered work spans from university classrooms in the United States to rural communities abroad. As an educator at the University of Colorado, she worked as a faculty member for the INVST Community Studies Department where she trained community leaders to work for the benefit of humanity and the environment. Jamie is a practicing attorney at Scheitler & Rezmovits, PC in Denver, Colorado.

Shanah Trevenna has been leading and guiding leaders of companies and non-profit organizations in the impact space for over 15 years. Shanah's unique style as an executive and leadership coach bridges her broad academic and professional experience with a honed intuition that helps leaders connect with their true nature and create their most fulfilling life and business. Her PhD focused on evolving business and the global economy, so she speaks and consults globally on diverse topics such as B Corps, women's empowerment, blockchain for good, and conscious entrepreneurship. Shanah currently works with 100 global coaching clients.

Shana Rappaport has worked actively for over a decade as a cross-industry convener to advance sustainability solutions. Over the last five years, as director of strategic programs for GreenBiz Group, Shana has helped build and scale the VERGE global event series, focusing on how technology accelerates the clean economy. Shana previously served as Director of Education for Bioneers, and as a nationally recognized community leader during her time as an undergraduate and graduate student at USC.

PREFACE

Seana Lowe Steffen was the creative and strategic visionary behind this book and a beautiful soul. Tragically, she was killed in car accident near Longmont, Colorado, on September 16, 2017, before it could be published, but her light has shined bright as a guide through my completion of this project on her behalf.

I remember Seana calling me in the fall of 2016 with the news of her book proposal having been selected for publication. She was giddy with excitement and pride — enough so that just the tone of her voice made me giggle, too. She had a way of doing that — of sharing in such an authentic and embodied way that I couldn't help but want to get involved. That was one of Seana's most powerful gifts — the ability to inspire those around her to work with her in service to the possibility of a better world.

Before she died, Seana was on a mission to answer the guiding question, *"How do we bring out the best of our diverse humanity to ensure a sustainable future?"* She believed in humanity's potential to meet the environmental and social challenges facing our planet in a way that would result in wondrous outcomes. This book and the process for its creation are a reflection of all that Seana held good and true, from the collaborative nature of the writing process to what she believed in the core of her being would be the impact of having this resource exist in the world. She was very proud of it.

Seana intended that this book empower individuals, organizations, and communities with practical tools and actionable insights to manifest the vision of a future where all life can thrive. Specifically, she hoped to:

- *Awaken the world* to the potential of this pregnant moment in global history — inspiring recognition that our generation is the first, and possibly last, with the ability to meaningfully address these pressing global challenges.

- *Inspire belief in what's possible* in and for our world — bridging the divide between urgency and agency.

Seana celebrated her 50th year of life just a couple of weeks before her untimely passing. She spent the week of her birthday in the same way she lived her life every single day, expressing delight and profound gratitude. The last words of her birthday reflection convey the very essence of her being:

> *Infinite blessings to name and celebrate [...] I am so grateful for the gift of my life every moment of every day, and wish the deep contentment of a fulfilled heart to all. Onward.*

I hope you will find this book as meaningful and relevant as Seana knew it could be.

Jamie Rezmovits
Co-Editor

INTRODUCTION

Seana Lowe Steffen and Jamie Rezmovits

On September 25, 2015, the 193 countries of the United Nations (UN) General Assembly adopted the United Nations' 2030 Agenda for Sustainable Development in what Elizabeth Cousens, the Deputy CEO of the UN Foundation, described as, "the most inclusive process the UN has ever seen" (E. Cousens, personal communication, February 3, 2017). Indeed, the agenda itself, which is a plan of action for people, the planet, and prosperity "to shift the world onto a sustainable and resilient path" states that, "Never before have world leaders pledged common action and endeavor across such a broad and universal policy agenda" (United Nations [UN], 2015b).

As if on synchronous cue, that week Mark Carney, head of the Bank of England and chair of the International Financial Stability Board, named climate change the "tragedy of the horizon" during his London City Dinner speech to Lloyd's Register, a 325-year-old behemoth in the insurance industry (Carney, 2015). In the face of unprecedented change, Carney issued a "carbon bubble"[1] warning shot over the bow of the future of a sustainable global economy with the threat of US$100 trillion in stranded assets. Back in New York, Paul Polman, CEO of Unilever, publicly broadcast from the UN General Assembly a welcome to the launch of the B Corp movement in the UK describing it as, "an important part of the shift toward a more inclusive purpose-driven economy which is unquestionably needed" (B Corp UK, 2015). Polman stated that "This is an exciting time to be in business. I am proud that Unilever will do its bit to help the B Corp movement scale so that one day all companies will compete not only to be the best in the world but be best for the world" (B Corp UK, 2015).

1

Each of these remarkable examples reflects an emergent trend in leadership with individuals, organizations, and communities answering a uniquely twenty-first century call to greatness. It is a call from metrics and movements demanding a response to breached critical thresholds. In 2016, the world experienced its hottest year on record – again. The global average temperature was the highest since global records began in 1880 (NOAA, 2017). According to the UN Millennium Ecosystem Assessment, rising human population has polluted or overexploited the majority of the ecological systems on which life depends, and humanity is straining the ability of the Earth's ecosystems to sustain future generations (Millennium Ecosystem Assessment, 2005). A majority of scientists concur that every major ecosystem in the world is in decline, and many believe that the sixth great extinction has begun (Ceballos, Ehrlich, & Dirzo, 2017). From a scientific perspective, this is now the Anthropocene epoch,[2] ushered into existence by human-induced changes, such as climate change, which are global in scale (Zalasiewicz et al., 2008). Globally, in 2015, 736 million people lived in extreme poverty, with one in five people in developing regions living on less than USD 1.90 per day (World Bank, 2018).

Our understanding of the significance of sustainability threats and the implications at all levels – global, societal, and individual – has only begun. By 2050, the direction of this turning point will already be known, but from a systems perspective, the story itself is being written today through a collection of individual acts and leadership choices being made moment by moment.

In these uncertain times of unprecedented environmental, economic, social, and political change, the world needs leadership capable of charting a future of global sustainability and collective wellbeing. Beyond asking why the changes are happening *to* us, we also have the opportunity to question why they are happening *for* us. In other words, how are we being compelled to evolve our leadership, and who are we being called to become?

THE UNITED NATIONS' TRANSFORMING OUR WORLD: 2030 AGENDA FOR SUSTAINABLE DEVELOPMENT

History was made when world leaders stepped up and pledged unifying commitments to secure a sustainable future "where all life can thrive" by adopting the United Nations' 2030 Agenda for Sustainable Development (the 2030 Agenda). The plan for developing the 2030 Agenda was created in June of 2012 in Rio de Janeiro, Brazil, at the United Nations Conference on Sustainable Development (Rio + 20) as part of a three-year multi-lateral and multi-stakeholder process. The heart of the 2030 Agenda is the 17 Sustainable Development Goals (SDGs). The SDGs succeeded the Millennium Development Goals (MDGs), created in 2000, which endeavored to meet the needs of the world's poorest people by eradicating global poverty by 2015 (UN, 2015a). The MDGs established measurable objectives for addressing hunger, achieving universal primary education, promoting gender equality, and avoiding child and maternal mortality, among others. The final MDG report found that the 15-year attempt was "the most successful anti-poverty movement in history" reducing the number of people living in poverty by more than half (UN, 2015a).

The SDGs build on the extraordinary progress begun by the MDGs while also addressing areas where, despite best efforts, progress was not sufficient. In addition, while the MDGs only applied to developing countries, the SDGs will apply universally to all UN member states. The SDGs broadened the content, scope, and scale of the MDGs with a particular emphasis on environmental sustainability as central to the achievement of all goals. While the MDGs were more narrowly focused on reducing poverty in all its dimensions, the SDGs were developed with an explicit understanding of the relationship between environmental sustainability and two other dimensions of sustainable development: the economic and the social.

Designed by collective intelligence and diverse inputs from grassroots to the government, the 2030 Agenda (UN, 2015b) is a brilliant plan that emboldens local to global engagement and supports aligned momentum throughout the world. It charts a "sustainable and resilient path" designed to leave no one behind, and reach "those furthest behind first" (UN, 2015b). The 17 STGs and their 169 associated targets are "integrated and indivisible," balancing economic, environmental, and social dimensions to achieve a vision of our world where:

- All human beings are free from poverty and hunger and "can fulfill their potential for dignity and equality and in a healthy environment."

- "All human beings can enjoy prosperous and fulfilling lives [...] in harmony with nature."

- The planet itself is free from degradation to be able to support present and future generations.

The SDGs address global challenges that are vital to the survival of humanity, tackling environmental issues such as climate change and clean energy and covering a wide range of social needs like health and wellbeing, education and access to livable wages, and job opportunities. In addition, the goals address core obstacles to sustainable development such as gender inequality and economic disparity. The goals are meant to be conceptualized holistically with the understanding that they address root problems in a systematic and interrelated way. The goals recognize that either progress or deterioration on one goal affects progress or deterioration on other goals as well. We cannot eliminate poverty (SDG 1), for example, without decent work and economic growth for all (SDG 8). We cannot take action to combat climate change and its impacts (SDG 13) without addressing responsible consumption and production (SDG 12). This profound interconnection makes the agenda the most significant global effort so far to advance sustainable development.[3]

Bridging the Leadership Gap

The outcomes of such universal and unanimous commitments are inspired and inspiring, yet what will it really take to bridge the leadership gap between a plan of action and unprecedented progress? The world's leaders have made a promise, and now they and the rest of the world's social actors need access to the best leadership guidance and resources available to accomplish what has never been done: to translate the bold vision of what is possible for humanity to a sustainable reality.

In response, *Evolving Leadership for Collective Wellbeing: Lessons for Implementing the United Nations Sustainable Development Goals* aims to provide that guidance in the form of a useful resource designed to heighten leadership effectiveness through access to vanguard theory and practice. This collection highlights stories and insights from leadership practitioners and scholars around the world and offers invaluable lessons, models, and practices to draw upon. Case and place-based chapters bridge theory and practice to empower diverse actors around the world.

PART I: EVOLVED LEADERSHIP FOR A SUSTAINABLE FUTURE

Part I of this book offers various perspectives on the leadership qualities and capacities necessary to achieve the UN SDGs. Liberating the power of our leadership potential starts with embracing our innate capacity to shape our world. When we are mindful that each action and inaction impacts the web of life, our choices can align with and evolve for the impact that we intend. The unprecedented opportunity before us to co-evolve a future of global sustainability and collective wellbeing requires leaders that understand that leadership matters. The choices that we make with our unavoidable influence on the web of life impact the present as well as the future. We have a profound opportunity and responsibility to look beyond our time and make choices that keep future generations in our minds and hearts.

Achieving the SDGs requires an integrated approach because the SDGs themselves are interrelated. Thus, leading for sustainable development means leading with the awareness of the interconnection of both our global challenges as well as their potential solutions. We begin our exploration of leadership qualities and capacities with Seana Steffen's chapter on the "Emergence of Restorative Leadership," a holistic approach to leadership that specifically recognizes the interconnectedness of all life and acts for the highest benefit to all. This chapter introduces the research-based guiding framework of restorative leadership and helps to answer this book's guiding question: *How do we bring out the best of our diverse humanity to ensure a sustainable future?*

The greatest threats to a thriving future of global sustainability and collective well-being are cynicism and resignation. We can and must offset attitudes of impossibility with inspired voices and compelling demonstrations. The next two chapters in the book offer both. In Chapter 2, "Humanistic Leadership for Sustainable Transformation," Barry A. Colbert, Jessica Nicholson, and Elizabeth C. Kurucz provide an empirical case study of Sustainable Waterloo Region (SWR), an environmental, social enterprise headquartered in Waterloo, Ontario, Canada. The authors demonstrate both the necessity and effectiveness of leading from a humanistic perspective – one that remembers that our shared humanity has the capacity to bind us together despite differences in geography, cultures, faiths, and conditions. In Chapter 3, "Collective Impact Through Regenerative Development: Lessons from Green and Healthy Home Repair," Elizabeth A.

Walsh tells the story of how the Austin Housing Repair Coalition embodied the principles of regenerative design and development and succeeded in furthering the progress of at least three SDGs in their work providing green and healthy home repair services in Austin, Texas.

Sustainability, which is by definition forward thinking, can be used as a lens through which to navigate our rapidly changing world. In order to ensure a sustainable future, leaders must be able to adapt to changes in a way that moves progress forward toward the achievement of the SDGs. The freedom and power of conscious choice are innately available to us as human beings. When we live and lead with clarity of intention, breakdowns, and hardships can become ingredients for breakthrough progress – even beyond what would have been possible had those circumstances not occurred. Ebere Morgan explores these ideas in Chapter 4, "Achieving a Sustainable Future Through Adaptive and Strategic Leadership." This chapter provides a framework for assisting leaders in learning to bring complex challenges to the surface as a tool for developing the skills necessary for leadership for the twenty-first century.

We complete this portion of the book with Wanda Krause's Chapter 5, "Leadership Lessons from Women in High Risk Environments," which asserts that women from locations other than the West should not be viewed as victims but as central actors in moving humanity toward sustainability. From them, we can learn how to embody qualities such as resiliency, trust, persistence, and hope – qualities which are vital to the achievement of the SDGs.

PART II: LEADING FROM ALIGNED VALUES

This extraordinary time brings us unique challenges and opportunities that call us to envision and manifest like never before. Translating bold visions to new levels of positive impact requires breakthroughs in design and practice. Understanding how to connect shared values for a common vision is essential in inspiring the vigorous, positive action that is needed to achieve the SDGs. Part II of this book explores the importance of value alignment and provides methods, frameworks, and examples for aligning values with action.

In Chapter 6, "Fossil Fuel Divestment: The Power of Positively Deviant Leadership for Catalyzing Climate Action and Financing Clean Energy," Abigail Abrash Walton highlights the process and impact of leaders and organizations' engagement in fossil fuel divestment whereby financial investments in the world's largest fossil fuel extraction companies are reinvested into clean energy. Her chapter provides tangible methods for organizational leaders and others who want to improve institutional capacity in an effort to address climate change.

In Chapter 7, "Aligning Your Team's Vision with the World's Bold Goals," Adriana Salazar, David García, and Mariana Quiroga present a strategic framework for guiding organizational actions toward addressing the world's most pressing problems developed by Mexican-based Cirklo, a social innovation consulting company. Their Team Alignment Tool provides a method specifically for aligning organizational values with the UN SDGs.

Finally, in Chapter 8, Karen Cvitkovich tells the story of lessons she learned in Standing Rock, North Dakota, where she joined a group of activists working to stop the construction of the Dakota Access Pipeline in 2017. "Perspectives and Possibilities: Aligning for Social Change" describes how political, cultural, and informational differences between people on the same side of a social and environmental change initiative can serve as powerful tools for sustainable change.

PART III: RELATIONSHIPS AND THE HEART OF OUR SHARED HUMANITY

While the SDGs provide a global plan of action, they also require local participation and involvement to achieve them. Working together, individuals, not-for-profits, institutions, businesses, and governments must come together to ensure a sustainable future for all. At the core of coming together is the ability to relate. The ability to relate – to others, to ideas, to challenges, and to solutions – is critical for addressing the complex environmental, social, and economic aspects of sustainable development. Part III of this book examines the role of relating and relationship in the context of bringing out the best of our diverse humanity to ensure a sustainable future.

Dung Q. Tran and Michael R. Carey examine Pope Francis' 2015 encyclical, *Laudato Si'* in Chapter 9, "Relational Leadership and Laudato Si': Pope

Francis' Call to Care for Our Common Home." When Pope Francis described the environmental crisis in the context of spiritual and moral viewpoints, he demonstrated his belief that the ideas are inextricably interconnected. *Laudato Si'* overtly relates poverty, for example, to environmental degradation and addresses the need for integrated solutions to the world's most pressing challenges.

Chapter 10, "Thriving as One Global Family: Leadership Beyond the Nation State" by Ejaj Ahmad and Hugh O'Doherty, inspires leadership that encourages breaking away from relating through tribalism and the idea that we are separated by ethnicity and nationality. They assert that if we are to achieve the SDGs, we need to look at the world's challenges with the lens that each of the challenges affects all of us, and thus each challenge requires the cooperation of actors on a global scale. If we can look at others and see and feel our shared humanity, we are better able to make choices that bring about the highest benefit to all.

In "How to Negotiate for Sustainable Relationships and Prosperity," Chapter 11, Mehrad Nazari shares a practical method of negotiation in which parties move beyond self-interests by harnessing the innate desire of the human spirit to connect, communicate, and co-create optimum results. Moving beyond self-interests is critical for achieving the SDGs as solutions to challenges like poverty and climate change necessitate seeing beyond ourselves to the heart of our shared humanity and profound interrelatedness.

PART IV: THE MORAL AND ETHICAL IMPERATIVE OF AN INCLUSIVE ECONOMY

Although the MDGs helped to bring more than one billion people out of extreme poverty (UN, 2015a), deep inequalities still exist in the global economy. Inclusion is at the heart of the 2030 Agenda. It is echoed in the pledge to leave no one behind and in the vision of a "just, equitable, tolerant, open and socially inclusive world in which the needs of the most vulnerable are met" and "a world in which every country enjoys sustained, inclusive and sustainable economic growth and decent work for all" (UN, 2015b). Creating an economic system that works for all is a moral and ethical imperative. This section of the book explores how we might co-evolve business and the economy in ways that increase economic health for all, even the most vulnerable, while at the same time honoring people and the ecological limits of the planet.

Chapter 12, "The Living Company: A Systems Approach," by Jennifer M. Chirico and Anette M. Nystrom, explores how adopting an integrative systems perspective, which allows us to think in terms of contexts, relationships, and patterns, can help us to better understand the current resource and humanitarian crisis, and lead to greater equality, improved human rights, a healthier earth, happier people, and increased long-term financial success. In the context of the 2030 Agenda, when we use a systems approach to imagine new ways of doing business or building an inclusive economy, we can see how business and the economy are simply parts of an even larger interconnected system that includes ecological systems and social systems. In this way we can understand how shifts in the way we think about the economy affect other parts of the system — or in the case of the SDGs — other goals and targets.

Shanah Trevenna then provides a framework for co-creating a unified global political-economy with a values-based cryptocurrency that empowers our collective wellbeing in Chapter 13, "Guiding Principles for Co-Creating a Sustainable Economy and for Leveraging Blockchain for Collective Wellbeing." The path we are currently on as a global community, she warns, will ensure that a small number of individuals and companies wield the power to keep much of the world's population underpaid, underutilized, and unfulfilled. By creating a global polity united in using Deep Democracy on Blockchain, we can instead harvest the best of all of humanity's diverse ingenuity to co-design our future.

The global emphasis on the gross domestic product (GDP) as the primary indicator of societal well-being is a major culprit in fueling climate change and collective malaise. While GDP identifies the monetary value of the economy, it does not help us to understand whether our lives are actually improving. When disaster and war are essential to growth, and collective happiness and wellbeing do not count at all, we can see how our system is set up for producing outcomes that are misaligned with what most of us say is most important. In Chapter 14, our last chapter in this part of the book, "Gross National Happiness: A Powerful Instrument for Positive and Sustainable Global Change," Elżbieta Jabłońska explores the Bhutanese paradigm of development which recognizes the need for holistic development from the individual to the societal level. By, bringing spiritual, emotional, and cultural well-being into balance with material well-being, this paradigm builds economic inclusivity into the very foundations of development.

PART V: GROWING OUR FUTURE LEADERS

With this final section, we explore education and training as key levers for systemic transformation and the foundation on which to build peace and sustainability. Education and training are critical for the achievement of sustainable development because, in order to address the SDGs, leaders must possess the knowledge, skills, and experiences necessary to make SDG-aligned choices and changes. The chapters in this section provide best-practice case study examples of successful education and training for sustainable development which can be emulated by practitioners all over the world.

Envisioning and being able to imagine a better future is an essential skill for leaders engaged in sustainable development work (Tilbury & Wortman, 2004). In Chapter 15, "Prototyping in the Anthropocene: A Case for Optimism from the Young Southeast Asian Leaders Initiative," Christina Monroe and Lance C. Boyd describe how the skill of prototyping, which involves envisioning possible solutions to a challenge, allows us to improve ideas at an early stage before large-scale resources are used.

In Chapter 16, "Evolving leadership for a sustainable future — Ceeds of Peace," Maya Soetoro-Ng and Kerrie Urosevich examine the Ceeds of Peace program in Hawaii, USA. By inspiring the next generation of leaders to meaningfully contribute to building a more sustainable and resilient future, the program has identified seven leadership skills that they believe are essential for achieving just and sustainable communities: critical thinking, courage, communication, compassion, conflict resolution, commitment, and collaboration. Ceeds of Peace explicitly incorporates the SDGS into the design and content of their curriculum and internal processes.

Grace Hurford and Philippa Chapman describe the joy and fulfillment that arises from nurturing and supporting students to lead for sustainability in Chapter 17, "Let's Get Sustainable: A Five-day MBA residency adventure." As a result of their MBA program, they see significant results including students beginning to realize what is possible in, and for, our world — bridging the divide between urgency and agency in their own communities with enthusiasm and skill.

The Future of Humanity is in our Hands

The twenty-first century is calling us to greatness and nothing less will do. It is our hope as editors that this book be a useful resource that deepens understanding about the potential and promise of this unique time in history. We have an unprecedented opportunity to co-evolve into a future of global sustainability and collective wellbeing. It is a journey of living transformative questions that awaken us to new possibilities and empower us to become our best selves. How will you help to bring out the best of our diverse humanity to ensure a sustainable future?

As the 2030 Agenda states, "The future of humanity and of our planet lies in our hands. It lies also in the hands of today's younger generation who will pass the torch to future generations. We have mapped the road to sustainable development. It will be for all of us to ensure that the journey is successful and its gains irreversible" (UN, 2015b).

NOTES

1. The 2015 Paris Climate Agreement to reduce greenhouse gas emissions and to avoid the most dangerous effects of climate change requires tremendous reductions in CO_2 emissions and nearly zero overall greenhouse gas (GHG) emissions moving forward. The cap on carbon emissions will render much of our fossil fuel reserves "stranded assets" (McGlade & Ekins, 2015), meaning that companies that own fossil fuels will not be able to use their reserves. Fossil fuel companies continue to invest in and develop new fossil fuel reserves despite their already stranded assets, presenting a significant financial liability and resulting in fossil fuel companies being overvalued, thus creating a "carbon bubble." For more information from the academic literature on the possible impacts of a carbon bubble on financial stability please see Weyzig, Kuepper, van Gelder, and van Tilburg (2014), Schoenmaker, van Tilburg, and Wijffels (2015), and Batten, Sowerbutts, and Tanaka (2016).

2. The International Union of Geological Sciences (IUGS) asserts that we are in the Holocene ("entirely recent") epoch, which began 11,700 years ago after the last major ice age. However, some believe that title is no longer in alignment with the current state of the planet. "They argue for 'Anthropocene'—from *anthropo*, for 'man', and *cene*, for 'new'—because human-kind has caused mass extinctions of plant and

animal species, polluted the oceans and altered the atmosphere, among other lasting impacts" (Stromberg, 2013).

3. For more information and a complete list of the SDGs, see https://www.un.org/sustainabledevelopment/sustainable-development-goals/

REFERENCES

B Corp UK. (2015, September 28). *Unilever's Paul Polman supports the launch of B Corps in the UK* [video file]. Retrieved from https://www.youtube.com/watch?v=5bzHGOxgXgg. Accessed on June 1, 2018.

Batten, S., Sowerbutts, R., & Tanaka, M. (2016). *Let's talk about the weather: The impact of climate change on Central Banks.* Staff Report Paper No. 603, Bank of England.

Carney, M. (2015, September 29). *Breaking the tragedy of the horizon – climate change and financial stability.* Speech presented at City Dinner in Lloyd's of London, London. Bank of England. Retrieved from https://www.bankofengland.co.uk/-/media/boe/files/speech/2015/breaking-the-tragedy-of-the-horizon-climate-change-and-financial-stability.pdf?la=en&hash=7C67E785651862457D99511147C7424FF5EA0C1A. Accessed on June 1, 2018.

Ceballos, G., Ehrlich, P., & Dirzo, R. (2017). Biological annihilation via the ongoing sixth mass extinction signaled by vertebrate population losses and declines. Proceedings of the National Academy of Sciences of the United States of America, PNAS July 25, 2017. 114 (30) E6089–E6096; published ahead of print July 10, 2017.

McGlade, C., & Ekins, P. (2015). The geographical distribution of fossil fuels unused when limiting global warming to 2°C. *Nature, 517*, 187–190.

Millennium Ecosystem Assessment. (2005). *Ecosystems and Human Well-Being: Synthesis.* Washington, DC: Island Press; 2005. Retrieved from https://www.millenniumassessment.org/documents/document.356.aspx.pdf. Accessed on June 1, 2018.

NOAA. (2017). *Global Analysis – Annual 2016.* Retrieved from https://www.ncdc.noaa.gov/sotc/global/201613. Accessed on June 1, 2018.

Schoenmaker, D., van Tilburg, R., & Wijffels, H. (2015). What role for financial supervisors in addressing systemic environmental risks? Sustainable Finance Lab working paper.

Stromberg, J. (2013, January). What Is the Anthropocene and are we in it? Retrieved from https://www.smithsonianmag.com/science-nature/what-is-the-anthropocene-and-are-we-in-it-164801414. Accessed on June 1, 2018.

Tilbury, D., & Wortman, D. (2004). *Engaging people in sustainability.* Gland: IUCN.

United Nations. (2015a). *The Millennium Development Goals Report 2015.* New York, 2015:1–75. Retrieved from http://www.un.org/millenniumgoals/2015_MDG_Report/pdf/MDG%202015%20rev%20(July%201).pdf (cited 2 August 2016). Accessed on June 1, 2018.

United Nations. (2015b). *Transforming our world: The 2030 Agenda for Sustainable Development.* Retrieved from https:/sustainabledevelopment.un.org/post2015/transformingourworld. Accessed on June 1, 2018.

Weyzig, F., Kuepper, B., van Gelder, J. W., & R. van Tilburg. (2014). *The price of doing too little too late; the impact of the carbon bubble on the EU financial system*, Green New Deal Series Volume 11, The Greens/EFA Group −European Parliament.

World Bank. (2018, September). *Poverty.* Retrieved from https://www.worldbank.org/en/topic/poverty/overview. Accessed on September 30, 2018.

Zalasiewicz, J., Williams, M., Smith, A., Barry, T. L., Coe, A. L., Bown, P. R., … Stone, P. (2008). Are we now living in the anthropocene? *GSA Today, 18*(2), 4–8. doi:10.1130/GSAT01802A.1

PART I

EVOLVED LEADERSHIP FOR A SUSTAINABLE FUTURE

1

THE EMERGENCE OF RESTORATIVE LEADERSHIP

Seana Lowe Steffen

The consensus agreement of all 193 member countries of the United Nations to adopt the 2030 Agenda for Sustainable Development on September 25, 2015, was historic. A plan for universal action, it is a stirring pledge that inspires belief in the best of all possibilities for humanity and the planet that we call home. Composed of 17 Sustainable Development Goals and 169 targets, the Agenda charts a global path toward a balanced future where all life thrives. The unprecedented agreement is the outcome of countless acts of restorative leadership, from grassroots to government, and reflects a global awakening to our universality: "The future of humanity and of our planet lies in our hands" (United Nations, 2015).

At the same time as world leaders gathered in New York City to launch the Sustainable Development Goals (SDGs), on the other side of the Atlantic, the B Corp movement was launching its official expansion to the United Kingdom. B Corps, which number in the thousands, are businesses emboldened by the mission of the not-for-profit B Lab to certify as standard bearers of the movement to redefine business as a force for good. Unilever CEO Paul Polman, who was in New York as a member of the UN Global Compact, took time out of UN activities to broadcast a YouTube message. Sharing his hopes and sentiments, Polman described the B Corp movement as "an important part of the shift toward a more inclusive purpose-driven economy which is unquestionably needed" (B Corp UK, 2015).

Leaders like Paul Polman and leadership teams like that of B Lab reflect an emergent trend in leadership as individuals, organizations, and communities answer a uniquely twenty-first century call from sustainability metrics and social movements worldwide. Together, they represent an awakened and aware leadership responding to what has become a pivotal question for all sectors and all societies: *How do we bring out the best of our diverse humanity to ensure a sustainable future?* It is the central question that informs restorative leadership and guides each aspect of its impact on the world. This chapter introduces the research-based guiding framework of restorative leadership and illustrates several principles in practice across government, business, and not-for-profit settings that include B Lab and certified B Corps like Biomimicry 3.8, the UN 2030 Agenda process, and the NGO World Pulse.

RESTORATIVE LEADERSHIP

Bringing out the best of our diverse humanity to ensure a sustainable future is the leadership challenge and opportunity at this time in the evolutionary story of humanity. It is the design question and the leadership imperative yet to be realized. Thankfully, there are emerging leadership distinctions that reveal what is possible for locally to globally resonant impact. For example, it is distinct to lead communities and organizations trust themselves and each other enough to examine and consciously abandon centuries-old social norms that have become incongruent with universal values; it is distinct to lead such that individuals and communities and organizations are inspired to engage in tens of millions of small acts that collectively transform livelihoods and bio-regions; and it is distinct to lead for unprecedented inclusivity and collaboration such that universally relevant risk is transformed to hopeful possibility.

At once ancient and modern, restorative leadership is an emergent framework that captures the nature of these emerging distinctions in order to guide us to fulfill our evolutionary potential. Restorative leadership has been discerned through a grounded theory process analyzing data from individual interviews, participant observation, and primary source media.

Over 40 individual, organizational, and community case studies were chosen purposively for their record of positive outcomes on global sustainability and collective wellbeing. Some have been clients. Through years of watching, listening, and reading, the emergent phenomenon of restorative leadership can best be described as a holistic approach to leadership that recognizes the interconnectedness of all life and acts for the highest benefit to all. Striving to do no harm and to heal the earth, our communities, and ourselves, restorative leadership cultivates the best and most balanced expression of universal values and natural laws.

PRINCIPLES IN PRACTICE

Restorative leadership is visionary, courageous, and infinitely creative in generating yet unfulfilled possibilities. Because it reflects a holistic perspective on leading and living, empowered action is accessible to anyone anywhere, starting wherever we are and with whatever we face. It is an approach to leadership that compels a level of positive impact unimaginable at earlier times, made possible by scaling across networks of connectivity with unwavering commitment and heart-centered resolve.

As an engaged way of being and doing that restores balance, restorative leadership embodies a sensibility of significance beyond oneself, one's community, and one's organization. There is a quality of remembering what has been forgotten and fulfilling on life's ultimate purpose. The effort to fulfill the highest potential for the highest good, while doing no harm and healing, reveals that there are several underlying principles reflected by restorative leadership in action.

The World is an Interdependent Web

As the world is an integrated whole, each action and inaction impacts. Each choice that we make as humans with our unavoidable influence on the web of life impacts the present and future. That capacity for influence reflects the innate leadership potential of restorative leadership. Each of us is uniquely positioned and endowed to have a positive impact that no one else can have.

Genius and Goodness Abound

Restorative leadership demonstrates a fundamental belief in human potential and faith in basic goodness. Humanity is replete with good hearts that care deeply and want to make the world a better place. Collective intelligence, innate knowledge, and universal wisdom are readily available with the guidance integral for a thriving balance.

Everything is Possible

In this world of infinite potential, wondrous outcomes are available with sustained vision and creativity. Restorative leadership orients toward a vast horizon of possibility and consistently evolves life's highest unfolding.

While these principles undergird restorative leadership generally, the data suggest that each gives rise to particular aligned practices for demonstrating restorative leadership in action. For example, because the world is an interdependent web of life, restorative leadership strives to:

- take the long view;

- be highly intentional with life's impact; and

- leverage the interconnection for cascading benefit.

From a belief that genius and goodness abound, practicing restorative leadership means to:

- ask and listen, align, and co-create;

- scale across shared values; and

- go net generous.

And with a foundation that everything is possible, restorative leadership works to:

- create eddies of possibility by example;

- transform circumstances to aligned momentum; and

- live and learn the guiding questions.

This chapter will focus on three of the practices that are highly illustrative of restorative leadership principles in action.

THE WORLD IS AN INTERDEPENDENT WEB: TAKE THE LONG VIEW

For most, restorative leadership originates with an awakening to or a foundational understanding of the age-old insight and scientific fact that the world is an interdependent web of life and that the life cycle on Earth extends into deep time: both past and future. The past that we have to learn from is what Janine Benyus, founder of the certified B Corp Biomimicry 3.8, describes as, "3.8 billion years of brilliant, time-tested solutions" through life's evolution (J. Benyus, personal communication, July 23, 2010). The future that we have to consider is best illustrated by the cultural practice of the Haudenosaunee Confederation, or Iroquois, who "consider the impact on the seventh generation" when making decisions (Haudenosaunee, 2017).

Prime Minister Gro Brundtland, who was chair of the UN World Commission on Environment and Development that first introduced the idea of sustainable development in 1987, describes the perspective of leadership needed at this time:

> Leadership always means taking the long view, inspired by our common needs and a clear sense of shared responsibility for taking the necessary action. In our time, it means thinking even further ahead than leaders had to do one or two generations ago. Now we have the evidence to show us that our human activities, the footsteps of our own time, will affect negatively the lives and choices we leave to future generations in a potentially disastrous way, due to our own overstepping of planetary boundaries. We face a moral challenge to act and to act in time to protect the planet Earth and the livelihood for new generations. (G. Brundtland, personal communication, April 25, 2012).

That moral challenge that Brundtland describes is what compels the moral courage to engage in restorative leadership, whether demonstrated by the transnational leadership that launched the SDGs or the cross-sector leadership that is transforming business. The foundational principle of interdependence and the practice of taking the long view is embedded in the B Corp movement. As B Lab co-founder Andrew Kassoy states, "Having people behave and having leaders behave ethically in the recognition that their decisions and their actions have consequences because we are all interdependent, with an eye towards not themselves but the betterment of the whole society, is what we need now" (A. Kassoy, personal communication, May 17, 2013).

The B Corp movement may be the most important movement of the twenty-first century given the widespread impacts of business on the planet and the vast potential for business to be a force for good. Jay Gilbert, the founding voice for B Lab, left his US$250 million company in pursuit of the vision of a shared and durable prosperity for all. "B" is for "benefit," and together with B Lab's co-founders Bart Houlahan and Andrew Kassoy, Jay is a recipient of the Skoll Award for Social Entrepreneurship in recognition of the global benefits from B Lab's efforts. A certified B Corporation is to business what USDA Organic certification is to food. To become a B Corp, a business submits itself to a rigorous third-party assessment comprising the highest standards for social and environmental performance.

Collectively, B Corps lead a growing global movement of people using business to solve social and environmental problems across 50 countries and 130 industries around the world. The collective impact of their systems approach includes driving impact investment to companies doing well by doing good and establishing laws protecting businesses that want to serve triple bottom line interests of people, planet, and profit.

Because the world is an integrated whole, business is powerfully positioned in the nested interdependencies of the environment, society, and economy to take the long view and act with both current and future generations in mind. The emergence of this leadership role for business reflects a return to what has been forgotten about the inherently purpose-driven roots of being a company: to come together in the life-affirming exchange of meeting needs and sharing bread. To be a certified B Corp like Biomimicry 3.8 or Unilever's recent acquisition Seventh Generation is to institutionalize restorative leadership. If a business passes those highest standards to become a certified B Corp, the business signs the *B Corp Declaration of Interdependence* (B Corporation, n.d.) committing to strive for a global economy where business is a force for good and to operate from beliefs:

- That we must be the change we seek in the world.

- That all business ought to be conducted as if people and place mattered.

- That, through their products, practices, and profits, businesses should aspire to do no harm and benefit all.

- To do so requires that we act with the understanding that we are each dependent upon another and thus responsible for each other and future generations.

GENIUS AND GOODNESS ABOUND: ASK AND LISTEN, ALIGN, AND CO-CREATE

Embracing an ethic of community, restorative leadership strives to do no harm, to serve collective wellbeing, and to bring the highest benefit to all. It is leadership that is community-minded, engaging networks to forward and sustain hopeful possibilities. Inviting, listening for, and building from local and innate knowledge, both around and within, results in innovative and wondrous outcomes. The genius of collective intelligence is widespread and available with wise guidance when we trust in human and natural communities. In essence, as Meg Wheatley says, "Whatever the problem, community is the answer" (personal communication, May 17, 2011). As a fundamental practice of restorative leadership, the participatory approach to engage genius is astoundingly simple: ask and listen, align, and co-create.

The universal commitment of all the world's nations to the SDGs was the result of unprecedented listening, aligning, and co-creating. To get to that moment when, "Never before have world leaders pledged common action and endeavor across such a broad and universal policy agenda" (UN, 2015) took patient and persevering restorative leadership emboldened by what is so evidently possible and so significantly at stake. It was a success made possible by standing on the shoulders of widespread community genius and decades of Millennium Development Goal progress. In service to the highest benefit to all, two years of intensive engagement with people around the world, and listening particularly to the voices of the most vulnerable, resulted in breakthrough ideas like "common but differentiated responsibilities" and reaching those "furthest behind first" (UN, 2015).

Globally, those furthest behind tend to be women. An innovator in the space of women's empowerment is the World Pulse digital media network, which was founded by Jensine Larsen to empower every woman and girl to believe in the power of her voice and to use it to build a world where all life thrives. Believing that digital technology is the fastest route to uniting and empowering women, World Pulse is a growing network of 25,000 active members in over 190 countries that connect from internet cafes in conflict zones to cell phones in rural villages to boardrooms in Fortune 500 companies.

With its community-centered approach, World Pulse engages network members to forward and sustain hopeful possibilities locally to globally. Larsen and World Pulse demonstrate restorative leadership through their mission and methodology. "In our theory of change, step number one is 'invite,' and you have to ask the question. You have to specifically put a call out to women about whatever issue or topic because too often women don't necessarily think it's for them or that their opinion matters [...] So you have to put out a special call saying, 'We want to hear from women specifically on this'" (J. Larsen, personal communication, September 25, 2015). The World Pulse experience of feeling witnessed and valued inspires members to self-authorize for the benefit of their communities and the unmuting of women's leadership potential everywhere. Jensine describes the World Pulse participatory practice as, "[...] crowdsourcing the feminine intelligence of the planet" (J. Larsen, personal communication, September 25, 2015). World Pulse channels those voices and solutions to influential forums and decision-makers globally to impact initiatives benefiting all women – and with that, the state of the world.

Neema Namadamu, a disability activist from the Democratic Republic of Congo, was empowered by her World Pulse experience and training to launch women-only Internet centers in the DRC and to build an online movement of hundreds of "Hero Women" ("Maman Shujaa" in Swahili) speaking out on World Pulse. In response to a rebel attack threat, the Maman Shujaa wanted their solutions about how to stop the violence to be heard at the White House. World Pulse partnered with Change.org and the Enough Project to launch an online appeal which delivered over 100,000 signatures to the White House petitioning the government to appoint a US special envoy to the region. As a result of the support and envoy response, the women were emboldened to create a US$10M human rights-based development plan to deliver to the World Bank. Whether supporting community-based initiatives or facilitating demand-driven development policy, World Pulse demonstrates restorative leadership by recognizing the genius of typically unheard interests, and ensuring that the diverse insights of those furthest behind can actively participate in transforming global problems.

While the restorative leadership demonstrated by World Pulse culls and channels the collective intelligence of women's often silenced voices, Janine Benyus taps into the voiceless wisdom that surrounds us. Expanding beyond humans to engaging the rest of nature, Benyus, together with Dayna Baumeister and their team, co-founded the certified B Corp Biomimicry 3.8 to help innovators solve human problems through the brilliance of nature's design. Because nature's genius among us can date back billions of years, Janine urges us to ask and listen, align, and co-create with our competent elders: "The oldest are the blue greens, the blue green algae. They are 3.8 billion years old! We're 200,000 years old. Billion versus thousand. Two-hundred thousand. Three point eight billion. It's staggering. [...] It turns out that the model for one of the most sophisticated machines right now, the fuel cell, is the most ancient organism, and I think that's pretty poetically beautiful" (J. Benyus, personal communication, July 23, 2010).

Biomimicry, defined out of Benyus' quest to meet human design needs harmlessly, is "learning from and then emulating nature's forms, processes, and ecosystems to create more sustainable designs" (Biomimicry 3.8, n.d.). Janine has been recognized widely for the impact of her restorative leadership, including as a *Time Magazine* "Hero for the Planet," as a *BusinessWeek* "Most Influential Designer," and as the Smithsonian Institution's Cooper-Hewitt National Design Mind Award recipient. Biomimicry 3.8 itself has an impact that spans five continents and 25 industries. The Biomimicry 3.8 team models restorative leadership in an evolutionary design process that starts with deep listening for what a design is intended to do. As Janine explains, "That's a very powerful thing when you get to the level of city. What do you want your city to do? So then once you're at function, you can biologize the question" (J. Benyus, personal communication, July 23, 2010). Once the design challenge has been biologized, the participatory practices engage nature's genius with the guiding question: What in the natural world has already solved this challenge? In other words, what would nature do? From asking and listening:

> We realize that all our inventions have already appeared in nature
> in a more elegant form and at a lot less cost to the planet. Our most
> clever architectural struts and beams are already featured in lily
> pads and bamboo stems. Our central heating and air-conditioning
> are bested by the termite tower's steady 86 degrees F. Our most

stealthy radar is hard of hearing compared to the bat's
multifrequency transmission. And our new "smart materials" can't
hold a candle to the dolphin's skin or the butterfly's proboscis.
(Benyus, 1997, p. 6)

The highest impact restorative leadership outcomes emerge from a partici-patory process that iterates and builds on an evolving understanding and application of collective intelligence in service to the common good. Capacity and knowledge are coevolved in the process, thereby illuminating community assets and validating collective intelligence to further build upon. At Biomimicry 3.8, that co-creative process brings the intelligence of what they call "nature's champion adaptors" into deep conversations with humans for learning. The champion adaptors specifically, and life's design principles generally, inform the iterative process. For example, in working together with the founding B Corp Seventh Generation, they asked and lis-tened for what sea cucumbers, mustard plants, and bombardier beetles could teach about packaging. As Janine explains, "[…] we keep on going back to the natural world for information at every level. […] and all in the service of creating breakthrough products and processes that are sustainable, that are inherently and deeply sustainable" (J. Benyus, personal communication, July 23, 2010).

Whether transforming the nature of relationships among species or nations, or transforming information technology to relationship technology, restorative leadership demonstrates humility, a curiosity that borders on wonder, and confidence in the genius that abounds while swimming in the space of hopeful possibility. Restorative leadership facilitates and guides rather than commands and directs, empowering individuals and groups to come together in shared vision on common ground to co-create truly bril-liant outcomes of highest benefit. There is immense trust in the wisdom of the community, in the integrity of universal values, and in the prospect of facilitating positive momentum with any circumstances. For some in leader-ship, it requires what Wheatley calls a "conversion moment […] when you realize that it's not all up to you, and that other people are as competent and capable and creative as you are" (M. Wheatley, personal communication, May 27, 2011). In essence, an asset-based approach, restorative leadership, empowers others to see and apply their knowledge and skills and to embrace their collective assets as relevant and applicable to diverse local and global priorities.

EVERYTHING IS POSSIBLE: CREATE EDDIES OF POSSIBILITY BY EXAMPLE

To stand up in the current of existing norms with our voices for and examples of possibility grants others permission and empowers space to do the same. From that, waves of inspiration and courage ripple. Leading by example and being the change we wish to see are timeless lessons for demonstrating all that is possible when existing norms and models limit perceptions. In restorative leadership, creating eddies of possibility by example is a highly strategic leadership choice to embolden norm change and to galvanize those who have forgotten or doubt the vastness of life's potential.

When Paul Polman broadcast his B Corp message, it was a milestone moment in the movement to redefine business as a balancing force for good. Viewing business as part of an integrated whole, Polman consistently champions the unquestionable need for system change toward an inclusive, purpose-driven economy. He demonstrates restorative leadership not only by taking the long view of disrupting quarterly reporting norms on behalf of long-term value creation but by authorizing Unilever to create very visible eddies of possibility. Under his restorative leadership, Unilever certified Ben & Jerry's as the first publicly owned subsidiary B Corp in 2012 and purchased the founding certified B Corp Seventh Generation in 2016. Securing a certified B Corp like Ben & Jerry's was a strategic target in fulfilling B Lab's theory of change, which specifies building a credible community of certified B Corps. Jay Gilbert describes certified B Corps as "lighthouse brands" intended to accelerate cultural shift such that all businesses are empowered to "be like a B Corp," a top 5 trend recently named by *Forbes Magazine* (Harnish, 2015).

Building a credible community of certified B Corps that embolden the collective voice of responsible business to be heard illustrates how eddies of possibility can have a benefit multiplier effect. Andrew Kassoy explains, "The B Corp brand is helping create a collective voice for a different kind of behavior. So that then flows into the demonstration effect, which I think over time will be the bigger impact. The message is starting to resonate with the 70 million consumers who care about buying from companies that they believe in, and having the collective voice of [the B Corp] community starts to make that possible (A. Kassoy, personal communication, May 17, 2013)." In addition to the widespread impacts from the combined efforts of B Lab and Unilever, the moments that founding B Corp Patagonia became the first registered benefit corporation in the world's sixth largest economy, California, and that Rally became the first certified B Corp to go public were milestones that sent waves of inspiration throughout the movement to redefine business as a force for good.

A member of the B Corp movement, Biomimicry 3.8 itself creates eddies of possibility by nature's example, representing nature's intelligence at design tables with trained biologists who can guide bio-inspired design that then creates further demonstration effect. Biomimicry involves relating to nature as a mentor, as well as our model and measure of success. Through education, innovation consulting, and public speaking, Biomimicry 3.8 intentionally propagates possibility through compelling evidence and outreach that highlight the impact of nature's guidance. Both strategic and generous, their offshoot biological intelligence service asknature.org offers inspiring design examples of sustainable solutions informed by nature's brilliance.

As Janine Benyus says, "This is the era of demonstrating that it's possible!" (J. Benyus, personal communication, July 23, 2010). For example, it is possible to learn from the humpback whale's tubercle fins and evolve the aerodynamic design of an airplane's wings for 32% fuel savings and 62% better lift; it is possible to follow the guidance of the kingfisher to redesign the nose of a bullet train like the nose of a highly evolved diving beak to reduce electricity costs by 15% and eliminate a sonic boom problem; and it is possible to use CO_2 as a feedstock like plants do and use it to make biodegradable plastics (Bioneers, 2015). According to Biomimicry 3.8, by 2030, there could be as much as US$1.6 trillion contributed to the global GDP by bio-inspired, and therefore more sustainable, products and services (Biomimicry 3.8, n.d.).

World Pulse, alternatively, trains and spotlights women's leadership with the express intent to amplify voices and movements for positive change that will embolden others. Through transformational media and storytelling, World Pulse works to, "unleash the potential of the half of humanity that is currently being repressed" (J. Larsen, personal communication, September 25, 2015) with a ripple effect of self-authorized leadership. Jensine Larsen and the World Pulse team highlight the stories of "[...] the many Malalas" (Malala's Story, n.d.) like Chi Yvonne Leina who, after finding World Pulse and gaining the courage to speak out, successfully inspired a national move-ment to end breast ironing in Cameroon:

> *Leina's story is an example of the power of one woman's voice, where there is a tremendous silence around a very damaging tradition called breast ironing in Cameroon. It affects three to four million women and girls. It's where mothers and grandmothers will heat up hot stones and pulverize the breast tissue of their daughters and granddaughters. Now they do this in an attempt to protect them from the severe rates of sexual violence that exist, and they are not fully aware of the detrimental health impacts and psychological impacts that result. So she started writing her story about escaping the practice and how she wanted to crusade to end it. We had never heard of it, so we spotlighted that story and soon enough CNN saw it and spotlighted it on their site as number one for that week. (J. Larsen, personal communication, September 25, 2015)*

Leina participated in the World Pulse platform and training program, broke a stigmatized silence, and made international headlines, gained visibil-ity and followers, and received awards and financial support to take her leadership vision to the next level. Her model and message emboldened more than 30,000 other women and girls in Cameroon to stand up in the current of the breast ironing tradition and vow not to participate. After the government learned about what she was doing with and through World Pulse, they were moved to support Leina on a campaign that now includes working together with celebrities and men to eradicate the practice of breast ironing across Cameroon.

CONCLUSION

Engaging in restorative leadership is to bring renewed confidence and resolve to the ancient and enduring leadership practice of empowering the commu-nity to fulfill its leadership potential. Restorative leadership is an approach that helps us remember what we have forgotten, drawing on the best of 3.8 billion years of evolution and bringing out the best of diverse humanity to ensure a sustainable future. In this twenty-first century context, restorative leadership engages in the explicit and worthy effort of restoring balance and sustaining diverse and abundant life on Earth. Restorative leadership also extends and seeks the wise participation of society's diverse margins and what Biomimicry 3.8 calls the "30 million soft-spoken species" (Biomimicry 3.8, n.d.).

In the presence of restorative leadership, there is a quality of deep connection and caring, intuitive in its insight and grounded in its love, respect, and even reverence for the intelligence, effort, and diversity of the life force present in our communities and nature. From a restorative leadership perspective, we have a profound opportunity and responsibility with our leadership influence as conscious actors to remember what life itself teaches us about how to answer the 21st century's call to greatness and play our part healing and transforming the state of the world moment by moment.

REFERENCES

B Corp UK. (2015, September 28). Unilever's Paul Polman supports the launch of B Corps in the UK [Video File]. Retrieved from https://www. youtube.com/watch?v=5bzHGOxgXgg. Accessed on June 1, 2018.

B Corporation. (n.d.). *The B Corp Declaration*. Retrieved from https://www. bcorporation.net/what-are-b-corps/the-b-corp-declaration. Accessed on June 1, 2018.

Benyus, J. (1997). *Biomimicry: Innovation inspired by nature*. New York, NY: Harper Collins.

Biomimicry 3.8. (n.d.). "What Is Biomimicry?" Retrieved from https:// biomimicry.net. Accessed on June 1, 2018.

Bioneers. (2015). "Janine Benyus — What Life Knows?" [Video File]. Retrieved from https://www.youtube.com/watch?v=OSlKh-8XoCs https:// biomimicry.net/what-is-biomimicry/. Accessed on June 1, 2018.

Harnish, V. (2015, December 15). 5 Key Business Trends to Master in 2016. Retrieved from http://fortune.com/2015/12/15/key-business-trends-2016/. Accessed on June 1, 2018.

Haudenosaunee. (2017). "Haudenosaunee Confederacy." Retrieved from http://www.haudenosauneeconfederacy.com/values.html

Malala Fund. (n.d.). "Malala's Story." Retrieved from https://www.malala. org/malalas-story. Accessed on June 1, 2018.

United Nations. (2015). Transforming our world: the 2030 Agenda for Sustainable Development. Retrieved from https://sustainabledevelopment.un. org/post2015/transformingourworld

2

HUMANISTIC LEADERSHIP FOR SUSTAINABLE TRANSFORMATION

Barry A. Colbert, Jessica Nicholson and
Elizabeth C. Kurucz

L'avenir est comme le reste: il n'est plus ce qu'il était.
—Paul Valéry (1948, p. 135)

(The future, like everything else, is no longer what it used to be.)

Human societies, governments, and organizations are facing unprecedented challenges from multiple directions. Macro-global problems of food and fresh water security, clean energy provision, and sustainable livelihoods are playing out within the context of explosive population growth and a changing climate. This presents an extraordinarily complex set of challenges. As populations, temperatures, and oceans continue to rise over the next century, the challenges will be even greater. In such a complex, unpredictable environment, what compass should leaders hold? What *kind* of leadership does the world need at this juncture to help ensure we bring forth the best of our shared humanity to provide a sustainable future for all, and for each? The *UN 2030 Agenda for Sustainable Development* (*"Transforming our World"*) calls for deep change to the ways we address such social, economic, and ecological challenges to improve the lot of every person. There are growing calls for placing humanity at the center as we navigate and design our future in the face of increasing sustainability challenges (Dierksmeier, 2016) and exponential technological changes (Tegmark, 2017).

In this chapter, we suggest that an emphasis on *humanistic leadership* will serve us best as we collectively navigate the remaining decades of this century. Beneath rich cultural diversities, our shared humanity is our most basic common denominator, and the evolving task of leadership is to return humanity to the center of our conceptions of a viable society. Leadership in this century must be focused on helping people across diverse geographies, cultures, faiths, and conditions to comprehend that the dignity and well-being of each individual should be our primary objective. Achieving that goal depends on learning how to act collectively, deliberately, and reflectively to flourish in a changing biosphere (Kurucz, Colbert, Lüdeke-Freund, Upward, & Willard, 2017). We are all individual human beings seeking to define and to live "a good life." In addition, although we are individuals, our definitions and realizations of a good life depend greatly on our sociability – our physical, psychological, and cultural interdependence with other humans within ecological contexts. Humanism centers upon the dignity and well-being of each individual person (Dierksmeier, 2011) as the primary objective and compass for policy-making and institutional design rather than blunt aggregate measures of economic churn such as gross domestic product (Stiglitz, Sen, & Fitoussi, 2010). Humanism is enacted in organizations and institutions through *humanistic leadership* (Lawrence & Pirson, 2015; Melé, 2016; Waddock, 2016), a model of leadership that works to advance such integrally human needs and aspirations. Bringing out the best of our diverse humanity to ensure a sustainable future begins with placing a high value on the dignity and well-being of each person.

A vibrant and vigorous civil society will be critical to positioning humanity at the center – leaving that to governments or corporate interests will not do (Mason, 2015) – and models of social entrepreneurship are particularly well designed to realize a humanist ethos (Pirson, 2009). In this chapter, we draw upon a case study in social enterprise to illustrate some core components of humanistic leadership. We begin by sketching the outlines of a humanistic perspective, based on ideas from a growing movement toward humanism in management, and take an elemental model of humanistic leadership from Lawrence and Pirson (2015) as an organizing framework. We then apply this framework to our focal case of Sustainable Waterloo Region (SWR), an environmentally focused social enterprise that has been operating in a tri-city region in Ontario, Canada, since 2009. Following the SWR story, we add some ideas from other leadership theories that emphasize an ethic of care (Gilligan, 1982; Held, 2006; Noddings, 1984) and the importance of social transformation as the context for leadership work (Burns, 2003). We describe the work of SWR in relation to a humanistic leadership framework and contend that such a framework better explains the success of SWR to date than does a conception of leading and managing rooted in a traditional economic paradigm. We then suggest how these ideas might be incorporated into the intentional engagement and transformation processes of such "third sector" organizations, and conclude with implications for similar organizations looking to catalyze multi-sector collaboration for sustainability through humanistic leadership. This kind of collaboration is critical for addressing the UN SDGs – indeed, Goal 17 is explicitly aimed at strengthening partnerships for sustainable development. In this case, the work of SWR directly impacts SDG 9 (building a resilient infrastructure and fostering innovation), SDG 13 (combatting climate change), and SDG 16 (building inclusive societies and accountable institutions).

HUMANISM AND HUMANISTIC MANAGEMENT

Humanism is a contemporary label for a long thread of ideas running from ancient India, China, Greece, and Rome through the medieval Islamic world to the seventeenth-century Enlightenment thinkers, and to neo-Pragmatists today. The common element is that the locus for meaning creation and social design is the dignity (i.e., inherent worth) and welfare of each human being, guided by reason (Cherry, 2009). Humanism is essentially a belief in natural forces and human responsibility for our well-being, without praise or blame attributed to gods or spirits, or appeal for supernatural intervention in human affairs. Under humanism, we work with what we've got, we lay in the beds we make, and we strive to make tomorrow better than today for every person through social care and ecological stewardship. As Pragmatist philosopher Richard Rorty described it, in rejecting the quest for "truth" that has dominated analytic philosophy, and defending the humanistic perspective running through the work of William James and John Dewey, "[...] what matters is our loyalty to other human beings clinging together against the dark, not our hope of getting things right" (Rorty, 1980, p. 727). Nineteenth-century movements branded as rationalist, freethinker, atheist, secularist, naturalist, and positivist loosely coalesced under the banner of humanism with the publication of the *Humanist Manifesto* in 1933, and humanism has since evolved into a contemporary worldview offering a positive, ethical framework for everyday life (Cherry, 2009). Definitions and manifestations vary, but four key elements of any humanistic framework are a belief in *progress* (human capacity for advancement and refinement); *reason* (embracing knowledge, learning, and justified belief); *inclusiveness* (universal acceptance into dialog with all persons capable of reason); and a focus on *individualism* (the idea that each person is inherently valuable, regardless of collective identities defined by race, ethnicity, national, or religious affiliation) (Nida-Rümelin, 2009).

Calls for a move toward humanistic management refute the limited and distorted caricature of a person prevalent in classical economics. This view presented the individual as simply a "materialistic utility maximizer, who values individual benefit over group and societal benefit" (Pirson & Lawrence, 2010, p. 553). This mythical *homo oeconomicus* only engages in an exchange with others to further his or her gain, an assumption that has shaped business and management education, leaving business schools open to the charge of doing more harm than good for management practice (Ghoshal, 2005). Humanistic management scholars accept the power and usefulness of markets, but instead of holding economic growth as the primary objective, they urge a transition to a "life-conducive economy" that places the dignity and well-being of each person at the center (Pirson, 2017, p. 2). Human beings are not merely the means to an end of shareholder value creation, but an end in themselves, as articulated in the conclusion of the *Humanistic Management Manifesto* (Humanistic Management Network, 2005):

> *Since human autonomy realizes itself through social cooperation,*
> *economic relations and business activities can either foster or*
> *obstruct human life and well-being. Against the widespread*
> *objectification of human subjects into human resources, against the*

common instrumentalization of human beings into human capital and a mere means for profit, we uphold humanity as the ultimate end and principle of all economic activity.

Lawrence and Pirson (2015) offered a useful perspective on humanistic leadership built on a "Renewed Darwinian Model" of human drives (Lawrence & Nohria, 2002). Darwinism is often misrepresented as a model of domination where only the strong persist in the survival of the fittest; Darwinism more accurately is about the survival of the *fitting* — those organisms and traits most adaptive to their environment are naturally selected to continue (Clark, 1984). Pirson and Lawrence (2010) make the argument that economism holds only two human behavioral drives as primary: the drive to acquire (dA), that is, the drive to obtain what is needed to survive and have progeny — food, water, shelter, mates — and the drive to defend (dD) what we have acquired. A humanistic view puts forward two further drives as primary: the drive to bond (dB) — to form lasting, mutually caring relationships with other human beings — and the drive to comprehend (dC) — the need to make sense of the world around us and its many relations to ourselves. In economism, dB and dC are considered to be secondary drives, hierarchically in service of the drives to acquire and defend. Humanism takes these two drives as independent and primary, just as important to human dignity and well-being as the first two, a perspective supported by recent neuroscience research (Lawrence & Pirson, 2015). Humanistic leadership attends to all four drives, supporting human flourishing and engendering a life-conducive economy. This is the foundation for bringing out our diverse humanity to ensure a sustainable future.

We now briefly describe the case of Sustainable Waterloo Region, drawn from one of our current research projects on multi-sector collaboration. The success of the organization to date cannot be adequately explained under two-drive economism — clearly, the latter two drives have played the larger role in the organization's progress. Observing such real-world success stories can help us draft narratives to propel movement to a humanistic economy, as suggested by Dierksmeier (2011): "Instead of deducing unrealistic theories from unsupported assumptions about a hypothetical *homo oeconomicus*, economics should rather observe the real, socially and culturally embedded, and morally oriented human being" (p. 24).

ILLUSTRATIVE CASE: SUSTAINABLE WATERLOO REGION

Sustainable Waterloo Region (SWR) is an environmental, social enterprise operating in Ontario, Canada, about an hour's drive west of Toronto. Waterloo Region is a tri-city area that has a population of approximately a half-million people, and the Waterloo—Toronto corridor is marketed as "Silicon Valley North." There is an entrepreneurial culture in the region, established on twin foundations of the early settlers' Mennonite heritage, with its communitarian ethos, and the international success of its technology sector: The modern smartphone was invented and commercialized from Waterloo in the 1990s through Research in Motion's (RIM) *Blackberry*. While RIM was eventually eclipsed by Apple, Samsung, and others in the smartphone market, it helped to inspire a start-up culture in the region that has birthed and grown hundreds of other companies along with a supporting innovation ecosystem. In 2009, SWR was founded by two environmentally conscious business school graduates, Mike Morrice and Chris DePaul, along with a small army of friends and volunteers, as a voluntary carbon emissions reduction program for local organizations. Mike and Chris had worked at some of the local offices of major technology companies like RIM and Microsoft and saw great potential for improvements in emissions reductions. Because there was an absence of meaningful carbon regulation at all levels of government in Canada, they decided to try to build a collaborative non-profit organization that would work with business and other partners in an experiment in self-governance for positive change. SDG 13 calls for "urgent action" toward addressing climate change, and it was that sense of urgency that Mike and Chris were feeling, but not seeing in action on the ground. SWR was launched with one program, *The Regional Carbon Initiative* (RCI). The RCI was a reduction pledge framework designed in collaboration with representatives from prospective local organizations, with Gold, Silver, and Bronze categories depending on the depth and timeline of reduction commitments. To help member organizations make good on their commitments, SWR began convening learning and networking forums, some on topics that were generally educational around environmental issues, and others more specific to the technical aspects of carbon accounting and mitigation. Within a couple of years, SWR was holding about eight such forums each year, and hosting 400 people at an annual Evening of Recognition to celebrate successes, distribute awards, and build positive momentum for further work.

In 2014, Mike transitioned out of SWR to scale out the original RCI program to eight other Ontario cities as *Sustainability CoLab*, and Tova Davidson was hired as Executive Director. Tova has led the growth of SWR in breadth and reach: what started as a single carbon mitigation program with three participating organizations in 2009 has grown to a network of over 70 regional organizations engaged in a suite of multi-sector collaborative programs involving local business, government, academic, and other civil society partners. Members pay an annual fee to participate, based on company size, to cover the operating costs of SWR, with a supplement from government programs and foundations. The work of SWR directly addresses elements of SDGs 9, 13, and 16: fostering collaborative innovation and building more accountable institutions, all pointed toward urgent climate action.

The RCI was replaced in 2016 by the *Regional Sustainability Initiative* (RSI), expanding to include water use and waste diversion alongside carbon mitigation as areas where members could make voluntary reduction pledges. SWR also manages *TravelWise*, the regional government's transportation demand management program, organizing transit options, carpooling, and promoting biking and bike lane infrastructure. *ChargeWR* is a program to convene multi-sector players to advance the region's electric vehicle infrastructure and promote the adoption of electric vehicles. Through an initiative called *ClimateActionWR*, SWR persuaded the three local city councils to set Canada's first regional carbon reduction target and is facilitating plans to help achieve it. Most recently, SWR led the development of *Evolv1*, a 120,000 square foot, net-positive energy, multi-tenant office building intended to serve as a demonstration site for building technology, a lever to influence local building code policy, and an incubator space for clean technology start-ups. SWR brought together the builder, the site on the University of Waterloo campus, and the anchor tenant; it is leading the fundraising for the incubator space and will manage the learning commons in the building. The Federation of Canadian Municipalities is supporting the project financially and is using it as a model for other cities looking to shift building practice and policy. Plans for *Evolv2* are already underway.

All of this work is powered by a small, dedicated SWR staff of eight, and a volunteer contingent of about 10 times that — a level of engagement that other volunteer-driven non-profits in the region have called astonishing. Many of the volunteers have other full-time jobs and bring considerable skill and experience to SWR. Volunteers we spoke with attributed such high commitment to three main factors: the purpose and mission of care for the environment is important to them, and not something they necessarily get from their day jobs; they are given meaningful, impactful work to do; and they are treated as full human beings by Tova and her staff. These volunteers are valued for their contribution, respected as peers, and celebrated as critical to the operation, as reported by several of our interview participants.

LEADERSHIP AND THE FOUR DRIVES AT SWR

Can a two-drive (to acquire, to defend) economistic perspective adequately explain the growth and success of SWR? Certainly, each of their programs, and the organization as a whole, must maintain financial viability. Their pitch to member organizations is also grounded in the economic business case for making commitments, which ranges from tangible energy cost-savings to less-tangible value-adds like reputational gain and attractiveness to prospective talent when hiring. However, in our interviews with SWR staff and many of their stakeholders in the region, we heard a great deal about the value of being part of a local learning network. We heard about the empowering feeling of being part of a solution and not just part of the problem on issues like climate change and the transition to a more sustainable world. We also heard about the importance of connecting with other like-minded people in the region, and the good feeling that this engenders. Bringing out our diverse humanity for a sustainable future depends entirely on valuing and including the real contribution of committed people.

These motivators were put forth as primary, and the economic component was merely a condition that had to be met, given the practical constraints of doing business. They were not described by our participants as secondary drives in service of making money. One respondent referenced "something I read in a management book: Profit to a business is like oxygen to a person—you need it to live, but it's not *why* you live" (Peter Drucker often gets credited for a version of this quotation). The drive to bond (dB) was met through participation in the network, by meeting regularly with like-minded people and feeling as though they were accomplishing something important together, and by supporting each other through caring practices and policies. The drive to comprehend (dC) is made manifest in the connections people in the region are drawing between their work and global issues like climate change. Interestingly, there is not a much imminent threat to Waterloo Region from climate change – it is a long way from coastal waters, and extreme weather events are rare in the area. The concern and the action come less from a drive to acquire and defend personal property, and more from the fact that people comprehend themselves as global citizens, and feel bonded to others who are in worse situations. A key function of SWR has been to catalyze and give form to the active and the latent environmental consciousness in the region. Many people clearly want to do the right thing, though often they don't know what action to take, and SWR has provided leadership and a direction for these humanistic impulsions. Shortsighted *homo oeconomicus* would not behave like the people in the SWR network. There is much more going on.

BONDING AND COMPREHENDING IN OTHER LEADERSHIP THEORIES: CARING AND TRANSFORMING LEADERSHIP

Lawrence and Pirson (2015) emphasize the independent importance of the latter two drives, the drive to bond and the drive to comprehend. These are critical to bringing forth our diverse humanity, so it is worth expanding on these two to underscore their importance to leadership for sustainability. Other fields of leadership study, each with a similarly humanistic ethos, have taken these ideas as their central focus. Notions of an ethic of care (Eisler, 2007; Gilligan, 1982; Noddings, 1984) arose out of feminist theory to challenge the predominant ethics of justice and efficiency, both of which emphasize individuality and rationality, but disregard the kind of "growth-in-connection" (Fletcher, 2012, p. 87) that we see in the SWR story. While humanism takes reason and a focus on individual dignity as foundational, it also admits context and emotion as important to defining a person's sense of worth. A caring perspective brings into high relief our fundamental human orientation toward others and the larger society as critical to our self-construction in those relationships. We develop as relational beings through our caring relations with others (Nicholson & Kurucz, 2017). Noddings (2002) distinguishes between *caring for* and *caring about*. Caring for

pertains to caring practices in real human encounters that are present, immediate, and felt; caring about is more general and abstract – caring about a
cause or principle, such as animal welfare, social justice, or environmental
issues. We see both at play in the SWR story, and both are attended to
deliberately.

Volunteers and staff are driven by their *caring about* the ecological environment, and they are humanly engaged by the *caring for* practices enacted
by Tova and her team. Some study participants we spoke to highlighted this
as a strength of the organization. They compared it to other cause-driven
non-profits they had worked for that had unsustainably "burned out their
people in pursuit of the cause". Ciulla (2009) defines care in leadership as
"attention to what is going on in the world and emotional concern about the
well-being of others" (p. 3). That is clearly the ethos at SWR, and it has
allowed the organization to compound its reach and impact. The primary
drive to bond (dB) is played out through leadership in *caring for* practices in
relations with others.

Transforming leadership, defined by James MacGregor Burns (1978), is
effectively aimed at describing the leader's role in helping others meet the
drive to comprehend (dC) – to position our sense of self and our actions in
a moral, social context. Interacting with others inherently raises ethical questions of what is good and right, though not all leadership theories adequately
address those questions. Lawrence and Pirson (2015) assert that humanistic
leadership is moral leadership (i.e., ethical questions are primary and are
judged on humanistic values); misguided leadership is amoral leadership
(ethics are neither consciously considered nor deliberated); and evil leadership is immoral leadership (where anti-humanistic practices are enacted).
Burns' notion of transforming leadership is inherently moral, and so for him
the assertion that a ruthless dictator could be called a transforming leader is
nonsense: "Transforming leadership ultimately becomes *moral* in that it
raises the level of human conduct and ethical aspiration of both leader and
led, and thus has a transforming effect on both" (1978, p. 20). It is also
inherently social, in that leadership performance is judged on whether societal conditions are improved for all people. Burns casts leadership as a relational process, invoked to bring about positive change rooted in humanistic
values, and he holds that criteria as the ultimate judge of a leader's performance. Leaders should be judged, according to Burns, on:

> *[...] values of honor and integrity — by the extent to which they advanced or thwarted fundamental standards of good conduct in humankind. They would have to be judged by the end-values of equality and justice. Finally, in a context of free communication and open criticism and evaluation, they would be judged in the balance sheet of history by their impact on the well-being of the persons whose lives they touched. (1978, p. 426)*

In meeting the drive to comprehend (dC), a transforming leader advances a humanistic ethos by helping people to self-construct their identity and the meaning of their work in relation to the good it is creating for broader society. *Transforming* is a verb. It denotes process: a process of learning and meaning creation that is relationally embedded, socially inclusive, and societally focused. Transforming leaders engage others in learning how to make the world better.

THE ROLE OF SOCIAL ENTERPRISE IN SUSTAINABILITY TRANSFORMATION: ACTIVATING AND LEGITIMATING ALL FOUR HUMAN DRIVES

Humanistic leadership means treating all four drives as primary, yet most of our business models and systems are built on assumptions of two-drive economism — the drive to acquire (dA) and the drive to defend (dD). The drive to bond (dB) and the drive to comprehend (dC) can be met through leadership practice that is informed by ideas of caring leadership and transforming leadership. Caring leaders exhibit *care for* the dignity and worth of every person they encounter, treating their motivations, emotions, physical, and mental wellbeing as inherently valuable, with an objective of preserving the caring relation. These leaders can also work to make the organizational mission and impact something that people *care about*. In a complementary way, transforming leaders help connect people to the societal value of their work, to comprehend their connections to the world and the wellbeing of others.

Social enterprises like SWR are built with that societal purpose, but that does not guarantee success. The facets of humanistic leadership we have observed at SWR, particularly the attention to the drives to bond and to comprehend, have allowed them to have an impact in the region disproportionate to their size. SWR is not only exhibiting humanistic leadership inside the organization but is also modeling it in the community. SWR has led in shifting the nature and content of the region's "sustainability conversations" (Kurucz, Colbert, & Wheeler, 2013): Respondents told us that it is no longer legitimate to contemplate a new public policy, business venture, or building project without demonstrating authentic consideration of social and ecological impacts, and whenever possible engaging the community on those terms.

Respect for SWR is high across the region. They have raised the aspirations of the people and those leading local institutions and created space for those aspirations to flourish. In the early years, SWR saw it as a great success to get a local politician to attend one of their events; at the most recent Evening of Recognition, two of the region's mayors were on stage receiving awards and recognition for their cities' growing sustainability programs. With an unabashed emphasis on all four primary drives, SWR and other such third sector actors can also effectively work to awaken and activate those drives within people and make them legitimate within the public discourse. This kind of local leadership is essential to realizing the United Nations Sustainable Development Goals and their aim of transforming our world.

The past, present, and future work of SWR contributes directly toward addressing several of the UN SDGs, in particular, SDG 9 (building a resilient infrastructure and fostering innovation), SDG 13 (combatting climate change), and SD 16 (building inclusive societies and accountable institutions). Their explicit focus is on acting as an "innovation intermediary" (Howells, 2006): building effective multi-sector partnerships, and fostering innovation toward mutual accountability and action. They have found that the most effective way to do this is to bring forth the diverse humanity in people through practicing humanistic leadership − caring, including, and connecting people toward building a more sustainable future.

Leadership for sustainable transformation is humanistic, pluralistic, contextual, and inclusive. It is aimed at building dignity for people and stewardship for our planet. Humanistic leadership can serve to make these legitimate things to talk about, legitimate themes to integrate into the discourse that shapes our civic institutions and governance policies. If the future is not what it used to be, if the coming challenges are sure to be increasing in complexity and severity, then a humanistic moral compass will be our most indispensable guide.

REFERENCES

Burns, J. M. (1978). *Leadership*. New York, NY: Harper and Row.

Burns, J. M. (2003). *Transforming Leadership*. New York, NY: Atlantic Monthly Press.

Cherry, M. (2009). The humanist tradition. In H. Spitzeck, M. Pirson, W. Amann, S. Khan, & E. Von Kimakowitz (Eds.), *Humanism in Business* (pp. 26–51). Cambridge: Cambridge University Press.

Ciulla, J. (2009). Leadership and the ethics of care. *Journal of Business Ethics*, *88*, 3–4.

Clark, R. W. (1984). *The survival of Charles Darwin: A biography of a man and an idea*. New York, NY: Random House.

Dierksmeier, K. (2011). Reorienting management education: From homo oeconomicus to human dignity. In W. Amann, M. Pirson, K. Dierksmeier, E. Von Kimakowitz, & H. Spitzeck (Eds.), *Business Schools Under Fire: Humanistic Management Education as a Way Forward* (pp. 3–18). Hampshire: Palgrave Macmillan.

Dierksmeier, K. (2016). What is 'humanistic' about humanistic management? *Humanistic Management Journal*, *1*, 9–32.

Eisler, R. T. (2007). *The real wealth of nations: Creating a caring economics*. San Fransisco, CA: Berrett-Koehler Publishers.

Fletcher, J. K. (2012). The relational practice of leadership. In M. Uhl-Bien & S. M. Ospina (Eds.), *Advancing relational leadership: A dialogue among perspectives* (pp. 83–106). Charlotte, NC: Information Age Publishing.

Ghoshal, S. (2005). Bad management theories are destroying good management practices. *Academy of Management Learning and Education*, *4*(1), 75–91.

Gilligan, C. (1982). *In a different voice*. Cambridge, MA: Harvard University Press.

Held, V. (2006). *The ethics of care*. New York, NY: Oxford University Press.

Howells, J. (2006). Intermediation and the role of intermediaries in innovation. *Research Policy, 35*, 715–728.

Humanistic Management Network. (2005). *The Humanistic Management Manifesto*. Retrieved from http://humanetwork.org. Accessed on September 27, 2017.

Kurucz, E., Colbert, B., Lüdeke-Freund, F., Upward, A., & Willard, B. (2017). Relational leadership for strategic sustainability: practices and capabilities to advance the design and assessment of sustainable business models. *Journal of Cleaner Production, 140*, 189–204.

Kurucz, E., Colbert, B., & Wheeler, D. (2013). *Reconstructing value: Leadership skills for a sustainable world*. Toronto: University of Toronto Press.

Lawrence, P., & Nohria, N. (2002). *Driven: How human nature shapes our choices*. San Francisco, CA: Jossey-Bass.

Lawrence, P. R., & Pirson, M. (2015). Economistic and humanistic narratives of leadership in the age of globality: Toward a renewed Darwinian theory of leadership. *Journal of Business Ethics, 128*(2), 383–394.

Mason, P. (2015). *Postcapitalism: A Guide to our future*. London: Penguin Random House.

Melé, D. (2016). Understanding humanistic management. *Humanistic Management Journal, 1*, 33–55.

Nicholson, J., & Kurucz, E. (2017). Relational leadership for sustainability: Building an ethical framework from the moral theory of 'ethics of care'. *Journal of Business Ethics*. Retrieved from https://link.springer.com/article/10.1007/s10551-017-3593-4

Nida-Rümelin, J. (2009). Philosophical grounds of humanism in economics. In H. Spitzeck, M. Pirson, W. Amann, S. Khan, & E. Von Kimakowitz (Eds.), *Humanism in Business* (pp. 15–25). Cambridge: Cambridge University Press.

Noddings, N. (1984). *Caring: A feminine approach to ethics and moral education.* London: University of California Press.

Noddings, N. (2002). *Educating moral people: A caring alternative to character education.* New York, NY: Teachers College Press.

Pirson, M. (2009). Social entrepreneurship: A blueprint for humane organizations? In H. Spitzeck, M. Pirson, W. Amann, S. Khan, & E. Von Kimakowitz (Eds.), *Humanism in Business* (pp. 248–259). Cambridge: Cambridge University Press.

Pirson, M. (2017). Editorial: Welcome to the Humanistic Management Journal. *Humanistic Management Journal, 1*(1), 1–7.

Pirson, M. A., & Lawrence, P. R. (2010). Humanism in business – Towards a paradigm shift? *Journal of Business Ethics, 93*(4), 553–565.

Rorty, R. (1980). Pragmatism, relativism, and irrationalism. *Proceedings and Addresses of the American Philosophical Association. 53*(6), 719–738.

Stiglitz, J., Sen, A., & Fitoussi, J. P. (2010). *Mismeasuring our lves: Why GDP doesn't add up.* New York, NY: New Press.

Tegmark, M. (2017). *Life 3.0: Being human in the age of artificial intelligence.* New York, NY: Alfred A. Knopf.

Valéry, P. (1948). *Reflections on the world today.* F. Scarfe (trans), New York, NY: Pantheon.

Waddock, S. (2016). Developing humanistic leadership education. *Humanistic Management Journal, 1,* 57–73.

3

COLLECTIVE IMPACT THROUGH REGENERATIVE DEVELOPMENT: LESSONS FROM GREEN AND HEALTHY HOME REPAIR

Elizabeth A. Walsh

Scholars in planning and leadership increasingly recognize that collaborative efforts of diverse stakeholders are required to meet the fundamental challenge of bringing out the best of our diverse humanity to collectively ensure a sustainable future. Often, these scholars have emphasized the importance of well-designed and facilitated public processes in supporting effective cross-sectoral change, implying that if planners get the process right, the desired outcomes will emerge (Christian Rammel, 2007; Healey, 2007; Innes, & Booher, 1999, 1999, 2010; C. O. Scharmer, 2009; Snowden & Boone, 2007).

In recent years, a theory of "Collective Impact" ("CI," to distinguish the theory from common parlance) introduced by John Kania and Mark Kramer in 2009 has become increasingly referenced as a successful process model to support collaborative change. Their 2011 article "Collective Impact" in *Stanford Social Innovation Review* has been cited over 1000 times.[1] In it, Kania and Kramer assert that diverse stakeholders can collaboratively achieve desired outcomes in the face of complex problems by establishing five necessary conditions in a facilitated stakeholder process.

This chapter challenges theories that a good participatory process design, a neutral facilitator, and the five conditions of CI are necessary or sufficient conditions for collective impact toward sustainable development goals (SDGs). Drawing on a participatory action research case study of a diverse coalition of actors who succeeded in advancing three SDGs through the integration of their green and healthy home repair efforts in Austin, Texas, this chapter asserts that collective impact toward SDGs is best achieved through a process of *regenerative development*. In contrast to sustainable development which aims to sustain economic growth by minimizing its social and ecological harm, regenerative development is defined as a place-based process of cultivating the ability in people, communities, and other living systems to renew, evolve, and thrive (Hes & Plessis, 2014; Plaut, Dunbar, Wackerman, & Hodgin, 2012). Although process design and facilitation techniques are important, the case study suggests that regenerative ways of *being* are just as important as regenerative ways of *thinking* and *doing* in the practice of regenerative development. The chapter identifies five leadership practices that support diverse actors in evolving their leadership for collective impact through regenerative ways of being, thinking, and doing.

The findings from the case study offer propositions for regenerative design and development employed by Austin Housing Repair Coalition (AHRC) members that can be applied by other practitioners working toward collaborative solutions to enhance environmental justice in the face of complex challenges in coupled social–ecological systems. Lessons learned are particularly relevant to those who are practicing CI or other forms of collaborative, adaptive, and co-management of complex systems. The case study also highlights the value of home repair programs as an intervention to advance three SDGs:

- Goal 3: Ensure healthy lives and promote well-being for all at all ages;

- Goal 11: Make cities and human settlements inclusive, safe, resilient, and sustainable; and

- Goal 13: Take urgent action to combat climate change and its impacts.

AHRC: A STORY OF EVOLVING LEADERSHIP FOR COLLECTIVE WELL-BEING

The story of the AHRC reveals how a diverse group of individuals evolved from an atomistic assembly of actors working in isolation to a high-performing ecosystem of leaders working creatively and collaboratively to ensure that people of all ages could enjoy healthy lives in healthy homes. Operating as an ecosystem, the AHRC succeeded in enhancing the well-being of low-income homeowners throughout the city by providing integrated green and healthy home repair services. Their story demonstrates the potential of regenerative ways of being, thinking, and acting to advance collective social and ecological well-being. This section presents a summary of the story based on an in-depth participatory action research case study conducted between 2010 and 2015 (Walsh, 2015).

The narrative of the AHRC begins in 2005 when grassroots community organizers in Austin, Texas with a predisposition for systems-thinking recognized three related problems:

(1) There were many residents living in homes in desperate need of health, safety, and energy efficiency improvements in central urban neighborhoods – needs that were exacerbated by increasing pressure from gentrification as well as intensified heat and flash floods from climate change (implicating SDGs 3, 11, and 13).

(2) There were many different governmental and nonprofit programs providing various types of home repair and services to these populations, but no single organization could oversee a complete process of home repair, let alone reach all the homes in need of support.

(3) Not only was the level of service by the providers unable to reach the demand, but also these organizations sometimes "undid" one another's work.

Further complicating these organizational challenges, governmental funding for home repair was separated into many funding streams (e.g., weatherization, architectural barrier removal, lead abatement, emergency home repair, and so on), each with its own application process. Even so, when confronted with these challenges, these community organizers saw the potential for integrated, coordinated service delivery across the diverse organizations.

Two organizers, Ruby Roa and Johnny Limon, imagined that if these diverse actors could work together, they could: (1) expand resources available for home repair and (2) invest resources more effectively through an integrated approach to green and healthy home repair. In doing so, they could help all their city's most vulnerable homeowners to save money on utility bills and medical costs. This was particularly important in Austin, a fast-growing city facing rising costs of living as well as rising temperatures and flood risks associated with climate change.

Roa and Limon soon found that bringing these diverse, *independent, isolated actors* together was easier said than done. Time and money were in short supply and existing home repair organizations struggled to sustain themselves. Yet, in time, this group of actors developed into a *strong negotiating network* that succeeded in securing $5 million in municipal bond funding for a public home repair program in 2009 to address gentrification (the first program to achieve such funding in the nation).

As trust, reciprocity, and an expanded awareness of potential assets and allies in the city grew, by 2010, they came to discover shared values and a vision of coordinated service delivery that would allow them to achieve more as a collective than they ever could when acting as independent actors. In time, united in their diversity by this vision, they evolved together into a *high performing, collaborative, innovative, and adaptive ecosystem* of actors committed to doing their part in service of collective efforts to provide integrated green and healthy home repair. As shown in **Figure 1**, 15 different programs (each with a range of actors including program leaders, contractors, volunteers, and trainees) operating in the non-profit, public, and private sectors came together so that they could contribute the best of their diverse capabilities to advance a sustainable future collectively (e.g., SDGs 3, 11, and 13). The group resisted establishing formal officers because the non-hierarchical, self-organizing governance form worked well for them. Even when they adopted officers and the elected chair was the head of one of the core home repair organizations, the underlying organizational culture of shared governance persisted. Their approach to shared governance also included willingness to share data and create structures for feedback through performance evaluation. Internally, they used evaluation to adapt their approaches to better achieve desired outcomes. Externally, these evaluations demonstrated the AHRC's collective impact and accountability.

As a high-performing learning network operating with collective awareness, the AHRC achieved a high level of adaptive capacity that empowered its members to direct flows of resources where they were needed most and track performance outcome measures. Between 2010 and 2012, AHRC members leveraged $5 million of bond funding with over $2 million in

Fig. 1. Key Members and Niches in the Austin Housing Repair Coalition Ecosystem.

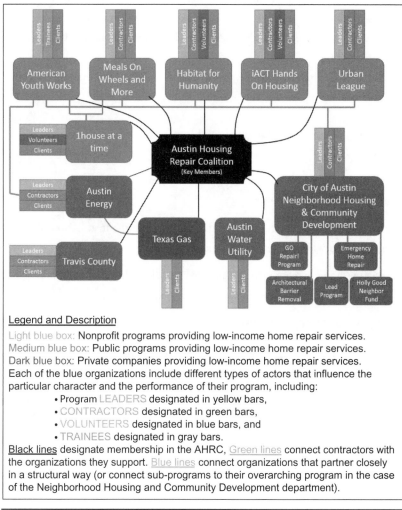

Legend and Description
Light blue box: Nonprofit programs providing low-income home repair services.
Medium blue box: Public programs providing low-income home repair services.
Dark blue box: Private companies providing low-income home repair services.
Each of the blue organizations include different types of actors that influence the particular character and the performance of their program, including:
• Program LEADERS designated in yellow bars,
• CONTRACTORS designated in green bars,
• VOLUNTEERS designated in blue bars, and
• TRAINEES designated in gray bars.
Black lines designate membership in the AHRC, Green lines connect contractors with the organizations they support. Blue lines connect organizations that partner closely in a structural way (or connect sub-programs to their overarching program in the case of the Neighborhood Housing and Community Development department).

additional funding sources, volunteer resources, and in-kind donations. These leveraged resources allowed the AHRC to more holistically repair 320 homes of Austin's most vulnerable, low-income homeowners. In that period, 68% of AHRC home repair clients were senior citizens, and almost 50% were people with disabilities. All households earned less than 80% of median family income (MFI), and over half earned below 30% of median family income.[2] The average home repair client lived alone on a fixed income of approximately $600–$1,200 per month, making it very difficult to invest in home repair and pay rising energy bills, especially in light of increasingly hot summers. Moreover, most had lived in their homes for several decades in neighborhoods where the cost of living was rapidly rising due to gentrification.

The AHRC's integrated green and healthy home repairs directly improved clients' lives and advanced SDGs 3 and 11 by:

- enabling low-income individuals and families to remain in the homes they love;

- creating healthier, safer home environments, and the potential for multigenerational benefits;

- lowering utility costs through weatherization and the installation of energy- and water-efficient appliances;

- assisting homeowners facing regulatory hurdles related to outstanding permits and work done without permits; and

- minimizing construction disruption through coordinated service delivery.

Additionally, the adaptive capacity of the AHRC as an ecosystem of home repair providers helped it combat climate change and its impacts (SDG 13). For Austin, climate change implies an increased risk of floods and fires as well as heat waves. In 2013, when devastating floods caused exceptional damage to the homes of 750 low-income families in Austin's Dove Springs neighborhood, AHRC leaders quickly responded, working to coordinate caseworkers from various agencies to assess urgent repairs, needs for special accommodations, and insurance limits, and then to assign priorities and match residents with different groups for relief in the form of home repair services, goods, and logistics (Messer, 2014).

Furthermore, as the threat of heat waves increases along with price of energy, the importance of energy-efficient home cooling also increases as a climate adaptation strategy (SDG13). Austin is known for its city-led green building program, and the city's investments in integrated green and healthy home repair for low-income households have supported workforce development. For instance, one of the AHRC home repair providers, American

YouthWorks, trains disadvantaged youth in the green building trades through its Casa Verde Builders program.

UNDERSTANDING AHRC'S SUCCESSES

Given this success story, how did the AHRC bring out the best of its diverse members and clients to cocreate a more just and flourishing future? What propositions about practices, processes, and principles does this case offer to those committed to evolving leadership for a sustainable future and collective well-being? The summary of AHRC's story above not only demonstrates a practical application of putting SDGs 3, 11, and 13 into practice, it also reveals the importance of regenerative ways of thinking, doing, and being to achieve collective impacts towards those goals.

Cultivating Regenerative Modes of Thought and Action

Early on, from their vantage point as community organizers with the capacity for systems-thinking, Roa and Limon were able to see the home repair system as a whole, including patterns of resources flowing between different agencies and actors. They were also attuned to the larger patterns in Austin's political landscape and the potential to include home repair as part of the historical bond issue for affordable housing. This knowledge emerged through their relationships with diverse stakeholders. These relationships of trust also enabled them to help other stakeholders come to see themselves as part of a larger whole and identify new opportunities for action to advance shared goals. When I joined the AHRC as a doctoral student in community and regional planning, my research on holistic approaches to green and healthy home repair furthered the coalition's capacity to identify vital niches and leverage points through which we could generate multiple community benefits. As a regenerative designer, I drew on practical tools, heuristics, and practices to support systems-thinking and build adaptive capacity, including the LENSES[3] framework of the Center for Living Environments and Regeneration (CLEAR) and literature on adaptive co-management, collaborative rationality, and CI. As important as these models for thought and action are, the case study revealed that they, alone, are insufficient to generate collective desired impacts.

Cultivating Regenerative Social Fields and Ways of Being

The AHRC story revealed that its impressive collective impact was less attributable to adherence to best practices or "structure-specific steps" (Kania & Kramer, 2013) than to the regenerative ways of being that evolved, shaping the leadership culture of the high-performing ecosystem. As shown in Figure 2, when the AHRC was first convened by community organizers, its leadership culture was that of an atomistic assembly, where actors mostly focused their attention on sustaining their organizations with little awareness of other actors. In time, the leadership culture evolved into a negotiating network with increasing political power, and ultimately a high-performing collaborative ecosystem achieving desired collective impacts to advance multiple SDGs.

Ultimately, operating as a collaborative ecosystem, individuals increasingly took inspiration from each other, tried new things, and learned together from their own sense of internal motivation, a higher sense of purpose, and sense of trust and belonging with others. Improved performance emerged through the interactions of all of such inspired leaders. These actors

Fig. 2. AHRC: Evolution of a Resilient, Collaborative Ecosystem.

Phase 1: Atomistic Assembly (2005–2007)
Community advocates frame problem & convene key stakeholders

Phase 2: Negotiating Network (2007–2009)
Emerging network of competitors negotiate and collaborate to leverage & expand resources for low-income home repair
- Austin Housing Repair Coalition officially formed (2008)
- Housing Bond Funding Secured (2009)

Phase 3: Collaborative Ecosystem (2010 –)
Collaborative partners engage in mutually supportive innovation ecosystem
- Organize around vision of whole-home approach to repair
- Members see selves in whole & pursue collective goals
- Mutually supportive relationships & referral network
- Reform of bureaucratic program guidelines
- Flexible response to emergent opportunities as well as crisis
- Develop channels for feedback (e.g., performance evaluation)

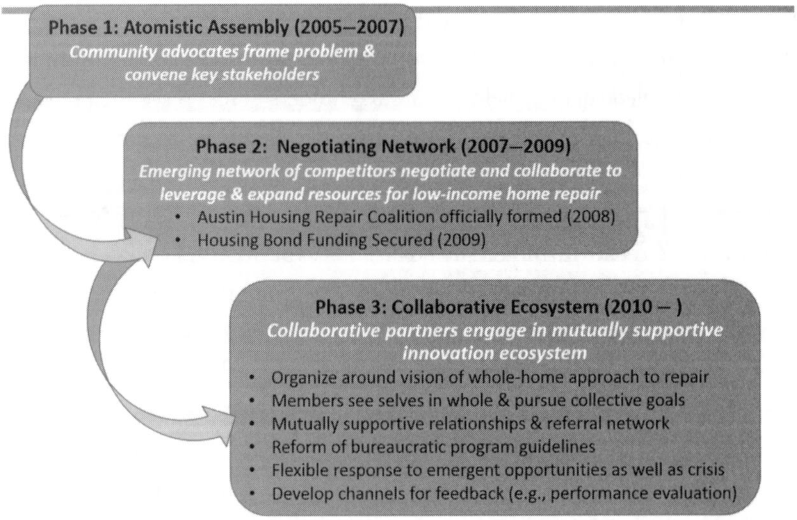

afforded one another a supportive environment in which to stretch or take a leap of faith.

The collective impact model advanced by Kania and Kramer (2011, 2013) does not explain this success. The AHRC achieved collective impact, but it did so *without* first establishing each of the five pre-conditions named by Kania and Kramer (2011, 2013): a common agenda, shared measurement, mutually reinforcing activities, continuous communication, and backbone support. Kania and Kramer (2013) argue that if these conditions are in place, collectively desired outcomes will "emerge." The case of the AHRC highlights two related problems with this model.

First, although many of the conditions are analogous to the evolution of AHRC's collective impact, they are not exactly the same. Kania and Kramer's definition of "backbone support" specifically requires "a separate organization with staff and a specific set of skills to serve as the backbone for the entire initiative and coordinate participating organizations and agencies" (2013, p. 1). The AHRC did not have a separate, neutral organization to coordinate its members. Instead, coordination was achieved through a collective, horizontal leadership approach characterized by a high level of trust and integrity among members. Even when the AHRC eventually chose to elect a board of officers, this neither created a hierarchical organization in the group nor a neutral backbone organization. Although the chair of the AHRC was the head of one of the major home repair organizations, other organizations trusted him and he honored their trust. Therefore, although an effective coordination function may be needed, it does not necessarily need to be a "backbone organization."

Second, in presenting these elements as *pre-conditions* of collective impact and emergence, Kania and Kramer fail to recognize that these elements may *themselves* be emergent outcomes. In the case of the AHRC, each of these elements emerged as individuals engaged together with a common sense of calling and increasing trust in one another. By presenting the five elements they observed as a replicable, top-down, reductive checklist for a collaborative process, they miss the underlying *regenerative ways of being* that contributed to the AHRC's collective impact.

Although Kania and Kramer's theory does not explain AHRC's collective impact, theories of awareness-based processes of collaborative social change do shed light on the AHRC's evolution into a high-performing ecosystem. As Otto Scharmer and colleagues have suggested through *Theory U*, when actors engage with one another in increasingly attuned, mutually supportive ways, they are more likely to achieve the outcomes their hearts' desire (C. O. Scharmer, 2009; O. Scharmer & Kaufer, 2013, 2015). AHRC's evolutionary dynamics progress into what Scharmer calls "deepening social fields of emergence," which I refer to as deepening *regenerative social fields.*

Scharmer identifies four such social fields associated with progressively more open and engaging qualities of awareness and intention:

(1) In Field 1, participants operate with "habitual" awareness, usually in their own silos;

(2) In Field 2, participants operate with "ego-system" awareness, striving to ensure their own survival in competition with one another;

(3) In Field 3, participants operate with "stakeholder" awareness, recognizing opportunities to negotiate with would-be competitors to achieve common goals;

(4) In Field 4, participants operate with "ecosystem" awareness, attending to their contribution within a larger co-creative ecosystem with aligned purpose.

When operating from Field 4 awareness, participants *engage with an open mind, heart, and will* and often experience a high level of creative energy. Theory U suggests that when a collective of actors evolve from Field 1 to Field 4 awareness, collectively desired outcomes emerge from the interactions of these self-organizing actors with aligned purpose, distinct roles, and personal motivation. This appeared to be the case with the AHRC. Through mutually supportive actions and aligned intentions to serve a greater whole, AHRC members were able to achieve more as a collective than they ever could act as independent actors. They were supported by the *regenerative social fields*, and they cocreated as they evolved into a high-performing collaborative ecosystem.

FIVE LEADERSHIP PRACTICES FOR REGENERATIVE DEVELOPMENT

Although there are no blueprints or recipes for constructing invisible, regenerative social fields and no outside designer or single leader can design and implement them, every actor in a social system has the capability to intentionally shape the evolution of these social structures to support collective well-being. This central premise of "theory U" is supported through observations from the AHRC study, through which many different actors contributed to a leadership culture conducive to collective impact. The case study suggests that there are principles and practices that support such regenerative development. As they are practiced and embodied by members of a group, the group may deepen into regenerative social fields. This section highlights such leadership practices derived from the cases.

Practice 1: Cultivating Intention, Attunement, and Integrity

The story of the AHRC suggests that when individuals engage consistently with transparent intentions, attunement to others, and integrity with regard to commitments given, they are likely to inspire the same in others and build the power of the social learning communities of which they are part.

This practice was particularly demonstrated by Ruby Roa and Charles Cloutman who played important roles as convening leaders of the AHRC. The clarity of Roa and Cloutman's intentions and enlightened self-interests[4] coupled with the consistency of their actions served to enhance the leadership capacity of the greater network. They kept their word. Furthermore, when Cloutman broke his word (or circumstances led to his word being broken), he addressed it with the group, took responsibility, and allowed the conflict to be resolved through open communication. Roa and Cloutman let their intentional, enlivened action speak in ways that inspired trust and leadership in others. As more and more people listened empathetically to others, freely expressed their intentions, and followed through with their commitments, the relational power of the network continued to grow. Members were able to learn from one another and elevate their collective performance.

Practice 2: Leveraging Power of Privileged Positions through Powerful Conversation

Because all institutions and social structures are made up of individual human beings, movement leaders can engage in powerful conversations to help individuals in positions of influence step beyond their assumed limitations into levels of performance they had not previously seen as possible.

Individuals may not be in a position to recognize their own agency, their deeper sense of purpose and possibility, or their potential role to play in a greater whole. Shifts can happen when a leader who has practiced overcoming such limits engages with them empathetically yet directly and helps them see an alternative pathway forward. Such powerful conversations require:

(1) working knowledge of the mechanisms and structures of power and positions of influence;

(2) the emotional intelligence that allows one to relate empathetically to individuals operating within those systems; and

(3) the courage to call those individuals out and, just as importantly, to *call them in.*

In the case studies, this capacity is clearly demonstrated by Roa and Cloutman. Their strong relational understanding of people and institutional systems helped them locate agency in systems and pull for accountability and integrity at the individual and system levels. This was not always a comfortable process, but it tended to enhance effectiveness and vitality. During a celebration in which Roa was recognized as Austin's volunteer of the year, individuals from various sectors testified to Roa's powerful requests of them. I have a personal, visceral memory of her putting me on the spot, looking me in the eye, and naming the leadership role she saw that I needed to step into to move the AHRC to its next level. Through strategic and soulful conversation, she helped many people discover the power to do the right thing.

Practice 3: Establishing Holding Spaces for Regenerative Social Fields

The AHRC case reflects the importance of creating an environment conducive to dialogue, deeper social learning, and self-organization. This "environment" becomes a bounded, intimate holding space for authentic, vulnerable, and generative conversation. Practices #1 and #2 enable this space, as does consistent meetings and face-to-face engagement.

In the AHRC, members collectively created a holding space for social learning and self-organization through its monthly face-to-face meetings. Roa and Johnny Limon initially cultivated this space through powerful invitations to diverse stakeholders in one-on-one conversations (e.g., practice #2). These individuals, representing 17 different organizations, came to the monthly meetings imagining that their perspective was valued and that they might join with others to address an important community need. In the course of these meetings, trust among participants grew, with an increasingly rich web of collaborative relationships. The holding space grew increasingly stable as more individuals showed up fully present and in service of common vision. There was no official "head" of the group, or hierarchy, but there were often clearly defined roles.

Importantly, although the AHRC did not have an independent backbone organization that could mediate conflicts among stakeholders, this holding space for self-organization and self-governance fulfilled the essential functions of a backbone organization identified in CI. The group valued its horizontal relations of power and instinctively resisted establishing officers and official memoranda of understanding, before ultimately establishing both to put them in a better position when applying for funding from outside organizations.

Even when the group decided to adopt a more formal structure and Cloutman assumed the role of chair, he set a respectful, focused, and familial tone for the monthly meetings that supported the non-hierarchical holding space. He cultivated an individual relationship with other participants, coming to understand them as both human beings and as professionals operating with particular strengths and agency in the larger home repair ecosystem. By engaging in a manner consistent with more deeply regenerative social fields, Cloutman further inspired others to generate a social field for the AHRC that was gracious enough that actors could ask direct and sometimes challenging questions about potential conflicts of interest among collaborators and other sensitive issues. The monthly circle of coalition members became a holding space that facilitated feedback and cultivation of collective intelligence.

Practice 4: Aligning with Collective Vision and Building Collective Recognition

The AHRC case suggests that the framing of a collective vision and "story of us" that aligns the intentions of individual organizations strengthens the potential for regenerative social fields conducive to CI. A strong collective identity helps individuals recognize their part within the whole, and also helps those on the outside recognize the collective and its parts. Discovery of common ground and common interests is facilitated by holding spaces for social learning in which actors (individual and institutional) feel safe to share their needs and aspirations (practice #3). Discovery of a common frame also depends on the individual(s) who are:

(1) inclined to listen for unity in diversity,

(2) adept in holistic, systems-thinking, and

(3) capable of presenting a vision of the whole in ways that diverse actors can see their place in a bigger picture.

Once collective intentions are stated, and coordinated actions are taken to advance them, recognition of the group's identity as a collective strengthens both internally and externally. Internally, the consistent action builds a sense of solidarity and social capital. Externally, the consistent action builds recognition and political capital in the larger community. This in turn expands possibilities for effective action, further reinforcing growth and self-efficacy of the collective.

For example, the AHRC case revealed the catalyzing potential of a common vision and collective story of success that depended on each member, and that no member could achieve independently. Although the group formed in 2006 with a general purpose of leveraging shared resources to achieve greater collective impact for suffering low-income homeowners, it wasn't until March 2010 that it adopted a clear statement of vision and mission that called for the contributions of all in the network. This alignment process was accelerated when a doctoral student in Community Regional Planning (this author) joined the group, originally to research the health impacts of weatherization in low-income homes in Central Texas. Trained as systems-thinker and facilitative leader, I was well-situated to observe the form and function of an emerging ecosystem focused on expanding access to green and healthy homes. Once the vision crystallized and was formally adopted, the vision statement helped actors who had once interacted out of either competition or in the oblivion of one another develop a heightened sense of collective identity and agency.

Practice 5: Generative Listening

A critical discipline underlying the successful practice of each of the four practices named above is that of "generative listening," defined as listening with an open mind, heart, and will (Hanlon & Rigney, 2011). This kind of engaged listening is different from the neutral listening of an impartial backbone organization or mediator: "open" does not imply "impartial" or "detached." Instead, generative listening is often at once both open and intentional: the listener may be listening from (or *for*) a common commitment or vision. Although such listening is intentional, it is not *attached*. Instead, the quality of openness pertains to the curiosity, compassion, and courage that individuals bring to their listening, as they attempted to advance a common vision while working in a dynamically changing landscape.

For example, I actively practiced generative listening and found that it increased my capacity to engage as a purposeful yet open and flexible facilitative leader of collaborative action inquiry.[5] The practice helped me to revisit consistently my own intentions (and the frames underlying them) as I became more open, attuned, and responsive to collaborators and the dynamic systems of which they were part.

Summary of Individual-level Practices Contributing to Regenerative Development

Together, these five interrelated leadership practices support the evolution of collaborative leadership to achieve collective well-being. They underscore the relationship between the interior condition of individual participants and the exterior dynamics of group interactions. As these individual-level practices and principles were embodied by members of the AHRC, others increasingly adopted them. Regenerative ways of being are contagious and build cocreative energy for collective action. These practices, along with regenerative ways of thinking, also resonate with the overarching theory of "restorative leadership" developed by Seana Lowe Steffen, especially with regard to the importance of "systems thinking, participatory engagement, unwavering commitment, and generosity of spirit" (2012, p. 21).

CONCLUSION

In conclusion, the principles and practices of regenerative design and development can be applied to focus the attention and energy of a collaborative group in ways that bring out the best of our diverse capabilities to collectively support thriving living systems.

Regenerative ways of thinking, doing, and being helped the AHRC achieve greater collective impact toward SDGs than would have been possible by any organization working alone. Through regenerative thinking, they were able to design green and healthy home repair programs as a leverage point to advance inclusive, multigenerational urban environments that support the health and well-being of vulnerable individuals and increase resilience to climate change (SDGs 3, 11, 13).

Additionally, the case emphasizes that cultivation of regenerative social fields enables collective impact. Embracing regenerative development as a developmental, coevolutionary process to support well-being is an important paradigm shift from conventional models of development. The practice of regenerative development helps us recognize the moment by moment choices we have about how we show up in the world. Such awareness influences both our experience of life and our capacity to positively influence our material conditions. The principles and practices of regenerative development support our collective well-being as we work to advance a sustainable future.

NOTES

1. A GoogleScholar search on May 30, 2018 revealed that the article had been cited 1,226 times.

2. In 2012 in the Austin-round Rock Metropolitan Area, below 30% MFI implied a family of four making less than $22,750 in a year.

3. Living Environments in Natural, Social and Economic Systems

4. As discussed in Walsh's dissertation, Roa and Cloutman had a clear sense of vocational calling to the work of providing home repair. They were not driven by a desire to "look good," to prove something, or to survive personally. Their sense of urgency

came from a source that called them to be the best that they could be in service of an endeavor that was much bigger than they could do alone.

5. My generative listening practice was reflected in my practice of note-taking. In addition to recording the "facts" of what was said and had happened for meeting minutes (derived from open-minded listening), I frequently made note of my interpretation of interpersonal dynamics (from open-hearted, empathetic listening), and my intuitions about what might be emerging in the collective will (from open-willed listening).

REFERENCES

Christian Rammel, S. S. (2007). Managing complex adaptive systems – A co-evolutionary perspective on natural resource management. *Ecological Economics*, (1), 9–21. doi:10.1016/j.ecolecon.2006.12.014

Hanlon, D., & Rigney, J. (2011, February). Generative Listening: Subtleties to prepare your inner-self for the art of receiving. Retrieved from http://www.therightmind.com.au/FileUpload/files/DHJR022011-1%20.pdf

Healey, P. (2007). *Urban Complexity and Spatial Strategies: Towards a Relational Planning for Our Times* (1st ed.). New York, NY: Routledge.

Hes, D., & Plessis, C. du. (2014). *Designing for hope: Pathways to regenerative sustainability* (1st ed.). New York, NY: Routledge.

Innes, J. E., & Booher, D. E. (1999). Consensus building and complex adaptive systems: A framework for evaluating collaborative planning. *Journal of the American Planning Association*, 65(4), 412. Retrieved from https://doi.org/Article

Innes, J. E., & Booher, D. E. (2010). *Planning with complexity: An introduction to collaborative rationality for public policy*. Hoboken, NJ: Taylor & Francis.

Kania, J., & Kramer, M. (2011). Collective impact. *Stanford Social Innovation Review*. Retrieved from http://www.ssireview.org/blog/entry/embracing_emergence_how_collective_impact_addresses_complexity

Kania, J., & Kramer, M. (2013). Embracing emergence: How collective impact addresses complexity. *Stanford Social Innovation Review*. Retrieved

from http://www.ssireview.org/blog/entry/embracing_emergence_how_
collective_impact_addresses_complexity

Messer, K. (2014, December 26). Rising from the Halloween flood. *Austin
Chronicle*. Retrieved from http://www.austinchronicle.com/news/2014-12-
26/rising-from-the-halloween-flood/

Plaut, J. M., Dunbar, B., Wackerman, A., & Hodgin, S. (2012).
Regenerative design: the LENSES framework for buildings and communities.
Building Research and Information, 40(1), 112–122. doi:10.1080/
09613218.2012.619685

Scharmer, C. O. (2009). *Theory U: Learning from the Future as It Emerges*.
San Francisco, CA: Berrett-Koehler Publishers, Ebooks Corporation Limited.

Scharmer, O., & Kaufer, K. (2013). *Leading from the emerging future:
From ego-system to eco-system economies* (1 ed.). San Francisco, CA:
Berrett-Koehler Publishers.

Scharmer, O., & Kaufer, K. (2015). Awareness-based action research:
Catching social reality creation in flight. In H. Bradbury (Ed.), *The SAGE
Handbook of Action Research* (3rd ed.). Thousand Oaks, CA: Sage
Publications Ltd.

Snowden, D. J., & Boone, M. E. (2007, November 1). A leader's framework
for decision making. *Harvard Business Review*. Retrieved from https://hbr.
org/2007/11/a-leaders-framework-for-decision-making.

Steffen, S. (2012). Beyond environmental leadership to restorative
leadership: An emerging framework for cultivating resilient communities in
the 21st Century. In D. R. Gallagher (Ed.), *Environmental Leadership: A
Reference Handbook*. Thousand Oaks, CA: Sage Publishing.

Walsh, E. (2015, August). Home ecology and challenges in the design of
healthy home environments: Possibilities for low-income home repair as a
leverage point for environmental justice in gentrifying urban environments.
Dissertation, University of Texas.

4

ACHIEVING A SUSTAINABLE FUTURE THROUGH ADAPTIVE AND STRATEGIC LEADERSHIP

Ebere Morgan

INTRODUCTION

Leadership has been under intense and rigorous study for the past few decades. Its importance and significance are difficult to overstate. It is believed that competition and eventual success of communities and organizations in the twenty-first century's global economy will be fraught with complexities, challenges, and filled with competitive opportunities and threats (Ireland & Hitt, 2005). Additionally, the emergence and speed of international development have witnessed tremendous strides in our lifetimes. However, the world's poorest and most vulnerable regions and communities continue to face steep and seemingly unassailable challenges to date.

In 2015, the UN Secretary-General, António Guterres, declared that world leaders have collectively adopted the ambitious 2030 Agenda for Sustainable Development, with 17 Sustainable Development Goals (SDGs) at its heart. This Agenda stands as a shared plan to transform the world in 15 years and, crucially, to build lives of dignity for all. In assuming the 2030 Agenda for Sustainable Development, world leaders resolved and committed to free the entire humanity from poverty, secure a healthy global community for future generations, and to build and foster peaceful, diverse but inclusive societies as a basis for ensuring lives of dignity for all. As a guiding principle, this collective journey has embedded within its core a promise *to leave no one behind*.

This chapter highlights 2 of the 17 integrated and indivisible SDGs and targets embedded within the 2030 Agenda and its framework, namely:

Goal 1: End poverty in all its forms everywhere.

Goal 16: Promote peaceful and inclusive societies for sustainable development, provide access to justice for all, and build effective, accountable, and inclusive institutions at all levels.

Deliberate, audacious, ambitious, and transformational as this global agenda may seem, one thing is certain, leadership is a key vehicle and driver of its sustainable achievement as set forth by the collective international community. The leadership that is proposed in this global undertaking suggests that which is adaptive and strategic in approach in order to attain and actualize its stated targets and goals. It is also self-evident that good and effective leadership will no doubt bring about the desired results and outcomes that will change the world for the better, while chronically poor leadership will ensure the continuance and steady decline in the overall state of affairs in the global community as it currently stands today.

Additionally, this chapter explores scholarship on the various approaches and theories of leadership and working to gain an understanding through the collective insight into the various leadership theories and approaches is necessary to set forth a distilled understanding and strategy on leadership within the lens and framework of the contemporary leadership issues facing the twenty-first century dispensation and its peoples.

THE SUSTAINABLE DEVELOPMENT CONCEPT

There is no disputing that the international community has come a long way in reaching a common global viewpoint on the concept of sustainable development that now features prominently on the agenda of several international development initiatives, particularly at the UN level.

The year 2015 drew leaders from 193 nations together to face the future. The realities were daunting, presenting with global scales of famine, drought, wars, plagues, poverty, and varied forms of global disturbances and instability. Summed together, the world as it was understood by its leaders was in critical and chaotic crisis. Crisis, both at the micro and macro levels of diverse societies. This community of global leaders formulated a strategic plan known as the SDGs. These 17 goals envisaged a future that would be devoid of poverty, hunger, inequality, and safe from the impact of climate change. These goals also followed a systematic framework, approach, and action to bring about the change(s) that will set the world on a distinct course toward a beneficial future from a strategic standpoint.

Munasinghe (1996) proposed an apt illustration of a three-pronged approach which depicts the links and interactions among the economic, social, and environmental pillars of sustainable development. A cursory look at this approach in the light of the stipulated SDGs suggests that these three approaches are an effective lens to encapsulate and capture the span of the prevailing issues identified in the global agenda and its priorities.

The economic approach to sustainability is based on the underlying concept of optimality and economic efficiency applied to the use of scarce resources. The social approach of sustainability is people oriented and seeks to maintain the stability of social and cultural systems, including the reduction of destructive conflicts. Consequently, the environmental view of sustainable development focuses on the stability of biological and physical systems (Andrews, McConnell, & Wescott, 2010). These three-dimensional views have been adopted by various authorities as the lens through which sustainable development can be defined and evaluated for effective leadership intervention strategies.

Contextually, the commitment to end poverty in all its forms everywhere (SDG:1) and the promise of peace, justice, and strong institutions (SDG:16) are critical to Munasinghe's interactive framework. Both SDGs fundamentally embody the economic and social contexts of every society. While poverty derives from the economic status of a community or society, it does, however, fester and incubate a string of social dilemmas which in turn lead to economic disturbance, thus, creating a vicious cycle. Providing people in every part of the world the vital support needed to reduce and eradicate poverty in all its manifestations is the very essence of sustainable development. SDG:1 focuses on ending poverty through interrelated strategies, including the promotion of healthier economies, social protection systems, decent employment, and building the resilience of the poor (United Nations, 2017).

However, the promise of peaceful and inclusive societies for sustainable development (SDG:16) through access to justice for all and building effective, accountable, and inclusive institutions at all levels presents a daily social dilemma. How can communities successfully develop – how can its people exist – without peace? At the same time, how can communities experience and have peace devoid of justice, human rights, and good governance based on the rule of law? This SDG seeks to reduce all forms of violence and propose that governments and communities find lasting solutions to conflict and insecurity through strengthening the rule of law, reducing the flow of illicit arms, and bringing developing countries more into the center of institutions of global governance (United Nations, 2017). These multifaceted strategies fall within the social approach to sustainability as posited by Munasinghe.

LEADERSHIP AND SUSTAINABLE DEVELOPMENT CHALLENGES

The global community is confronted with significant challenges in three chief areas of sustainable development: economic, social, and environmental. There is no doubt that we are witnessing a significant paradigm shift in the major socioeconomic and geopolitical dimensions that shape the world as we know it. A huge proportion of the world's population is still living in extreme poverty, and income inequality within and among many countries has witnessed a strong astronomical climb. According to the United Nations report of the World Economic and Social Survey (2013), "achieving sustainable development will require global actions to deliver on the legitimate aspiration towards further economic and social progress, requiring growth and employment, and at the same time strengthening environmental protection" (p. v).

Eradicating all forms of poverty (SDG:1) is central to sustainable development. Poverty comprises basic deprivation and denial in various domains, including income, hunger, poor health, social exclusion, discrimination, and inaccessibility to basic services and necessities. It is critical to note that deficiencies in any of the identified domains can, in turn, aggravate the depth or duration of deprivations in one or more of the others causing a ripple effect. For instance, conflict, social disturbance, and war exacerbate poverty. According to the SDGs Report, conflict (regional and international) has become the most insurmountable barrier to poverty eradication and sustainable development. War, violence, and persecution worldwide led to the displacement of 65.6 million people from their homes by the end of 2016. This represents an increase of about 300,000 people since 2015 and the highest level recorded in decades (United Nations, 2017). Thus, suggesting that eradicating poverty (SDG:1) and promoting peace, prosperity, justice, and strong institutions (SDG:16) as SDGs in a changing world require a holistic approach that takes into account the interplay between the different dimensions of sustainable development and the strategic leadership to bring it to life. Additionally, it remains imperative that the international community takes bold and collaborative actions to accelerate progress in achieving the SDGs through effective leadership that will transcend the norm and convention in structure, form, function, and outcome.

THE NORTH–SOUTH DEVELOPMENT DIVIDE

While efforts seem to be geared toward achieving a collective sustainable future in the world, a staggering reality demonstrates the contrary.

For example, Orga (2012) wrote:

> The world has witnessed increased interdependence in the last two decades, thanks to globalization. The main driving forces of this process are technology, policy and competition and it subordinates domestic economies to global market conditions and practices. Developed nations are the beneficiaries of globalization as their share of world trade and finance has been expanded at the expense of developing countries. Thus, the process exacerbates inequality between the world's regions and poverty in the developing world. (p. 154)

According to the Royal Geographical Society (with IBG) (n.d.), in the 1980s, the Brandt Line was developed as a way of showing how the world was geographically split into relatively richer and poorer nations. Following this model, wealthier countries are almost all located in the Northern Hemisphere, except for Australia and New Zealand. However, poorer countries are mostly located in tropical regions and in the Southern Hemisphere. These include countries in Africa, Latin America, and developing Asia including the Middle East.

In his work, *Globalization: The Politics of Global Economic Relations and International Business*, Mimiko (2012) illustrated that the North mostly covers the West and the First World (developed, capitalist, and industrialized states), along with much of the Second World (former communist-socialist, industrial states), while the South largely corresponds with the Third World (collective states known as the developing countries of Africa, Asia, and Latin America). He posited that while the North may be defined as the richer, more developed region and the South as the poorer, less developed region, many more factors differentiate between the two global areas. Of those who live in the North, 95% have enough food and shelter. Additionally, the Global South lags in appropriate technology and has very limited political stability. Furthermore, the economies are disarticulated, and their foreign exchange earnings depend on primary product exports (Mimiko, 2012).

Despite very significant development gains globally which have raised many millions of people out of absolute poverty, there is substantial evidence that inequality between the world's richest and poorest countries is widening (Royal Geographical Society, n.d.). Mimiko (2012) asserted that in economic terms, the North — with one-quarter of the world population — controls four-fifths of the income earned anywhere in the world. Ninety percent of the manufacturing industries are owned by and located in the North. Conversely, the South — with three-quarters of the world's population — has access to one-fifth of world income. As nations become economically developed, they may become part of the "North," regardless of geographical location; similarly, any nations that do not qualify for "developed" status are in effect deemed to be part of the "South" (Therien, 2010).

Today's global community is much more complex than the Brandt Line depicted years ago as many poorer countries have experienced significant economic and social development. Nevertheless, inequality within countries has also been growing and some commentators now talk of a "Global North" and a "Global South" referring respectively to richer or poorer communities found both within and between countries. For instance, while India is still home to the largest concentration of poor people in a single nation, it also has a very sizable middle class and a very rich elite (Royal Geographical Society, n.d.).

BRIDGING THE NORTH–SOUTH CHASM

It is quite evident that while many parts of the world have advanced toward better and desirable political and economic stability and cooperation, the Global South, for the most, the part remains a cauldron of instability and economic deprivation (Nkurayija, 2011). The resulting poverty in this huge region has demonstrably varied underpinnings that include political, social, and economic constraints.

While the Global South continues with its chronic struggles with the encumbrance of its status quo, it continues to falter tremendously due to a lack of leadership and effective strategies to surmount the prevailing issues that appear to fester with no end in sight. Africa, for example, continues to lead the pack in this regional class. For more than four decades, Africa has been the sole recipient of countless development initiatives both at the local and international levels. Unfortunately, these initiatives have yielded many of the crises that Africa is experiencing today, such as the debt crisis, extreme poverty and political instability, and socioeconomic dilemmas within and across its borders. The goal to end poverty (SDG:1) and to promote peace, justice, and strong institutions (SDG:16) are aimed at effectively bridging the critical divide between the north and south. These two important goals fronted by global leaders is geared toward the creation of a common and unified global community that will promote less insular and isolated cooperative development among a select few regions of the world rather than the global community as a whole.

Nkurayija (2011) identified four critical strategies necessary for bridging the chasm that exists between the global north and south. These include (1) peace and security for development, (2) governance and leadership, (3) positive economic growth, and (4) global interdependence. These four primary opportunities and integrative elements can be adopted and exploited by the Global South in order to assail the challenges it currently faces. Additionally, peace, justice, security, and political stability would be required to enable the Global South to adopt good governance and leadership in building lasting institutions that promote sustainable development, thus accomplishing the strategic imperatives of a more united global community in dealing with the challenges facing a significant proportion of its people.

A NEW KIND OF LEADERSHIP FOR SUSTAINABLE DEVELOPMENT

The contemporary pervasiveness of constant pressure of change presents a significant challenge for leaders of the twenty-first century in every framework of human activity and social exchange. It has become clear that surviving and thriving under the immensity of such change demands skillsets and competencies that transcend beyond the norm that was readily obtainable a few decades ago. Today, regional and institutional successes require a whole new mindset, toolset, and skillset.

The 17 SDGs form a cohesive and integrated package of global aspirations the world commits to achieving by 2030. Building on the accomplishments of their predecessors the Millennium Development Goals (MDGs), the SDGs address the most pressing global challenges of our time, calling upon collaborative partnerships across and between countries to balance the three dimensions of sustainable development – economic growth, environmental sustainability, and social inclusion.

Following the adopted 2030 Agenda for Sustainable Development and the shared SDGs among global leaders, the 17 new SDGs, also known as the Global Goals, collectively aim to end poverty, hunger and inequality, take action on climate change and the environment, improve access to health and education, promote peace and justice, and build strong institutions and partnerships.

Contextually, the true success of any country, in quest of achieving SDGs, largely depends on leadership. A leadership type that is innovative, adaptive, strategic, and most importantly effective. This form of effective leadership translates into practical public policy formulation, management, and implementation, as well as decent public service delivery, to meet the needs, goals, and objectives of the world and its people.

Leadership is fundamentally essential and central to sustainable development. In the same vein, achieving the SDGs will require the concerted efforts of governments, the business sector, civil society, and individuals in general. Innovative leadership and management will be vital for organizations in all sectors to integrate these development goals into strategic plans and operational activities in service of realizing the 2030 aspirations (Iftakhar & Bahauddin, 2018). In dealing with the mission to end poverty (SDG:1), and to promote peace, justice, and strong institutions (SDG:16), the ominous task remains a daunting challenge that only a new revolutionary leadership can undertake and implement strategically. Iftakhar and Bahauddin (2018) further posited that leadership for achieving sustainable development is rooted in a living processes paradigm, rather than a mechanistic paradigm. They contend that complex living processes demonstrate sustainable properties and patterns and can suggest important strategies for effective leadership. Accordingly, qualities of functional living processes include resiliency, adaptability, awareness, creativity, and relationships. Considering that our world is inherently paradoxical, that multiple realities exist, and that living beings organize and adapt according to their environments, leadership must be adaptive and strategic (flexible, self-renewing, resilient, willing to learn, intelligent) – attributes only found and resident in living systems (Iftakhar & Bahauddin, 2018).

In today's global community, the critical challenges for attaining sustainable development are complicated, interconnected, and will require the collective efforts of all to strive toward creating a more sustainable future. Thus, leaders, instead of solely providing dramatic solutions need to become creators and facilitators – creating opportunities for people, fostering and facilitating the needed synergistic collaborations in coming together to generate their intelligent solutions and answers. However, our new kind of sustainable development leaders should not only bring people together and build creative collaborations, but should also help people embrace a relationship with uncertainty, chaos, and emergence of the times. It is, however, important to note that simply collaborating to solve problems, even when values are common and shared, can be an arduous and challenging process. At the same time, leaders must recognize that the tension, conflict, and uncertainty that come from differences and diversity can provide great potential for the creative emergence of viable solutions (Iftakhar & Bahauddin, 2018).

The goals to end poverty and advance peace and justice are quite visceral, and so is addressing and implementing them. The global community needs effective leadership that is adaptive and strategic for sustainable development. This form of leadership requires an intrinsic process, in which a leader must first be grounded in an appreciation of self (self-awareness) and a relational (relationship management) perspective of the world, in order to effectively work with others to bring about transformative and sustainable change. Additionally, self-awareness and self-reflection are processes in understanding one's skills, knowledge, and values within the context of community groups. These reflective processes allow for feedback loops, and cycles of growth and change (Iftakhar & Bahauddin, 2018). Consequently, leadership at its core should thus be understood as an inclusive, collaborative and a reflective process rooted in values and ethics.

Eradicating poverty in all its forms everywhere (SDG:1), and installing peaceful and inclusive societies for sustainable development, and providing access to justice for all and building effective, accountable, and inclusive institutions at all levels (SDG:16) are not goals to be tackled unilaterally and on one single level. Contextually, to achieve the SDGs thus highlighted, leadership at both the national and organizational levels must adopt leadership styles that stimulate and promote a sense of shared responsibility toward the accomplishment of the goals, is focused on the long-term, and thus would create systems and structures that would persistently guarantee the pursuit and attainment of these goals in the future. Furthermore, leaders must recognize the need for concerted efforts at the national and grassroots levels, be willing to imbibe, exhibit, and encourage ethical behavior and standards among all stakeholders (Iftakhar & Bahauddin, 2018).

In achieving the end of poverty and installing peace and justice, as SDGs, leaders must manage resources, be visionary and ethical, and focus on long-term goals without compromising values and principles (Iftakhar & Bahauddin, 2018). Likewise, leaders should be motivated by a vision to achieve the goals in the midst of changing environmental factors and involve all stakeholders in the governance process. It is suggested that the impact of this kind of leadership coupled with the synergy, coordination, and involvement of all concerned will no doubt lead to advances in economic efficiency, social cohesion, and environmental responsibility. Essentially, these are the three basic indicators of sustainable development (Iftakhar & Bahauddin, 2018).

ADAPTIVE LEADERSHIP

Given the world's current state of turbulence and instability, leaders seem to frequently make the false assumption and blunder in attempting to solve complex problems with technical fixes or band-aid solutions. Typically, technical challenges have inherently clear definitions and clear solutions while adaptive challenges are more systemic and complex in nature, having not-easily-unraveled definitions, ramifications, and resolutions (Klonsky, 2010). In years past, we have seen the continuous failure and handicap in the leadership necessary to drive sustainable development both regionally and globally. More noticeable is the simplistic technical approach employed by most leaders which appear to understate the reality of the issues and challenges embedded in the achievement of the SDGs. For instance, the goal to end poverty (SDG:1) and to install peace, justice, and formidable institutions (SDG:16) does not present the common task of an exact science. This is because these goals are complex in themselves and require more intricate and, yet, convoluted means to attaining the desired results that will stand the test of time.

Adaptive leadership is instrumental in aiding leaders to learn to bring to the surface tough and complex issues and strategically devise new patterns of behavior necessary to achieve more innovative and intelligent sustainable solutions. In business environments, adaptive challenges are potential opportunities that arise that cannot be simply solved by the application of technical answers supplied by authority figures but require the collaborative dynamics of the whole group to seek new ways of addressing these challenges.

Adaptive leadership is essentially the act of being able to lead through different environmental conditions and circumstances that require altercation for survival in an altering and changing environment. It is described as the adaptive, creative, and learning actions that emerge from the interactions of leaders as they strive to adjust to resulting tension. Additionally, it is an informal emergence dynamic that occurs among highly interactive and intentional leaders and is not merely an act of authority (Bright, 2011; Heifetz, 2004). These collective skills lead to the creation of dynamic and agile leaders who are incredibly effective and consistent in the face of any changing environment. According to Bradberry and Greaves (2012), adaptive leadership skills are what set great leaders apart from the rest. It is a unique combination of skills, perspective, and guided effort that enhance sustainable performance and excellence. In general, these skills represent the otherwise intangible qualities that great leaders have in common which undoubtedly can take any leader at any level to heights of performance that others cannot attain. As the global community seeks to attain practical results in eradicating poverty and creating peaceful societies thriving under effective rule of law through social institutions that will drive common success, it is noteworthy that conventional leadership devoid of adaptive skills and competencies will continue to yield realities far removed from the desired outcomes representative and characteristic of the sustainable development goals for our world.

STRATEGIC LEADERSHIP

The second type of leadership necessary for driving success in sustainable development is strategic leadership. As stated, achieving global goals require a different of mindset, tool set, and skill set. The times and results of conventional leadership are past and no longer effective. The global community and its set goals and objectives are otherwise focused in a different direction to address newly adopted priorities while leading the world into uncharted territories.

Strategic leadership is defined as the embodiment of processes used by leaders to affect the achievement of a desirable and clearly understood organizational vision by influencing the organizational culture, allocating resources, directing policy and directives, and building consensus within a volatile, uncertain, complex, and ambiguous global environment (Goff, 2010). Strategic leaders are referred to as individuals who have the ability to think strategically by envisioning, anticipating, innovating, and maintaining flexibility and mobilizing others to adopt change (Guzman, 2007). According to Christensen and Foss (1997), strategic leadership is described as the ability on the part of leadership to anticipate, envision, maintain flexibility, think strategically, and work with others to initiate changes that will create a viable future. In organizational contexts, this type of leadership style when properly honed and established for long periods of time is known as a strategic competitive advantage.

While twenty-first century leadership requires a strong adaptive component, it also requires a strategic aspect to thrive successfully. The SDGs were birthed on the collective vision of the various leaders who identified a new focus and direction for our global community. However, the execution and implementation of sustainable development goals can only survive if leaders are successful in their communities. In other words, when one leader fails or falls short in his/her community, there is an ultimate failure in the efforts of the entire global community in reaching its objectives. Thus, it holds that individual leaders at the local or national levels should employ the strategy of vision, flexibility, and collaboration to achieve the goals to end poverty and install peace and justice in their communities. Without maintaining strong focus, flexibility, and deploying cooperative partnership strategies, there will be little or no success at the regional level in achieving sustainable development goals and the viable future anticipated for our global community as we move forward as a people.

CONCLUSION

Today's world is fraught with complexities, crises, challenges, and astronomical change. Achieving a sustainable future seems a far-fetched endeavor. Leaders are in great need of the tools and opportunities to succeed at various levels, both regionally and institutionally. These issues have also adversely affected and created dichotomous distinctions in our global environment, thereby leading to the challenge of inequalities on various fronts.

In an age of globalization and global community expansion, governance within and among countries is becoming more diffuse and complex. Critical steps for sustainable development include a collective and synergistic approach in eradicating poverty, promoting good governance, the rule of law, human rights, basic and fundamental freedoms, equal access to fair justice systems, as well as combatting corruption and mitigating illicit financial flows. In addition, effective and inclusive institutions are necessary to prevent all forms of abuse, exploitation, trafficking, torture, and violence to the global citizenry (United Nations, 2015). Improved global cooperation through the United Nations and other like-minded institutions is necessary to avert the spread of wars, violence, and extreme poverty as is now afflicting many countries in the economic south. Collaborative partnerships of all kinds will be essential to build effective, accountable, and inclusive institutions at all levels.

The goal to end poverty in all its forms everywhere (SDG:1), and to promote peaceful and inclusive societies for sustainable development, provide access to justice for all, and build effective, accountable, and inclusive institutions at all levels (SDG:16), presents an uphill challenge to today's leaders. While conventional leaders with conventional tools, skills, and mindsets continue to fail their various communities in the quest for sustainable development, it has become imperative that a new kind of leadership be employed for this global undertaking. A new leadership that is both adaptive and strategic in form and function is required to achieve the sustainable development goals amidst the prevailing global environment fraught with constant change and uncertainty. Most importantly, strong and effective leadership, a coherent implementation plan, and engagement of all government departments and diverse stakeholders are necessary to ensure that the SDGs are achieved at local, national, and international levels.

The ominous challenge to end poverty and to install peace, justice, and strong institutions through cooperative partnerships requires that leaders begin to imbibe effective practices that will assist them to achieve sustainability in regional and institutional success. Building adaptive and strategic leaders is essential in today's demands for development and competitive advancement. This new paradigm is critical if we as a global community are to achieve equilibrium and sustainability within and across all borders. The time is now, the place is here, and the stakes are high.

REFERENCES

Andrews, M., McConnell, J., & Wescott, A. (2010). Development as leadership-led change. *HKS Faculty Research working paper series, RWP10-009*, John F. Kennedy School of Government, Harvard University. Retrieved from https://dash.harvard.edu/bitstream/handle/1/4449099/andrews_ developmentleadership.pdf?sequence=1

Bradberry, T., & Greaves, J. (2012). *Leadership 2.0*. San Diego, CA: Talent Smart.

Bright, M. (2011). *An examination of adaptive leadership processes using action research* (Order No. 3491164). Available from ProQuest Dissertations & Theses Global (919007504). Retrieved from http://search. proquest.com/docview/919007504?accountid=165104

Christensen, J. F., & Foss, N. J. (1997). Dynamic corporate coherence and competence-based competition: Theoretical foundations and strategic implications. In A. Heene & R. Sanchez (Eds.), *Competence based strategic management* (pp. 287–312). Chichester: John Wiley & Sons Ltd.

Goff, L. G. (2010). *Strategic leadership development in the U.S. Navy: A phenomenological study of Navy Rear Admirals* (Order No. 3396506). Available from ProQuest Dissertations & Theses Global (305244778). Retrieved from http://search.proquest.com/docview/305244778?accountid= 165104

Guzman, P. M. (2007). *Strategic leadership: Qualitative study of contextual factors and transformational leadership behaviors of chief executive officers* (Order No. 3302617). Available from ProQuest Dissertations & Theses Global (304732510). Retrieved from http://search.proquest.com/docview/ 304732510?accountid=165104

Heifetz, R. (2004). *Leadership without easy answers*. Cambridge, MA: Harvard University Press.

Iftakhar, N., & Bahauddin, K. M. (2018). Why leadership is essential for achieving sustainable development goals. *International Policy Digest, 10*(1). Retrieved from https://intpolicydigest.org/2018/01/10/why-leadership-is-essential-for-achievingsustainable-development-goals

Ireland, R. D., & Hitt, M. A. (2005). Achieving and maintaining strategic competitiveness in the 21st century: The role of strategic leadership. *Academy of Management Executive, 19*(4), 63–77.

Klonsky, M. F. (2010). *Discussing undiscussables: Exercising adaptive leadership* (Order No. 3426112). Available from ProQuest Dissertations & Theses Global (761367319). Retrieved from http://search.proquest.com/ docview/761367319?accountid=165104

Mimiko, O. (2012). *Globalization: The politics of global economic relations and international business* (p. 47). Durham, NC: Carolina Academic.

Munasinghe, M. (1996). Environmental impacts of macroeconomic and sectoral policies. *International Society for Ecological economics*. Washington, DC: World Bank.

Nkurayija, J. C. (2011). *The requirements for the African continent's development: Linking peace, governance, economic growth and global interdependence*, Berlin, Germany. Retrieved from http://www.

culturaldiplomacy.org/academy/content/pdf/participant-papers/africa/Jean-De-La-Croix-Nkurayija-The-Requirements-For-The-African-Continent%27s-Development-Linking-Economic-Growth.pdf

Orga, J. I. (2012). *Globalization: The Nigerian experience. Review of Public Administration & Management, 1*(2), 154–179. Retrieved from http://www.arabianjbmr.com/pdfs/public/2.pdf

The Royal Geographical Society (with IBG). (n.d.). *The Global North/South Divide*. Retrieved from https://www.rgs.org/CMSPages/GetFile.aspx?nodeguid=9c1ce781-9117-4741-af0a-a6a8b75f32b4&lang=en-GB

Therien, J. (2010). Beyond the North–South divide: The two tales of world poverty. *Third World Quarterly, 20*(4), 723–742.

United Nations. (2015). *Transforming our world: The 2030 Agenda for Sustainable Development*. Retrieved from https://sustainabledevelopment.un.org/post2015/transformingourworld

United Nations. (2017). *The Sustainable Development Goals Report 2017*. Retrieved from https://unstats.un.org/sdgs/files/report/2017/TheSustainableDevelopmentGoalsReport2017.pdf.

World Economic and Social Survey. (2013). *Sustainable development challenges*. New York, NY: Department of Economic and Social Affairs. Retrieved from https://sustainabledevelopment.un.org/content/documents/2843WESS2013.pdf.

5

LEADERSHIP LESSONS FROM WOMEN IN HIGH-RISK ENVIRONMENTS

Wanda Krause

INTRODUCTION: EXPANDING OUR HORIZONS

The UN aims to end extreme poverty, protect the health of the planet, and create a future where every person lives with opportunity and dignity by 2030 through the Sustainable Development Goals (SDGs). The question then becomes: what qualities do we need to possess as leaders to achieve the SDGs? Biases and misconception related to what leadership qualities are needed, as well as who might be best suited to offer leadership lessons, limit our ability to answer this question. I propose that by overcoming these biases to learn how marginalized women empower themselves and others to create change, we gain valuable insights for all leaders implementing the SDGs for collective well-being.

A barrier to overcoming these biases comes from the Western worldview that often considers women in places other than the West (referred to as the *developing world*, the *global south*, the *third world*, or even the *fourth world* of communities within the West) as needing to be saved. Feminists, activists and "good-doers" are not immune to this mindset, and therefore may be biased in determining what approaches and forms of activism are needed and significant for empowerment. In other words, the West frames these women as victims, both by focusing on the disempowerment of women in particular geographical settings and also by situating Western thinkers and practitioners (sometimes including those who are Western educated) as the saviors in the dynamics of community development and empowerment initiatives. As a result, we often miss diverse forms of agency contributing to change in high-risk environments that would provide insights for a world which, I argue, is actually entirely at risk of similar chaos.

A key barrier to recognizing the agency and wisdom of non-Western women comes from an assumption, both implicit and explicit, that only the West can claim knowledge or understanding of "best practices" regarding sustainable development and peace. Another challenge is that Middle Eastern women are depicted as passive actors in the public domain (Hale, 1991, p. 31). An overview of the various initiatives in high-risk geographical areas reveals that power for change is often wielded by the "marginalized". Their struggles and activism are often missed "within the logic of subversion and resignification of hegemonic terms of discourse" (Mahmood, 2004, p. 155).

From the research I have conducted with women in the Middle East who have had to find innovative and creative ways to secure a more peaceful and sustainable future, I argue that women who have often been framed as victims and in need of being saved are often those who have much to contribute in terms of wisdom and practices for sustainable development globally. They are providing examples of how to chart a future for global sustainability through everyday practices and various forms of activism often unaccounted for. For example, the women I have studied create change within their systems by creating cultures of trust and reciprocity by significantly embodying these qualities. In the next section, I will provide more significant examples of actions and qualities needed to evolve leadership for the SDGs that have been demonstrated by these women, often deemed ill-suited as leaders for change.

This chapter aims to examine the forms of agency and processes of transformation demonstrated by a specific marginalized group: women in the Middle East. I will focus on women in the Arab Gulf, Egypt, Qatar, and the United Arab Emirates as representative of the North Africa and the Middle East (MENA) region. Their actions and embodied values will shed light on how women in these turbulent environments find innovative ways to circumvent oppressive structures and facilitate empowerment and change. They especially demonstrate the capacities we need to embody as we all enter greater turbulence and complexity globally.

A WORLD IN HIGH RISK

I am a citizen of the world.

— *Diogenes Laertius, Greek philosopher (CE 220)*

As Mark Gerzon observes, two millennia ago philosophers were proclaiming themselves citizens of the world (2012, p. xii). Yet then, as now, leaders communicate a belief that their states are separate from the world. As Gerzon points out, we are actually not citizens of the world strictly speaking as we do not carry global citizen passports; yet the truth is that we are *all* profoundly affected by the decisions and actions of people whose faces we may never see, whose language we may not speak, and whose names we would not recognize. They are also affected by us. Our well-being, and in some cases our survival, depends on recognizing this truth and taking responsibility for it as global citizens (Gerzon, 2012).

Recently, aboard an airplane flying along the British Columbia border between Canada and the US, I could see the edge of a forest fire with the plumes blowing in the direction we were flying. It was the first time I had ever seen actual flames of a forest fire. I learned soon that this fire was on the US side. But as we continued on, the smoke cover was everywhere. Bearing witness to this disaster was a powerful reminder that while we may not be citizens of the world in passport, we are all still in it together. Whatever fire literally and metaphorically appear to be on the other side of the border have direct influence on the side we might be on — and vice versa. Thus, we can no longer speak of empires or states as isolated entities. We can no longer think of high-risk environments without reflecting on how much we might *all* in fact be *at* high risk, as we are globally connected.

The current experience of humanity, both in the Western and non-Western world, is one of increasing turbulence and crisis (Ife, 2016, p. 9). Such accelerated changes require new ways of learning to address these challenges (Zuber-Skerritt, 2012, p. 4). We are a world in crisis together, and I again emphasize the point that the West does not hold the truth to the "good life," nor the only path to sustainable development. Instead, we need a different and much more fundamental approach to understanding and attending to turbulence, crisis, and change. This approach must include an understanding of the issues of disempowerment and empowerment and the capacities beyond traditional activism that enable freedom, peace, and prosperity in chaos. We need new ways of recognizing the agency of all actors, especially those long framed as "victims." Those who have struggled in high-risk environments have a great deal to teach the rest of us who are just beginning to see the effects of a world in crisis. Women, especially in places other than the West, are mostly left out of studies on change and transformation due to the biases of state-level politics and political change. Yet, I propose that these women have a great deal to offer the world in way of demonstrating how to lead change.

LEADERSHIP LESSONS FROM WOMEN IN HIGH-RISK ENVIRONMENTS

Much of the research and work I have been involved in over the past few decades in the Middle East has been with women living their everyday lives in some form of struggle within a high-risk environment. Often, their conception of the "good life" is embedded in circumstances that largely include poverty. Some of the women have no conception of what it is like to live in poverty, and yet their struggles arise from what some refer to as traditions or even "fabricated traditions." I had the honor of observing, working with, and studying women working for change in these regions. Some took to the streets in protest during the Arab uprisings. Others fought to change laws that marginalized and oppressed women, or secured laws for banning the trafficking of children. Others opened orphanages, hospitals, and schools or worked or volunteered in charities and numerous types of social and women's organizations. I believe we have much to learn from these women whose lives have been contextualized by socioeconomic and political repression and who, not merely despite these oppressive structures but *because* of them, have learned how to create resilience and work together. They illustrate the kinds of qualities humanity needs to end extreme poverty, protect the health of the planet, and create a better and more dignified future.

The women I participated with very often collaborated to empower others, whether in formal organizations or more quietly via avenues of networks. Examples include women who work around the clock to teach other women about their rights or simply teach skills to help women become more independent, such as how to read or develop skills for employment. Other examples include offering workshops that teach spiritual principles that help women get through tough times. They also facilitated networking so women could share provisions for mere survival in those tough times.

Beyond these actions, these women offer valuable lessons in how they *embody* leadership. They practice change and transformation by developing qualities like resilience, persistence, patience, trust, hope, and, importantly, a power derived from within and brought to the world through what I describe as 'spiritual activism', which is "creating change through bringing spirit, love and therefore light where needed through action" (Krause, 2013, p. 16). They taught me that the way forward to creating positive and sustainable change had everything to do with these inner transformations linked to the values they lived and embodied in practice. In this way, they create a politics of *hope* through activities that empower the marginalized and transform power relations. "Hope names the effort of prospective energy, self-creation looking forward, reliance on ourselves, and trust that we shall manifest better values in the world" (2006, p. 113).

Women often navigate change through innovative ways used to circumvent the system and in the process, create bonds of solidarity. For example, one group of women I worked with in the UAE founded the first women's shelter in Dubai. They did not do this as a registered group because they would have been viewed by the government as a threat to political order and squashed. Instead, they formed a network of solidarity with like-minded women and men who could take on different roles to help women and young girls who had escaped from trafficking. In this process, they saved hundreds and brought attention to the issues of trafficking to those in power positions who traditionally wrote these women off as prostitutes and punished them according to local laws. After creating the shelter, these women went on to implement the first laws on trafficking of children in the country. They did not do this by challenging the state overtly. Instead, they worked with specific individuals within the state who could understand what they were trying to do and had the power to create changes. Simultaneously, these women collected foodstuffs, clothes, and money to run the shelter. They offered workshops to these women and girls around resiliency and spiritual learning. They networked to offer tutoring to trafficked girls and helped families take these girls and some of the children to experience family life with their own children. This is but one of many examples.

Women also create change by refusing the *status quo* and finding other means to exercise their power. I listened to women who pushed themselves to learn to read and write in literacy classes tell me that they would now stand up to authority (i.e., husbands) because they can now read for themselves and can now access *correct* information that affects their lives. Many of these women experienced not only emotional but physical abuse by their husbands. According to the UN's SDG 5 progress 2017 report, "19 per cent of women between 15 and 49 years of age said they had experienced physical and/or sexual violence by an intimate partner [...]" By gaining literacy and information, women stepped into a more powerful position to address their situations. One means through which these women gained information to guide action to greater well-being was through women who taught them literacy skills and at the same time educated them on abuse. Thus, they demonstrate important leadership qualities including courageousness for refusing and circumventing the *status quo*.

To mitigate worsening economic circumstances, especially following the Arab Spring, the women explained that they rely more on the acts of reciprocation, sharing, and interdependence to meet the needs of the poor. As two interviewees exclaimed, they had never seen women with their children eating out of garbage cans in Egypt before the revolution and that the spiraling economic situation requires of women to do things they never did before. The need to pay attention to the economic aspect driving agency is more critical than ever. In this endeavor, it is also important to pay attention to the qualities these women embody in their quest to end extreme poverty, create opportunities, and enhance dignity. Some women networked to create their own economic well-being through the act of reciprocity where they traded their produce. Others pooled foodstuffs and used clothing so all could take what they needed and sell the rest. A group of women helped a women's organization get its start by taking turns babysitting the entire group's children so that each woman could eventually contribute her skills and experience. Such impactful contributions are often provided by women and rarely accounted for. In fact, the UN's 2017 SDG 5 progress report found that "[th]e average amount of time spent on unpaid domestic and care work is more than three-fold higher for women than men, according to survey data from 83 countries and areas. Available data indicate that time spent on domestic chores accounts for a large proportion of the gender gap in unpaid work" (UN Sustainable Development and Knowledge Platform, 2015).

Many of these women claimed that endurance was most essential since the revolution, and with the Muslim Brotherhood government destroying the economy further. With worsening conditions and no end in sight throughout the chaos and violence, women somehow found the *power within* themselves to renew their resolve for a better life for themselves and their children and continue their struggle. They saw no external indication that their economic situations would improve, yet the faith – a politics of *hope* – they relied on to sustain them and enable them to continue translated into a greater capacity to endure.

A mothering and nurturing proclivity was also noticeable and called into action. An interviewee told me, "I love to help people, especially the poor. It is something that fulfills me in life." Using a mothering proclivity as the motivator to action was evident when another participant stated, "I love to see everyone helping to protect children." In other words, one can argue that women's feminine nature of mothering and nurturing equips them to give of themselves, especially without traditional rewards for their efforts. For example, while numerous women expressed an understanding that their charity work carried out relentlessly still would not necessarily produce immediate results, they nevertheless continued their work. In other words, the feminine capacity for patience was exercised despite frustrations with worsening conditions. In all the multitudinous Islamic charities, not specific to women, I have entered in Egypt I have quickly noted that the ratio of women to men is almost always higher. Even women in charity organizations with dwindling donations continued to provide skills training for jobs despite a shrinking job market. In line with spiritual activism, they relied on an inner strength and kept going and developed the capacity for patience, sacrifice, and endurance through a desire to assist others.

Many women expressed that their motivation lies in simply doing *khair* (good deeds). A participant shared, "Allah created the souls with *khair*. Our ideology is to develop *khair* in people. *Khair* is a seed that you plant, but the growth of the seed depends on activism". Many women, thus, rely on an existential reward. It is important to understand the values that motivate women to participate from many sources including Islam. Ross argues, Islam has not impeded progress towards gender equality (2012, p. 89). Through meaning-making, women can *derive empowerment through religion* and can use interpretations to respond to practices and interpretations that constrain rights and threaten well-being. In a study on values in Qatar that influence change in organizations, Al Dulaimi and Saaid concluded that masculine aspects were negatively correlated with an effective commitment to change.

On the other hand, they stated that femininity better correlated with productivity and a readiness to embrace change (Al Dulaimi & Saaid, 2012, pp. 182–91).

In many places, I sat with women who mustered the courage, often at older ages, to learn to read, to learn religion that was previously pulled out of context to oppress them, or to communicate with other women about physical abuse they endured. In living rooms, makeshift shelters or inconspicuous buildings, these women helped one another, exchanged ideas, put forward innovative steps to create change, and enabled their own transformation and the empowerment of others. These women taught me that despite the bleakest of moments, together we have strength and capacity to make changes, even if at first small. They also taught me to find the strength within myself to question what I've been taught all along, or what I have not been taught all along. For example, mostly every time I come to the West from the Middle East I get some variance of the questions: "Did you feel you were in danger?"; "Did you have to wear the scarf?" or "What was it like as a woman?" Such questions are born out of curiosity around "otherness." Yes, sometimes I was in high-risk situations, but mostly when I chose to put myself in those situations for whatever objectives. Yes, I wear the scarf at times; yes, I have felt it oppressive in specific circumstances, and paradoxically it gives me power, freedom, and significant access in other situations.

Lessons learned from these women are valuable for leaders aiming to implement the SDGs. Particularly, SDG goal 5 aims to "achieve gender equality and empower all women and girls." This is also a central goal shared by the women studied in this chapter. As the UN reports, "[g]ender inequality persists worldwide, depriving women and girls of their basic rights and opportunities […] [a]chieving gender equality and the empowerment of women and girls will require more vigorous efforts, including legal frameworks, to counter deeply rooted gender-based discrimination that often results from patriarchal attitudes and related social norms" (Progress towards the Sustainable Development Goals, E/2017/66). Not unrelated to SDG 5 is SDG 8, which is to promote sustained, inclusive and sustainable economic growth, full and productive employment, and decent work for all. SDG 16 also relates as it strives to promote peaceful and inclusive societies for sustainable development, provide access to justice for all and build effective, accountable, and inclusive institutions at all levels. The women of this study share these goals and offer many useful lessons in their quest to create opportunities for empowerment, inclusion, and sustainable development (Progress towards the Sustainable Development Goals, E/2017/66).

WE CAN'T RECOGNIZE CHANGE WHEN WE CAN'T SEE IT

Our world requires even more concrete examples of women who are achieving change and sustainable development. However, we can't recognize change when we can't see it. To recognize the value of the various forms of agency demonstrated by women in geographically high-risk environments requires evolving the lens we use – a shift in thinking around what kinds of strategies and approaches serve to create change. This includes changing the emancipatory angle of a predominantly Western secular liberal politics framed as a shared feminist consciousness that marginalizes the often more significant means to creating sustainable change, well-being, and peace that women in the Middle East demonstrate in their activism.

Feminism and other disciplines have served to reproduce strong polarities between what it frames and categorizes as liberal and illiberal groups (Phillips, 2007, p. 25). For example, many Middle Eastern women cannot identify with the notion that Islam is the cause of their oppression and that they need to be freed from it. Instead, many of these women address a gender imbalance through embracing the precepts of Islam. The term "Islamic feminism" has gained some popularity and has been used to describe a sort of women's activism that works within Islam and questions aspects of traditional Islamic orthodoxy (Coleman, 2010, p. xxiii). Islamic feminism is, thus, a form of activism that references mostly Islamic sources and texts while sometimes questioning aspects of traditional Islamic jurisprudence, often using *ijtihad*, or the process of arriving at new interpretations of Islamic law through critical reasoning.

The women struggling for freedom in these countries also described a specific concern regarding Westernization corrupting their values such as around piety and/or posing a threat to traditional values and practices. Their struggle was around a shared view that society's principles and values have been lost, and it is values and principles that form the core to well-being of the world in which we live. This misappropriation of Western women's concerns and the biases of a Western secular discourse has marginalized many women's actual struggles and served to diminish their leadership potential.

To move beyond these limitations, we can recognize other examples of non-Western agency by aiming to learn from women who demonstrably influence change and redistribute power. Foucault explains that power cannot be understood merely within the framework of domination as something possessed and used by persons over others. Instead, it permeates life and produces new forms of desires, objects, relations, and discourses (Foucault, 1978, cited in Mahmood, 2004, p. 17). R. Eisler argues that as history has shown, it is not enough to change who controls the means of production and that one kind of top-down control will simply replace another (2007, p. 147). A lens whereby an oppressive force exercises *power over* only to produce either engagement or disengagement is a masculine rational dichotomous approach that serves to negate the existence of various other forms of power largely exercised by women. Other forms include *power to*, which is a generative or productive form of power that creates new possibilities and actions without domination or compliance. *Power with* "involves a sense of the whole being greater than the sum of the individuals, especially when a group tackles problems together" (Rowlands, 1998). For example, in a few poor neighborhoods, some women said that so many of the husbands were lazy or often drunk that from their perspective, women had but no choice to depend on one another, as means for a *power with*. Understanding *power with* as a core feature of leadership for sustainability and well-being for all is key. *Power from within* is the spiritual strength and uniqueness that resides in each one of us and makes us truly human. The capacities developed are self-acceptance and self-respect which extend, in turn, to respect for and acceptance of others as equals (Rowlands, 1998, 14). I add *power for* as a necessary ingredient for the recognition of changes in power relations and power exercised throughout society, in referring to the power one generates to help others and to empower.

We also must look beyond state-focused movements or specifically rights-based struggles to the agency of women within civil society and the economic and private spheres. It is in these spheres, thought to be *apolitical*, that a sense of being, desire, ideas, and a culture supportive of critical values are nurtured and contain great political value to change. They enable a different culture no longer based on fear and deprivation. In these spheres and networks, they learn to use principles that are, in fact, derived from their own culture and religion to see freedom from oppression as an imperative for well-being, even where the same religion is used to oppress them. For example, the women's shelter found that they could free those who had been jailed as prostitutes when dealing with power holders who could not understand their stance on the issue by citing Qur'anic passages that spoke to oppression and dignity of all humans. It is such a value system that becomes the seed for a more wide-spread critical stance and agency.

Interestingly, we miss everyday forms of participation when we are so focused on the state to provide economic provisions or rights. As the UN's progress report for SDG 5 also concludes, "[g]lobally, women's participation in single or lower houses of national parliaments reached 23.4 per cent in 2017, just 10 percentage points higher than in 2000" (Rowlands, 1998). According to the report, such slow progress suggests that stronger political commitment and more ambitious measures and quotas are needed to boost women's political participation and empowerment (Rowlands, 1998). Quotas are only one way to enhance political commitment and women's political participation. It is important to understand that skills development (SDG 8) and inclusion of all into the economy and higher levels of political governance (SDG 16) are steps that can enable true political empowerment and well-being. Many of the women I studied in powerful positions didn't have any idea of the struggles of poor women, for example. The realities of powerful women were often separated from those of most other women. Hence, establishing a quota system without understanding what contributes to bringing out the best of our diverse humanity to ensure a sustainable future includes might actually contribute to the greater marginalization of poor women. We must include providing support for collective efforts that include acts of selfless giving, collaboration, trust, and reciprocity, not just pursue quotas for participation rates of women at the state level of political participation.

We also miss effective leadership for change when we focus on only protests during times of change. I participated in the Arab Spring revolts in Tahrir Square and believe it is not only those who took to the streets in protest around basic rights violations whose forms of participation contributed towards changes. In the literature on politics, civil society development, and democracy, political activism or movements are often accorded priority as the primary sites of political agency (Krause & Finn, 2018), As such, a great deal of attention has been accorded to the time frame of the Arab uprisings. Such movements have value and place where a refusal of the political order must be articulated. I argue, however, that the expansion of values of reciprocity, trust, giving, collaboration, and solidarity[1] – core features of civil society and citizenship mobilization – are enabled by women participating in various unconventional forms of movements such as informal networks. Their pursuits generate change by people who do not see themselves necessarily as activists, but rather as "good doers." They create what A. Bayat calls "non-movements" (2013).

A critical understanding around the kind of agency that is needed to tackle global issues is one that can recognize and appreciate forms of participation that are not directed at just the state or men. To achieve empowerment where individuals, organizations, and societies flourish over the long term requires that we shift our thinking, practices, and consciousness around control and power to values-based thinking and strategies of civility, specifically focused on trust, reciprocity, tolerance, and collaboration, which are essential aspects of democratic thinking.

CONCLUSION

Today's global problems are created by short-sighted, mechanistic thinking of the current economic paradigm (Laszlo, 2006, p. 39). Furthermore, in imposing our epistemologies and frameworks, Westerners miss how the agency of others in especially the *non-developed world* is linked to our struggle and, as a result, miss what contributes to change in a world which, I argue, is actually entirely high risk. The West is not immune to the effects of socioeconomic, political, or environmental crisis and turbulence, and I argue that we have much to learn from women we have thought ill-suited for leading change.

Central to this learning is an integral perspective regarding diversity and a deeper understanding of what leadership capacities are needed to navigate a world in crisis. The women who feel this crisis more directly illustrate the capacities that must be developed. These include spiritual activism and solidarity through innovative and creative forms of collaboration. The women of this study illustrate that countering a global breakdown necessitates the transformation of consciousness that occurs through everyday practice and exercising agency towards the transformation of the self and of power relations. They also demonstrate that disrupting the *status quo* is not limited to protesting or taking to the streets, but by working in solidarity to create trusting relationships, reciprocity and enduring forms of collaboration. For example, the SDG 5 target on reducing violence occurs through such means as working through vertical and horizontal relationships built on trust and solidarity. As such, it is important to study, understand, and support the development of broader networks that can respond to crisis more quickly than can perhaps larger organizations. For example, while taking to the streets in protest forms one aspect of their activism, the women illustrate the centrality of everyday forms of participation and activism. These included fostering collaborations within networks to create a safe place for trafficked women and children, and enabling skills development and learning that embrace democratic and spiritual principles. Of significance are the qualities that these women embodied to persist even when change was not immediately evident. Regardless of whether the change would manifest from these efforts, women leveraged their *power from within* and created transformation by developing the inner qualities of resilience, fortitude, and patience. Achieving the SDGs by 2030 will rely on such persistence. It's also valuable to note that this differs from a *power over*, such as control or resistance practices.

As Koopman argues, "Pragmatism instead refocuses philosophy on the differences we humans can make. Hope is the mood in which we expect that we can make the requisite differences (2006, p. 111)." Indeed, these women provide us a deeper understanding of evolution and our place in the unfolding drama of life on this Earth. Their concerted efforts and the qualities they embody show us how to bring out the best of our diverse humanity to ensure a sustainable future, as is the focus of the SDGs. They pursue activities to support learning and teaching crucial skills to survive. They choose religious interpretations to respond to practices and interpretations that constrain rights and threaten well-being. They transform consciousness through working within principles and value systems that result in sustainable change.

These women deemed ill-suited to empowerment, and the creation of a sustainable future have much to teach the West as we all enter greater complexity and turbulence globally. Their impact on the world as a whole can be greater if we choose to understand that activism must begin now and not when we *feel* we are at high risk because we already are. We can choose innovative ways as these women do to create sustainable change. These women, although in few cases took to the streets to protest, seek refusal largely by working within their systems, not against them. We have much to learn and benefit from their creative ways of creating collaborative relationships with individuals who can also understand and share goals for empowerment and well-being of all. Significantly, we can learn leadership from these women in how to embody the qualities that will get us through the times of difficulty, such as resiliency, trust, persistence, and hope. We can similarly choose to nourish ourselves to continue our quest for achieving the SDGs through not only collaboration but through our own spiritual well-spring that resides in each of us to keep going in the midst of turbulence and crisis.

NOTE

1. The importance of mutual aid, solidarity building, and communitas for citizenship claims-making is grounded prominently in the work of Engin F. Isin. See Engin F. Isin. (2009). Citizenship in flux: The figure of the activist citizen, *Subjectivity*, 29, 367–388.

REFERENCES

Aldulaimi, S. H., & Saaid, S. Md. (2012). The national values impact on organizational change in public organizations in Qatar. *International Journal of Business and Management*, 7(1), (January), 182–190.

Bayat, A. (2013). *Life as politics: How ordinary people change the Middle East*. Cairo: American University in Cairo Press.

Canadian International Development Agency. 2012. Using research on the status of women to improve public policies in the Middle East and North Africa: A capacity toolkit for nongovernmental organizations. *Institute for Women's Policy Research*. Washington, DC: International Foundation for Electoral Systems.

Climate Change and Fire. Natural Resources Canada. (2017). Retrieved from http://www.nrcan.gc.ca/forests/fire-insects-disturbances/fire/13155

Coleman, I. (2010). *Paradise beneath her feet: How women are transforming the Middle East*. New York, NY: Random House.

Eisler, R. (2007). *Creating a caring economics: The real wealth of nations.* San Francisco, CA: Berrett-Koehler Publishers.

Foucault, M. (1978). *The history of sexuality.* New York, NY: Pantheon.

Gerzon, M. (2012). *Global Citizens: How our vision of the world is outdated, and what we can do about it.* London: Rider.

Global Peace Index. Measuring Peace and Assessing Risk. (2014). The Institute of Economics and Peace. Retrieved from http://economicsandpeace.org/wp-content/uploads/2015/06/2014-Global-Peace-Index-REPORT_0−1.pdf

Hale, S. (1991). *Gender politics in Sudan: Islamism, socialism, and the state.* Boulder, CO: Westview Press.

Ife, J. (2016). *Community development in an uncertain world: Vision analysis and practice* (2nd ed.). New York, NY: Cambridge University Press.

Isin, E. F. (2009). Citizenship in flux: The figure of the activist citizen. *Subjectivity, 29,* 367−388.

Koopman, C. (2006). Pragmatism as a Philosophy of Hope: Emerson, James, Dewey, Rorty. *Journal of Speculative Philosophy, 20*(2), 106−116.

Krause, W. (2013). *Spiritual activism: Keys for personal and political success.* San Francisco, CA: Turning Stone Press.

Krause, W., & Finn, M. (2018). Islamic and Islamist women activists in Qatar post-Arab uprisings: Implications for the study of refusal and citizenship. In H. Kraetzschmar & P. Rivetti (Eds.), *Islamists and the politics of the Arab uprisings: Governance, pluralisation and contention.* Edinburgh: Edinburgh University Press.

Kristof, N. (2017, August 26). There Once Was a Great Nation With an Unstable Leader, *Sunday Review,* Retrieved from https://www.nytimes.com/2017/08/26/opinion/sunday/caligula-roman-empire.html?emc=eta1

Laszlo, E. (2006). *The chaos point: The world at the crossroads.* Consett: Piatkus.

Mahmood, S. (2004). *Politics of piety.* Princeton, NJ: Princeton University Press.

Natural Resources Canada. (2017). Climate change and fire. Retrieved from http://www.nrcan.gc.ca/forests/fire-insects-disturbances/fire/13155

Phillips, A. (2007). *Multiculturalism without culture*. Princeton, NJ: Princeton University Press.

Ross, M. L. (2012). *The oil curse: How petroleum wealth shapes the development of nations*. Princeton, NJ: Princeton University Press.

Rowlands, J. (1998). A word of the times, but what does it mean? Empowerment in the is course and practice of development. In H. Afshar (Ed.), *Women and empowerment: Illustrations from the Third World*. New York, NY: St. Martin's Press.

Transparency International: The Global Coalition Against Corruption. (2016). Retrieved from https://www.transparency.org

Truth and Reconciliation Commission of Canada. Calls to Action. Winnipeg, Manitoba: Truth and Reconciliation Commission of Canada (2012). Retrieved from http://www.trc.ca/websites/trcinstitution/File/2015/Findings/Calls_to_Action_English2.pdf

UN Sustainable Development Knowledge Platform. (2015). Retrieved from https://sustainabledevelopment.un.org/post2015/transformingourworld

Wilkinson, R., & Pickett, K. (2010). *The spirit level: Why equality is better for everyone*. London: Penguin.

Zuber-Skerritt, O. (2012). Introduction to action research for sustainable development in a turbulent world. In O. Zuber-Skerritt (Ed.), *Action research for sustainable development in a turbulent world*. Bingley: Emerald Group Publishing.

PART II

LEADING FROM ALIGNED VALUES

6

FOSSIL FUEL DIVESTMENT: THE POWER OF POSITIVELY DEVIANT LEADERSHIP FOR CATALYZING CLIMATE ACTION AND FINANCING CLEAN ENERGY

Abigail Abrash Walton

INTRODUCTION

Climate change, or global warming, has emerged as one of the most significant dynamics of the Anthropocene Epoch (Zalasiewicz et al., 2008). The predominant contributor to climate change is the combustion of fossil fuels by humans (Heede, 2014; Melillo, Richmond, & Yohe, 2014). Sustainable Development Goals 7 (affordable and clean energy) and 13 (climate action) speak directly to addressing the challenge of averting the worst climate change impacts by transitioning to low-carbon energy systems. As the impacts of a changing climate become increasingly visible, world leaders have called for urgent action (European Parliament, 2017; Paris Agreement under the United Nations Framework Convention on Climate Change, 2015). Creating a sense of urgency is only the first step in a change process (Kotter, 2007). How do we mobilize the scale of climate action needed for tackling this challenge? We need effective change leaders, at all levels and in all sectors, both formal and informal, who can blaze new trails to address climate change, within their spheres of influence and do so with keen attention to sustainability and social justice outcomes.

This chapter highlights the actions of leaders pursuing fossil fuel divestment: selling financial investments in the world's largest fossil fuel extraction companies, and reinvesting those resources in clean energy. The chapter presents two new conceptual models: mission-aligned investing, at the organizational level, and mission-aligned leadership, at the individual level. These models exemplify and provide concrete structure for organizational leaders and others who seek to improve institutional capacity to address climate change (SDG target 13.3). How do our financial resources perpetuate fossil fuel combustion? How are we promoting clean, renewable, socially just energy sources? Learning from the experience of the change leaders studied here can deepen understanding of how organizational stewards can proactively, successfully, and effectively advance climate action and clean energy innovation by leveraging organizational assets.

TAKING COLLECTIVE ACTION: THE FOSSIL FUEL DIVESTMENT MOVEMENT

Since 2011, an active and expanding worldwide movement has emerged that is focused on divestment of all fossil fuel company holdings and reinvestment of those resources in climate solution-oriented approaches, including clean energy technologies. Pledged and/or already-divested global institutional assets are estimated at US$5.5 trillion (8 percent of global stock market value) (Arabella Advisors, 2016).

Members of the US philanthropic sector formally joined the movement in January 2014, when 17 foundations launched the Divest-Invest: Philanthropy initiative (Arabella Advisors, 2015; Dorsey & Mott, 2014). Members of the initiative span a spectrum of positions, including those with assets that are fully divested from fossil fuels and others that are at earlier stages of moving to complete divestment (Abrash Walton, 2018).

The Divest-Invest Philanthropy sub-movement approaches fossil fuel divestment based on arguments that moving resources away from the sources of carbon pollution is a moral imperative, financially prudent, and creates opportunities for innovative re-investment in renewable energy and other clean energy enterprises (Abrash Walton, 2018; Divest-Invest Philanthropy, 2017). The movement's approach is in sync with SDG Target

7.2: increasing the share of renewable energy in the global energy mix and its corollary indicator (7.2.1).

PHILANTHROPY AND CLIMATE ACTION: CHARTING THE BLUE OCEAN OF DIVESTMENT

This chapter provides firsthand reflections through in-depth interviews with 18 philanthropic leaders who are navigating the relatively uncharted blue ocean of fossil fuel divestment and clean energy reinvestment. Participants in the study were clustered primarily near Boston, MA; New York, NY; San Francisco, CA; Seattle, WA; and Washington, DC (see Table 1). The total combined organizational assets equaled US$3 billion and ranged from US$640,000 to US$801 million. Mean assets size was US$83 million.

The study examined leaders' motivations and actions in pursuing divestment, while simultaneously exercising their fiduciary duty to steward institutional assets. What explained the readiness of these leaders to engage in this unconventional investment behavior? What were the outcomes of divestment on leaders and their organizations?

A substantial body of research, scholarship, and theorizing has focused on the role of formal leaders in facilitating change within their organizations (e.g., Gilley, Dixon, & Gilley, 2008; Heifetz, Grashow, & Linsky, 2009; Kanter, 1999; Kotter, 2007; Quinn, 2004; Sirkin, Keenan, & Jackson, 2005). However, scholars have noted the need for more research that examines leaders' facilitation of pro-environmental behavior change within organizations (Metcalf & Benn, 2013; Robertson & Barling, 2013).

At a time in human history when we need catalytic change leaders, positive deviance has emerged as a leadership characteristic positively associated with environmental sustainability (Parkin, 2010). Positive deviance can be a key strategy for effective and lasting change. Positive deviance is defined as "intentional behaviors that depart from the norms of a referent group in honorable ways" (Spreitzer & Sonenshein, 2004, p. 832). Pascale and Sternin (2005) emphasized the innovative nature of positive deviants, noting that their "uncommon practices and behaviors enable them to find better solutions to problems than others in their communities" (p. 2).

Leading organizational change is not easy. Doing so to advance sustainability within the organization and globally is also challenging.

Table 1. Descriptors for Participants.

Participant Identifier	Total Institutional Assets (Millions US$)	Institutional Role	US Geographic Region
F1	<10	President	West Coast
F2	<10	Trustee	East Coast
F3	<10	Trustee	East Coast
F4	10–30	Board Chair	West Coast
F5	10–30	Executive Director	West Coast
F6	10–30	Executive Director	East Coast
F7	10–30	President	Mountain/Midwest
F8	10–30	President	East Coast
F9	10–30	Trustee	East Coast
F10	30–100	Executive Director	Mountain/Midwest
F11	30–100	Executive Director	East Coast
F12	30–100	Executive Director	West Coast
F13	>100	Executive Director	West Coast
F14	>100	Executive Director	East Coast
F15	>100	CEO	West Coast
F16	>100	Trustee	West Coast
F17	>100	Executive Director	East Coast
F18	>100	President	East Coast

Understanding leaders' positive deviance in pursuing divestment, an unconventional investing behavior, could yield insights that can advance understanding of effective organizational change leadership, particularly in support of climate action and clean energy.

Mission-aligned Investing

Leaders contextualized foundation divestment commitments within a broader movement toward mission-aligned investment decision-making. Divestment was, therefore, a specific investing behavior change, motivated by an awareness of and desire to address climate change, and informed by organizational leaders' desire to align institutional investments with an organizational mission (e.g., environmental protection; civic engagement and creating a socially just, sustainable, and peaceful society).

Leaders contrasted their mission-aligned investing stance with what they viewed as the norm for the philanthropic sector. One board leader's comments about the traditional disconnect between institutional investing and programming decisions were typical:

> There [are] still a lot of mental barriers. There [are] still a lot of people that are unwilling [...] or unable to get their mind around the idea that they don't need to have Exxon in their portfolio [...] [T]here is still a preponderance of investment people who have [...] the idea that [...] it's okay to make a mess over here. It just gives us more dollars to give away for cleanup over here. And that type of thinking [...] never really worked, but we allowed ourselves to believe it, and we should be smarter than that now. [F16]

Leaders used words such as "evolution" and "continuum" to describe the story behind the organization's divestment decision. This progression involved a shift in mental models.

One executive emphasized the shift as follows:

> [T]here's a realization that these are not two separate organizations, one that makes grants and one that makes investments and never the twain shall meet. [...] [T]he benefit is in understanding that your investments can serve your mission, or they can hurt your mission. You're either undercutting potentially your grants with your investments or being inconsistent values-wise, but you're also potentially leaving money on the table, leaving tools on the table that could be used in service of your mission. [F17]

Levels of Mission-aligned Investing

How did organizations move from a conventional investing stance to divestment? A key result of the study was a model of mission-aligned investing (see **Figure 1**), comprising six levels of investing. Readiness to pursue divestment was nested within this progression of institutional investing phases. Each level, beyond the baseline of Level 1 — in which investing decisions are separate from considerations of organizational mission, vision, values, and

Fig. 1. Conceptual Model: Levels of Mission-aligned Investing.

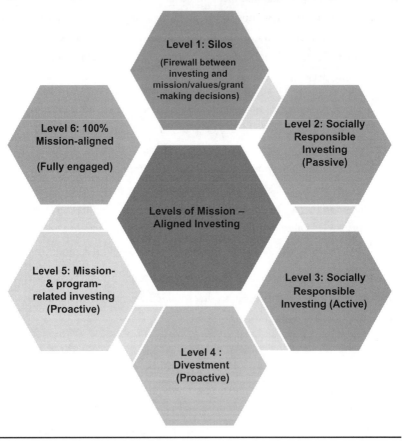

grant-making – represents an increasing degree of mission-aligned investing, moving from passive to fully engaged.

Level 1: Silos. Level 1 is conceptualized as a conventional investing stance. There is a complete separation between decision-making about investing and programs. Investing is not guided by the institutional mission, vision, and values. The investing priority is maximizing financial return. Grant-making is based on the conventional 5% annual payout generated from 95% of the institution's assets ("95/5 split"). Leaders used words including "firewall," "old school," and "traditional" to describe this level. As one executive described, "the goal of the investors and the Investment Committee is to make as much money as possible, which then allows a trickle-down effect of 5% payout for good. And that's still a very common and prominent belief" [F15].

Levels 2 and 3: Socially responsible investing (passive and active). Socially responsible investing included a range of actions. In Level 2, foundations adopted negative screening of investments (i.e., exclusion of specific types of holdings, such as corporations producing nuclear weapons or tobacco) to positive screens, based on environmental, social, and governance (ESG) criteria (e.g., community banks). In Level 3, foundation leaders actively participated in shareholder advocacy. Advocacy included voting with the foundation's proxies, signing onto shareholder resolutions, and meeting with corporate management to advance a mission-aligned change agenda.

Level 4: Divestment (proactive). Level 4 is self-initiated divestment where there may be no pre-existing screen available to inform investing choices. Divestment signals a shift to proactive institutional leadership engagement in "owning what you own." Divestment, in the words of one board leader, serves as a "gateway drug" to self-directed mobilizing institutional assets for change, based on mission, vision, values, and grant-making. Ceasing to invest in the continued extraction and combustion of fossil fuels is a major climate action commitment.

Participants viewed divestment as a clear departure from active socially responsible investing (Level 3) in the form of shareholder advocacy and engagement. Rather than continuing to engage with corporate management in the hope of changing the fossil fuel energy sector, divestment signaled a commitment to a new level of change leadership: intentional rejection of fossil fuel holdings.

When participants spoke about deciding to divest, they described feeling elation, relief, liberation, satisfaction, and pride. "[I]t felt exhilarating. It's just really one of those moments where you put your money where your mouth is [...] I feel very proud of them as a board and us as an institution," said one executive [F12]. Another board leader said:

> *[W]hen you think about [...] the philanthropic management of capital, the culture of wealth preservation or accumulation, the culture of our financial industry and the constraints that it puts on the expression of our values and what we're working towards in terms of a more just, healthy, diverse, rich world, [then] it's really*

*significant to liberate yourself from that to start to create something
different. [F3]*

One board leader's reflection indicated a twinge of regret at not having
divested sooner, "I wish we just had gone down this path earlier" [F16].

Level 5: Mission- and program-related investing (proactive). In Level 5,
the investing stance moves to proactively consider financial and social
returns, consistent with the institutional mission. This stance represents a
clear departure from the 95/5 split, as a greater percentage of institutional
assets are invested in mission- and program-related investments.

This "hands-on" capitalism involved a higher degree of proactive engagement in investing choices. As one board leader described, "[W]e're not independently operating a sustainable forestland acquisition and management
company, but we are making the decision to invest in those vehicles ourselves" [F3].

Level 6: 100% mission-aligned investing. In Level 6, investing is 100%
mission-aligned. Investments are based on financial and social returns. All
assets are deployed as tools for change. There may be a direct collaboration
between the foundation investment committee and program staff in decision-
making about investments as well as grant-making.

Mission-aligned Leadership

What were leaders thinking and doing as they pursued divestment? What
defined their change leadership? Leaders exhibited five key aspects of mindset and action: (1) owning what you own; (2) using assets as a tool for
change; (3) embracing change as an opportunity to catalyze innovation; (4)
communicating and collaborating with others to mobilize change; and (5)
engaging in learning and building a community of practice. These dimensions may be conceptualized as a model of mission-aligned leadership (see
Figure 2).

This model offers a guide for situating ourselves with respect to advancing breakthrough progress in addressing climate change. It invites us to consider in what ways we might — or could — be exercising our own mission-
aligned leadership.

Owning what you own. Leaders shifted to direct, decisive, proactive
engagement with institutional investing, punctuated by the divestment

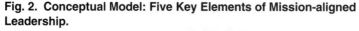

Fig. 2. Conceptual Model: Five Key Elements of Mission-aligned Leadership.

commitment and subsequent implementation. This change reflected leaders' new sense of responsibility for providing strategic and principled direction for the institution's investments. Leaders spoke about recognizing that they could "fire" their investment advisors and about feeling "liberated" from prior unquestioning reliance on those professionals. As one leader put it, "[A]re you owning what you own? You're responsible for those investments. You hire investment professionals to work for you. If they're not willing to [divest], then there's a question about whether they're the right investment professionals for you" [F17].

Taking a stand on divestment was a turning point in bringing leadership and mission consistency to a foundation's investments, matching behavior with values and beliefs. This engaged leadership stance, similar to the shift – at an organizational level – between Levels 3 and 4 of the mission-aligned investing model, was characterized by leaders' direct attention to actual investments and directing investment professionals. Leaders embraced this stance, even when acknowledging a lack of expertise in the investment domain. A board leader described his desire for the foundation to "put our money where our mouth is [...] it's time to stop talking and do something" [F16]. An executive acknowledged the uncertainty some might feel: "I can understand [being nervous about divesting], but at some point [...] you really have to, oh, boy, fish or cut bait" [F5].

Exercising investment leadership included overcoming the lack of will or imagination of investment advisors. As one leader noted, "[We] talked internally and to our financial advisors, and everyone said it would be too hard for us to do [...] Then we started paying more attention and said, well, how could we do it? What would we have to change?" [F9].

Leaders recognized that their focus on their own investments was not the norm for those in the executive role in the philanthropic sector. One leader described conversations with other foundation leaders in her region:

> [M]y biggest take-away [...] is that [...] many [...] CEOs who are
> running very large foundations don't understand investment
> decisions at all. They have ceded all of their responsibility and
> power to their [Chief Investment Officers]. So when their CIO tells
> them, we can't do it, they don't have either the willingness or
> knowledge to question how they arrived at that decision. [F12]

This leader reflected on the implicit role definition and power dynamics of the foundation executive's relationship with those guiding the institution's investments:

> [I]t is interesting that the [...] philosophy of many CIOs, which is,
> I'll make the money, you spend it, and don't bother me, actually
> has been integrated into how many CEOs think about their role.
> They're there as programmatic [...] and civic leaders but [...] they're
> not going to touch the investments. [F12]

Using all of your assets as a tool for change. Importantly, leaders' shift to proactive, decisive engagement included a shift in mindset to view all institutional assets as "tools for change." A board leader spoke about leveraging the philanthropic sector's assets as tools for change: "[T]here are other possibilities to create change with those assets than simply granting" [F4]. Another board leader emphasized the importance, for small foundations, of deploying all their assets in service of mission-aligned change:

> The conversation about divestment needs to be a precedent to a
> conversation about investment. And investment is a really
> important component of us allocating our resources in a way that
> maximizes the change that we can create. [...] Having 100 percent
> of our assets at work in enterprises that express our values is a 20X
> multiplier on just giving away 5 percent of our money in the form

of grants. And that's a really significant multiplier effect for a foundation [...] which has $7 million in assets. So are [you] a $350,000 a year foundation [...] or are [you] a $7 million foundation? How you think about yourself in that way is changed dramatically by your commitment to the divestment and investment process. [F3]

One chief executive noted that though the foundation had not engaged in climate change grant-making because the programming challenge seemed too overwhelming, board members recognized fossil fuel divestment as a significant means of acting within that foundation's sphere of influence to address climate change. Another executive articulated a range of institutional means, in addition to the foundation's financial investments and grant-making, for "contributing to the fight against climate catastrophe" [F18]. These included reputation, brand name, convening capacity, and intellectual assets.

Embracing change as an opportunity to catalyze innovation. Being able to see divestment as an opportunity to stimulate innovation was a key aspect that distinguished these leaders' approaches to understanding the benefits of divestment. Leaders viewed fossil fuel divestment as an act of leadership that was anticipated to send a signal to the financial services sector. This signaling, through a shift in demand, was expected to lead to fossil-fuel-free investing options as a norm. One leader's view of divestment exemplified this perspective:

I always said that I'm going to do some riskier investments [so] that when I'm done, my parents can do it through their teachers' retirement fund. [...] Transformational for us is investing in a solar industry that's nascent and through those activities bringing down the cost of solar. [F9]

Another leader noted that "part of the theory of change behind Divest-Invest Philanthropy was that we could support the larger movement [and] create demand for [investment] products that would then make it possible and easier for other institutions to join in" [F17]. A board leader spoke about the shift in investing as an urgently needed transformation process toward a more just and sustainable society. "[I]t's just so imperative that everything that we as a foundation do is either turning our back in every way we can on contributing to the destruction and beginning to build the groundwork, build the models, build the oases. [...] It's metamorphosis" [F2].

Communicating and collaborating with others to mobilize change. A distinctive aspect of mission-aligned leaders' divestment change process was their proactive external change leadership. This dimension of leaders' actions exemplifies SDG target 13.3 by building human and institutional capacity to address climate change. Some leaders not only talked with others within their organizations; many also reached out to engage colleagues at other institutions and to speak publicly about their organization's divestment decision. Some leaders also communicated about the change to grant-seekers and to their social and professional networks. This communication and collaboration with others catalyzed climate action by other organizations and individuals, thereby multiplying leaders' climate action impact.

Outreach was intended to create a demonstration effect on others that would shift social norms. This element was evident in one leader's statement about the importance of making the divestment commitment public. "[I]t's so important that folks get out there and say, it's okay. You can do this. To [...] be the early adopters who maybe make the mistakes or figure out how to make it work and give other people a reason and an example to follow" [F2].

Leaders took their change process to a new level by inviting and encouraging other foundations to join. One executive's organization was among the original 17 foundations to commit publicly to divestment. She described her outreach, beginning with the initial news coverage:

> *When the* New York Times *article came out in January of 2014, I posted it on Facebook. I tweeted about it. And I don't post and I don't tweet very often. [...] I was very proud of it. I've spoken on panels, and I've talked to people and made outreach to colleagues in foundations that I'm trying to get to join.* [F12]

This leader spoke about the impact — the ripple effects — of her change leadership outreach:

> *[T]wo [...] people that I talked with last year [...] a CEO and a general counsel [...] they've [...] said, okay, I think actually I need to learn about this [...] [The CEO is] looking at pulling together a pool of invest[ment] resources that would be*

earmarked for addressing climate change. And the general
counsel just called me last night and said, I wrote a report to the
board. They are going to begin an investigation and look at how
we can do everything within our institutional power to better
match our commitment to addressing climate change, including
looking at our investments. [F12]

Another leader spoke about her first forays into challenging her peers to "own what you own." As she described it, prior to the emergence of the divestment movement, at a meeting of foundations committed to funding environmental campaigns against coal as an energy source, she asked "who in the room is invested in coal. [...] And the room went quiet" [F17]. Her question was a professional challenge to colleagues to take responsibility for their institutions' investments in the very energy companies that their grant programs were challenging.

Once she had led divestment within her own institution, she did not stop. She proactively reached out to other foundation leaders to divest. "I've now talked myself to probably 40, 50, I don't know, more than 60 foundations," she said. "I've spoken to a lot of investment committees, and I've spoken to a lot of boards of directors" [F17]. She highlighted efforts that she and others had taken: "We [...] [all] sign[ed] a letter [...] to the 3,000 largest foundations in the U.S. saying, climate change is like no other issue. It means no business as usual. And we call on you to have this discussion" [F17].

Heightened engagement in communication went beyond philanthropic sector norms. One leader described the tension that he and board members felt in determining to what extent the foundation should be public with its divestment decision:

[W]e are always wrestling with that internal dynamic of, yes, we
want to be courageous and, yes, we want to be risk takers but [...]
no, we don't want our name on buildings and headlines and, no,
we don't want to be perceived as being self-aggrandizing, and we
prefer to be humble and quiet.[...] [T]here was that tension there.
And that's why when we made the decision in 2013, part of that
decision included support from the board for the notion that
I would be public with our decision process. [F15]

One of the evident ripples was the generative effect of the divestment decision, for foundation grantees. For example, one leader noted that her foundation had received a thank you letter from a grantee that said, "We can't tell you how much this inspires us and means to us and gives us energy for our work to know that we have allies in places like the foundations. It really matters" [F12].

Engaging in learning and building a community of practice. Analysis revealed a fifth key element of mission-aligned leadership: openness to new, networked, and continuous learning. Some leaders not only reached out to catalyze divestment by other organizations, they also intentionally developed a network for learning through a nascent community of practice. Participants spoke about the importance of blazing trails for other organizational leaders who are considering divestment. They cautioned others considering divestment not to "go it alone." This focus on sharing new learning with others was evident in these leaders' statements:

> [O]ne of the things I've encouraged the trustees to consider is that as we go through [making mission-aligned changes to our portfolio], and see whether we think there's something educable about it, that we publish it somewhere, someplace to share whatever we learn. [F14]

> [W]e want our effort [...] the challenges and the successes and the lessons we learned to be useful to others who are looking at the possibility of divestment. So we wanted to be very, very honest about this, and we want to be open and transparent. [F18]

Participants spoke about their desire to learn from and with others by participating in a community of practice. For one executive, the enriched learning environment created by other foundation leaders' creation of a community of practice was an advantage of joining Divest-Invest Philanthropy. "We talked about the fact that we would benefit from a community of practice that was developing among foundation experts around this issue" [F13]. Another board member noted, "I like the way I've learned about how it is impacting the fossil fuel companies. So, getting involved with that community has been very empowering" [F1].

For another leader, collective action and an ongoing community of practice were essential ingredients for success:

> [I]t was important that we do this as a cohort. One, there's safety in numbers, and philanthropy doesn't actually collaborate all that

much. So it was kind of unprecedented and particularly that it was on the investment side. [...] It would also create the basis of what we have called a community of practice [...] foundations could do this together and learn from each other, share information on the mechanics of divesting, share information on how to invest in climate solutions, and to [...] reinforce each other's journey. [F17]

Mission-aligned Leadership: Positive Deviance Outcomes

What can we learn about the impact of fossil fuel divestment – as a positively deviant act – on leaders, their organizations, and sectoral norms? Outcomes of participants' positively deviant mission-aligned leadership were evident at three levels: personal, organizational, and sectoral. These outcomes suggest the overarching benefits of pursuing mission-aligned investing, particularly through fossil fuel divestment.

Personal outcomes. Positive deviance is theorized to yield a sense of well-being for those who engage in it. A number of participants spoke about the way in which the divestment commitment and process had changed them, at a personal level. The personal change was apparent in one executive's reflection:

> *It energized me. [...] So did it change me? Yes. I learned a lot more about investments. I developed tremendous new relationships with foundation colleagues [...] I just have such tremendous respect for [...] the folks that have stood up and joined this in the philanthropic world. [F17]*

Another leader spoke about the positive and challenging aspects of the divestment commitment:

> *It has changed me. [...] [T]he whole experience has [...] deeply and powerfully reinforced my sense of personal commitment to the climate struggle and my dedication to our institutional contribution to this struggle, and it's done it in a way that has helped me feel an even more profound sense of responsibility and a more profound sense of community.*
>
> *I will also say it has some other effects that haven't been quite so wonderful. There are some colleagues in the foundation community who are not so happy to see me coming. [...] Their*

*stakeholders are not ready to take this step and even though they,
as foundation leaders, might wish that they could, they're
constrained. [F18]*

Organizational outcomes. A number of leaders spoke about the way in
which the divestment commitment – and moving to mission-aligned investing, more broadly – catalyzed changes within their organizations. For example, one leader noted that, while not foreseen or planned for, the evolution
to mission-aligned investing – and, specifically, the divestment decision –
had yielded important and generative organizational benefits. The outcomes
were financial savings, a newly energized board and staff, and a new norm
for the organization of removing the separation between investing and program decisions. As she described it:

*[E]mbarking on this mission-aligned approach overall did three
things. It ended up saving us money because we took such a deep
dive into our investments, we realized we were getting overcharged
and paying heavy fees. So we were able to actually save on
investment costs. Second, it energized our board about the
investments in a way that they hadn't been before. So it got excited
about the investments that otherwise were considered the boring
part of being on the board. And now our Investment Committee
meetings are much more [...] engaged, and they're much more
interesting. And, third, we now have our Investment Committee
and our program staff meeting together. So it also energized our
staff to think about what they could be doing with the investments,
whether it's through divestment, investment, asset activism like
shareholder resolutions or proxy votes. So it had very positive
consequences for our institution. [F17]*

None of the participants identified a drop in performance of the investment portfolio. Instead, participants spoke about the positive financial performance of their holdings, post-divestment. One leader's story was
representative of this trend. She shared, "We got out of coal before coal
tanked. We got out of oil before oil tanked. And since we have become mission aligned [...] [w]e're on average beating our benchmarks by 2%. So
we're doing great" [F17].

Financial sector outcomes. A number of leaders described the innovation
of an expanded set of investment options and financial services, which they

associated with the divestment movement and their own leadership. One executive's description of the impact of the foundation's divestment commitment on the foundation's investment advisors was similar to other leaders' statements. "[Our advisors] now consider this a niche business for them, so they're running with it as fast as they can" [F11].

Other participants spoke about the way in which their internal organizational shift to divestment and mission-aligned investment was mirrored by transformational change among conventional Wall Street investment firms. One leader related his perspective on this change:

> I don't know if you saw yesterday, Goldman Sachs bought Imprint Capital. [...] It's great for Goldman Sachs because they need to do something. [...] We took our foundation and moved it because they couldn't—not so much on the divest side, but even on the reinvest side—they really had very limited product offering. [...] [W]e probably weren't the only one. And so they went ahead and bought their way into the market. [F9]

Another leader's story revealed the way in which the learning and capacity-building generated by his foundation's process of divesting and moving to mission-aligned investing had contributed to new leadership roles for members of the foundation's investment committee:

> As a result in part [...] of his work on the [foundation's] investment committee [...] [one of our committee members] was named as the lead person at [his bank] to manage their ESG investment work [...] which demonstrates that one of the world's leading investment banks is changing as a result of what's going on in the marketplace and what they see happening in the future. [...] [T]he momentum is building and things are going to continue to rapidly change. I'm certain of it. [F18]

Another leader described the impact of her foundation's commitment to divestment. The foundation's investment advisor told her, "because you folks gave me the freedom to not focus on quarterly performance [...] your little $3 million foundation has influenced over $100 million worth of investments [from his other clients] into this direction" [F2].

CONCLUSION

How do we strengthen our own change leadership in tackling climate change? How might each of us engage in mission-aligned leadership and investing, within our own spheres of influence? Leaders in this study of fossil fuel divestment were pioneers of a new mission-aligned approach to institutional investing. They were also modeling mission-aligned leadership, engaging in positive deviance by departing from the norms of philanthropy and conventional asset investing to publicly commit to divesting from fossil fuels.

Some leaders were so far on the leading edge of this change that they were abandoning, and, in some cases, transforming Wall Street. They chose instead to place assets in investments that were more resonant with their institutions' values, mission, and programs and were seen as achieving social and/or environmental benefits and financial returns. These "hands-on" capitalists directed financial resources to proactively seek pro-climate solutions. Their motto might best be described, in the words of one leader, as owning what you own. As another leader put it, they were committed to "leveraging social change with all available tools" by aiming to deploy one hundred percent of their institutions' financial assets in service of mission.

My research suggests that organizational leaders can contribute to effective climate action and clean energy development (SDGs 13 and 7, respectively) by taking more direct responsibility for investment of institutional assets. In doing so, they may spark innovation and unleash new energy that enhances the well-being of the organization and its members and contribute to organizational and global sustainability. They may also experience a higher level of satisfaction, pride, happiness, and engagement with their organizational roles. They may flourish and contribute to others' flourishing. Positively deviant leadership focused on fossil fuel divestment can be effective change leadership for catalyzing climate action and financing clean energy.

REFERENCES

Abrash Walton, A. (in press). Positive deviance and behavior change: A research methods approach for understanding fossil fuel divestment.

Energy Research and Social Science: Problems of Method in the Social Study of Energy and Climate Change. doi: 10.1016/j.erss.2018.07.003

Arabella Advisors. (2015). Measuring the growth of the global fossil fuel divestment and clean energy investment movement. Retrieved from http://www.arabellaadvisors.com/wp-content/uploads/2015/09/Measuring-the-Growth-of-the-Divestment-Movement.pdf

Arabella Advisors. (2016). The global fossil fuel divestment and clean energy investment movement. Retrieved from https://www.arabellaadvisors.com/wp-content/uploads/2016/12/Global_Divestment_Report_2016.pdf

Dorsey, E., & Mott, R. N. (2014, January 30). Philanthropy rises to the fossil divest-invest challenge. *The Huffington Post.* Retrieved from http://www.huffingtonpost.com/ellen- dorsey/philanthropy-rises-to-the_b_4690774.html

European Parliament. (2017, October 4). COP23: The EU should ratchet up its climate goals. European Parliament Press Office. Retrieved from http://www.europarl.europa.eu/news/en/press-room/20171002IPR85129/cop23-the-eu-should-ratchet-up-its-climate-goals

Gilley, A., Dixon, P., & Gilley, J. W. (2008). Characteristics of leadership effectiveness: Implementing change and driving innovation in organizations. *Human Resource Development Quarterly, 19*(2), 153–169. doi:10.1002/hrdq.1232

Heede, R. (2014). Tracing anthropogenic carbon dioxide and methane emissions to fossil fuel and cement producers, 1854–2010. *Climatic Change, 122*(1–2), 229–241. doi:10.1007/s10584-013-0986-y

Heifetz, R. A., Grashow, A., & Linsky, M. (2009). *The practice of adaptive leadership: Tools and tactics for changing your organization and the world.* Boston, MA: Harvard Business Press.

Kanter, R. M. (1999). The enduring skills of change leaders. *Leader to Leader, 13*, 15–22. doi:10.1002/ltl.40619991305

Kotter, J. P. (2007). Leading change. *Harvard Business Review, 85*(1), 96–103.

Melillo, J. M., Richmond, T. C., & Yohe, G. W. (Eds.). (2014). *Climate change impacts in the United States: The third national climate assessment.*

Washington, DC: U.S. Global Change Research Program. doi:10.7930/
J0Z31WJ2

Metcalf, L., & Benn, S. (2013). Leadership for sustainability: An evolution
of leadership ability. *Journal of Business Ethics*, 112(3), 369–384.
doi:10.1007/s10551-012-1278-6

Paris Agreement under the United Nations Framework Convention on
Climate Change. (2015, December 12). Draft decision – CP.21. Retrieved
from http://unfccc.int/resource/docs/2015/cop21/eng/l09.pdf

Parkin, S. (2010). *The positive deviant: Sustainability leadership in a
perverse world*. London: Earthscan.

Pascale, R. T., & Sternin, J. (2005). Your company's secret change agents.
Harvard Business Review, 83(5), 72–81.

Quinn, R. E. (2004). *Building the bridge as you walk on it: A guide for
leading change* (1st ed.). San Francisco, CA: Jossey-Bass.

Robertson, J. L., & Barling, J. (2013). Greening organizations through
leaders' influence on employees' pro-environmental behaviors. *Journal of
Organizational Behavior*, 34(2), 176–194. doi:10.1002/job.182

Sirkin, H. L., Keenan, P., & Jackson, A. (2005, October). The hard side of
change management. *Harvard Business Review*, 37–45.

Spreitzer, G. M., & Sonenshein, S. (2004). Toward the construct definition
of positive deviance. *The American Behavioral Scientist*, 47(6), 828–847,
doi:10.1177/0002764203260212

Zalasiewicz, J., Williams, M., Smith, A., Barry, T. L., Coe, A. L., Bown, P.
R., ... Stone, P.(2008). Are we now living in the Anthropocene? *GSA Today*,
18(2), 4–8. doi:10.1130/GSAT01802A.1

7

ALIGNING YOUR TEAM'S VISION WITH THE WORLD'S BOLD GOALS

Adriana Salazar, David H. Garcia and Mariana Quiroga

INTRODUCTION

In 2015, the United Nations developed the 17 Sustainable Development Goals to focus diverse local and regional actions so that together we can collectively address worldwide needs and create a shared global future (UN, 2015). Yet, this shared agenda and our future require more than just written goals. It requires a higher level of engagement and action at the community level that can only be achieved by focusing on how people and teams connect to this vision and by fostering actions which will lead to accomplishing these goals. This is where Cirklo, a social innovation consulting firm, comes in. Using our expertise in human-centered design and innovation we have developed a process with clear steps and tools to align a diverse team´s vision within the framework of the SDGs. Called the *Team Alignment Tool*, this process can be used by diverse leaders to guide the community level actions required to reach observable and practical results aligned under the SDG goals.

The Team Alignment Tool provides a step-by-step guide for business groups and organizations to assess their motivations for change, individual expertise, and collective knowledge in order to identify the SDG(s) they want to address. Then the tool guides them through the subsequent actions necessary to integrate their vision into an impact strategy.

THE EMERGENCE OF OUR APPROACH – CREATING A COLLABORATIVE ECOSYSTEM IN MEXICO

Today, Cirklo is a leading social innovation consulting company in Mexico City that serves organizations and institutions from the private, public, and nonprofit sectors. We help them (1) develop, test, and implement purpose-driven innovative solutions for management services and (2) develop products that generate social, economic, and environmental impact throughout Latin America and internationally ("Cirklo, Impulsando Empresas," 2018). Cirklo first and foremost focuses on people, the motors of true social change, through the application of human-centered design strategies and innovation methodologies. First, we generate understanding amongst stakeholders. Then, we help them define the desired end-state. Finally, we co-develop test strategies and prototypes to meet the needs and objectives identified by both clients and other stakeholders.

It is important to recount Cirklo's roots to better contextualize the Team Alignment Tool´s approach and communicate important aspects of our company´s trajectory and the culture that influenced it. Cirklo evolved from being a small startup in the coffee shops of La Roma, Mexico City, to becoming a strategic partner for companies, institutions, and organizations that are looking for a human-centered approach to promote change and social impact. In 2011, Julio Salazar and Gabriel Martinez, two young aspiring entrepreneurs wanted an outlet to promote social impact through social innovation. They wanted to make a living doing it, so they founded Cirklo in Mexico City, a desert of social innovation at that time. While this initial vision may have seemed too simple or naive in 2011, it was magnetic enough to attract other motivated and talented future *Cirklos*, a term we use to refer to our team members. We found individuals among various sectors who shared similar views on how different approaches and tools from diverse innovation methodologies such as Design Thinking (Liedtka & Ogilvie, 2011), Cynefin Framework (Snowden, 1999), Human-centered Design (Ideo. org, 2015), Agile Methodology (Ries, 2013), and Collaborative Learning (Lee & Bonk, 2014) could be adapted to promote social impact (Acosta, 2017; Anzilotti, 2017; Duckworth, 2016; Elmansy, 2016; Laloux, 2014; Secretariat of Foreign Affairs, 2016; Sharratt & Planche, 2016).

We organized Mexico's first social innovation workshop with *Ojos Que Sienten* (Sight of Emotion),[1] an NGO dedicated to breaking social paradigms. They help improve the lives of individuals with blindness by providing different programs and services to increase community awareness of their unique issues in society. Ojos que Sienten allowed us to examine the organizational problems they were facing in the local, national, and global context. Through a collective thinking process between Cirklo and Ojos que Sienten, we realized we needed to answer one key question, *"What strategies can Ojos que Sienten use to decrease its dependency on donations?"* Together we formed a workshop to brainstorm and explore solutions. One idea involved maximizing the business potential of the individuals with blindness in the community by creating innovative businesses for them like Dinner in the Dark, Sensory Photography, etc. This experience, along with various projects that came soon after, allowed us to define our organization's vision and our way of working through problems with our strategic partners. We learned that we must listen, understand, and create a sense of community with the people and the resources that can bring about a positive impact where it is needed the most. Our chapter narrative is born from this early journey that narrowed our efforts to focus on the specific levers and processes, the "where" and the "how," that could make a measurable impact.

EVOLVING OUR BUSINESS MODEL FOR IMPACT ACROSS MEXICO

Mexico is the second largest economy and country in Latin America after Brazil (World Bank, 2017). Since the 1980s, Mexico has been an export-driven economy. But as the North American Free Trade Agreement (NAFTA) is currently being renegotiated and results are still uncertain, the need to innovate locally increases. Today, more than ever, there is a need to build and to foster resilience through social innovation and social entrepreneurship.

We developed our business model to function as a social enterprise by combining economic development strategies with innovative services to help our corporate clients incorporate social impact into their companies. The profits from these corporate clients continue to subsidize our work and projects that focus solely on creating a regional impact. This conscious reinvestment of our business model has become part of our company DNA and allows us to use profits and knowledge from corporate clients and transfer them into social impact initiatives. This allows Cirklo to maintain a sustainable organization while interchanging knowledge and best practices between the public, private, and nonprofit sectors.

We have made strong efforts to engage the private and public sectors in our work and vision by fostering an ecosystem around social innovation and social impact throughout Mexico. To achieve this, we collaborate and co-create with organizations in the social impact sector seeking to create social impact by integrating a triple bottom-line approach to create social, environmental, and economic value (see Figure 1). Our collective efforts have paid off. While seven years ago the term *social innovation* was not easily understood, it is now widely accepted in the mainstream industry and has become part of the national agenda for development. As a social innovation

Fig. 1. Collaboration and Co-creation between Multiple Stakeholders Is Key to a Sustainable Future.

ecosystem, we are adamant that the Mexican market and society, in general, has the potential to demonstrate that business-as-usual has no need to be avaricious and damaging to society. Instead, we strive to illuminate that the power of doing good in business is not only profitable from a bottom-line perspective; it is a mandatory role business must play to ensure our continued existence as a society.

WHY AND HOW CIRKLO ALIGNED ITS VISION WITH THE SDGS

With the broad goals of promoting social impact and positive social change nationally, Cirklo found itself at a crossroad in terms of how it could communicate its efforts across Mexico. As we were starting to reflect on our experiences developing projects, we recognized two main concerns: (1) each project was unique in its subject matter and process and (2) we were missing an overarching vision that could encompass all projects. By 2015, we had completed over 100 diverse projects including promoting better conditions for people with special needs, helping create innovative fundraising models for a multinational foundation, and supporting coffee cooperatives in Chiapas to develop outlets to reach new markets. It seemed like the team could take on any challenge. In theory, this sounds fulfilling, but this generated questions within the team. For an organization striving to generate systemic change, we were not really thinking systemically or strategically in terms of identifying our role and implementing our actions.

Cirklo's *Social Impact Division* recognized this challenge and sought out ways to focus our diverse team's passions, talent, and expertise. The one thing that united our team of twenty talented and extremely passionate consultants from all walks of life was our passion for social innovation and positive social change. How could we take advantage of this and leverage the one thing that brought us together to deepen our focus and impact? The idea of putting limits on the type of projects we would focus on seemed to counter the ambitious reasons that created Cirklo in the first place. Yet, a more critical analysis of our work up to that point forced us to recognize that we needed to focus if we wanted to make a more meaningful change.

By investigating systems and frameworks that could help us classify the past projects, we came across the United Nations Sustainable Development Goals (UN, 2015), and it was a moment of epiphany for us. This global agenda creates a framework for guiding our actions to address the world's most pressing problems, in effect creating a common language understood by both the public sectors and private sectors, and most importantly, is accessible for implementation at the individual, local, and regional levels. After some deliberation with the entire team, Cirklo entrusted the Social Impact Division to do extensive research and benchmarking in order to develop and carry out a rigorous process of integrating the human-centered strategies and innovation methodologies of the SDGs with the voices and perspectives of every Cirklo team member. In this way, we aimed to identify which SDGs we were best situated to align our efforts with. And we hoped to develop a meaningful process for focusing our efforts for measurable impact.

FOCUSING OUR ORGANIZATION'S DIVERSE EFFORTS USING THE SDGS

The result of this process was the development of an alignment process we now call the Team Alignment Tool. Its goal is to align the values and efforts of the organization with the SDGs to make a meaningful impact. To develop the tool, we first researched the UN SDG literature extensively to identify diverse perspectives related to each goal. We also interviewed Cirklo team members, as well as experts in Mexico and abroad. We asked them about their points of view and understandings of the SDGs, the implications related to their organization, and their desired organizational results. We then followed up that investigation with an analysis of the top 10 Foundations in Mexico ("Las 10 empresas," 2014), asking ourselves, *"How and where are they investing their funds?"* We mapped out their projects to gain a comprehensive picture of their main areas of influence and interest, then compared them with those of the corporations and the government in Mexico (see Figure 2). This mapping gave us a bird's eye view of the broad interests and efforts across the national ecosystem.

We then deepened our analysis by investigating institutions that have a global impact, including key players such as thought leaders, global financial institutions, and international organizations (see Figure 3).

We complemented this understanding by sifting through academic papers and reports like the Evaluation Report on Social Development Policy in

Fig. 2. A Comparison of the Main Area of Influence and Interest of the Foundations, Corporation and the Government in Mexico Based on the SDGs.

Prioritization of Secondary Research in Mexico

Mexico (National Council for the Evaluation of Social Development Policy [CONEVAL], 2012), which reported on different social program indicators by measuring social deficiencies in Mexico. We also familiarized ourselves with writings by international social leaders. Understanding these reports gave us an even better overview of the social sector ecosystem and further improved our understanding of how money and other resources were allocated across society and previously unseen trends emerged.

Once we had a broader understanding of the social sector, we went back to analyze our past and present social projects and asked the question, *"What type of experience and knowledge do we demonstrate through these projects?"* We then asked, *"What types of projects and areas do we want to be personally and collectively involved?"* We asked each team member to evaluate the root of their passions and their professional calling by answering, *"What areas of impact would you like to develop passionately the most?* By October 2016, we had enough understanding to facilitate an internal collaborative workshop aimed at narrowing our focus and aligning our efforts with certain SDGs.

Fig. 3. A Comparison of the Main Areas of Influence and Interest of Thought Leaders, Financial Institutions, and International Organizations in Mexico.

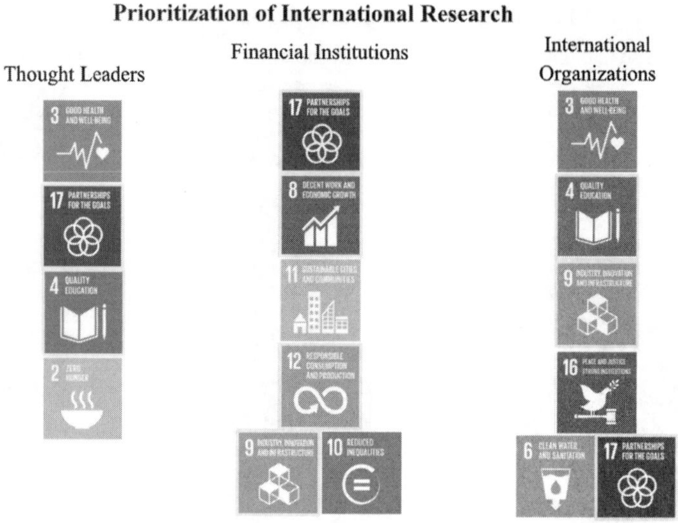

Prioritization of International Research

We first directed each team member to choose four SDGs best aligned with our present skills. Once the entire team had answered, we ranked and discussed the top four SDGs. From the four selected, we then led the team to choose two SDGs they would like to work on most passionately in 2018. The information from the workshop proved to be in sync with the individual surveys we had previously done and together they formed our team's interest criteria (see Figure 4).

USING THE LESSONS OF OUR APPROACH: THE TEAM ALIGNMENT TOOL

The steps described above show how any organization can align their efforts and vision with the SDGS. We found that they are especially useful for small organizations of about 20 people. For larger organizations, we suggest aligning in smaller teams first and then running strategic integration sessions. We also recommend documenting all the information collected on a

Fig. 4. A Comparison of the Main Area of the Interest of Previous Surveys and Team Members Chosen during the Workshop.

Prioritization of Team's Primary Research

Our Expertise

Team´s Interest

Note: As a result, we decided to focus on *SDG 4: Education, SDG 8: Economic Growth*, and *SDG 11: Sustainable Cities* (UN, 2015).

collaborative platform, like online spreadsheets, which then facilitate peer-to-peer collaboration with increased efficiency and transparency.

A. Setting the Groundwork with a Common Language

Before embarking on facing challenges and addressing them in a creative and collaborative manner, you need to have a common language. The complexity of making agreements is lessened when everyone involved is on the same page and shares a common vocabulary. How can you, your team, and your organization build a shared language towards a common vision?

- First, be aware of your work conditions. Listen to and be aware of your organization's motivations and integral human needs like physical, emotional, and psychological security.

- Second, map out your team's level of understanding, interests, and fears because those are driving factors in your organization's work.

While some of these aspects could be taken for granted by some, taking the time to ensure that the entire team is on the same page in terms of the processes is essential to ensure success and acceptance from the team.

B. Aligning Your Vision with the Sustainable Development Goals

Step 1: Research how others have aligned their visions with the SDGs. For us, this meant researching partners and organizations that inspired us at the national and international level, which we will detail later in this chapter.

Step 2. Understand the SDGs. Take time to understand each of the Sustainable Development Goals (UN, 2015). Each SDG has its own process, targets, and indicators. For us, this meant deep-dive synthesis and analysis sessions to discuss each of the development goals.

Step 3: Understand the local context. Since the SDGs work on a global scale, it is vital to understand their role on a national and local scale as well. What are the needs and challenges specific to your context? Each country has its own pressing issues. Identifying and understanding them helps to plan actions that will have a greater impact. Some ideas for conducting local-level research include:

o Identifying the trends and relevance of each SDG in your country;

o Pinpoint the central topics, agenda, and budget allocations of local foundations;

o Investigate the projects being run by the local corporate social responsibility sector;

o Research your government's agenda and initiatives towards the UN agenda for 2030. For example, your country might have an open government partnership;

o Interview local experts, thought leaders, and academic authorities;

o Open conversations focused on the SDGs within your network of allies, friends, and even with strangers.

Step 4: Understand the international context. Gain inspiration and understanding of the central topics and agenda held by institutions such as:

o global foundations,

o multilateral development banks and other financial institutions,

o international projects implementing the SDGs in your sector, and

o international thought leaders´ publications and movements.

We found that apart from researching and evaluating published information, reaching out directly to people and teams at these institutions generated tremendous insights.

Step 5: Review and reflect on your organization's practical experiences. Guide your team to review and reflect on your company or organization's experience. Prompt the discussion with the following questions:

o Do we understand and agree with the SDGs?

o Does our organization's vision align with the SDGs? Directly? Indirectly? How?

o What current or future projects align with the SDGs?

Reflect on how your organization creates, captures, and delivers value. Ask:

o Does our value proposition align with the SDGs?

o What points in your supply chain or business model relate to specific SDGs?

Step 6: Envision your team's purpose for the future. Conduct interviews with your team members to better understand your team's interests and future goals. Follow up by facilitating a collective workshop. First, host individual dialogues with your team members discussing their beliefs on positive impact and their professional career objectives. Ask:

o What sustainability topics deeply interest you?

o What types of projects would you like to be working on in one, five, or even fifteen years from now?

o How would you like the organization to evolve?

o What do you like about our leadership style?

○ What and how can we improve regarding our leadership style?

Second, plan and organize a collaborative workshop with your team. Schedule at least three hours to learn, reflect, and develop a rich conversation. We suggest the following activities:

○ Do an icebreaking exercise that works to eliminate potential team barriers.

○ Present the ongoing investigation efforts and current results for alignment with the SDGs.

○ Review your organization's vision and values.

○ Revisit the different SDGs and explain their targets and indicators.

○ Work to pair the individual employees' and the group's goals with the SDGs.

○ Share personal reflections and lead a collective conversation about these positively-correlated relationships with the SDGs.

○ Have the team members choose four SDGs they want to discuss.

○ Cluster the team's ideas and reflections.

○ Collectively narrow down the number of SDGs your team will focus on.

Step 7: Bring it all together. At this point, you should have plenty of information and understanding to build upon. Use the block icons designed by the United Nations for each SDG to help you visualize the information. Create categories of analysis that synthesize findings, such as local context, global context, and team context. Subdivide the categories by different roles and stakeholders. For example:

○ *local context*: foundations, corporations, government;

○ *global context*: thought Leaders, MDBs, international organizations; and

○ *team context*: our experience, our interests.

To visualize this information, we recommend ranking each SDG by relevance and frequency for each of the mentioned groups within a category. This can be done digitally or manually on a board in the office.

Step 8: Identify the Most Aligned SDG(s). The last step is to analyze patterns of strengths and interests. Organize them into categories that best map onto one or more SDGs. Then identify, discuss and agree on the SDG(s) that best align with those categories

Step 9: Develop Strategy. To develop strategy, ask the following question for each identified SDG:

o Where do we want to have an impact as an organization? (purpose perspective)

o Where should our money and funds be allocated? (business perspective)

o What is missing in our local context? (needs-finding approach)

o What is our area of expertise? (highlighting individual and group strengths)

o What do we love to do and how do we want to move forward? (crafting the future you want to be part of)

Our Results from using the Team Alignment Tool

Our team at Cirklo identified alignment with three SDG goals: quality education (SDG 4), decent work and economic growth (SDG 8), and sustainable cities and communities (SDG 11). Since completing this process, we have been actively engaging in projects within these three areas and have added impact indicators, which we've continually measured. For example, we were working on inclusive and equity education when we reflected on SDG 4, Quality Education (UN, 2015). We realized we needed to broaden our focus to move the needle on this SDG, so we decided to delve into initiatives outside the formal education sector including early childhood development, teacher training, and programs for the twenty-first century skills. This allowed us to focus our efforts on education in a more impactful way.

Six months after aligning ourselves to the SDGs, we started a project to define key metrics and indicators to measure the impact of public-private alliances with the Mexican Agency for International Development Cooperation (AMEXCID)[2] and the German Agency for International Cooperation (GIZ).[3] We've also recently started collaborating with the

BMW Foundation[4] to create communities of corporate foundations and enterprises, with the ultimate goal of building resilience in Mexico through a network that can be aligned actively with the SDG indicators.

LEVERAGING SDG ALIGNMENT FOR COLLECTIVE IMPACT

Putting the SDGs into practice allowed us to begin conversations and form alliances with a collective understanding of our needs and the needs of others. This allowed us to exert our combined influences to transform systems at the local and national level (see Figure 5). Below are examples of three collaborative projects pertaining to our three chosen SDGs.

Fig. 5. Putting the SDGs into Practice Allowed Us to Begin Conversations and Form Alliances.

Promoting Quality Education for SDG4 through Continuous Collaboration with the LEGO Foundation, Mexico

The LEGO Foundation's educational initiatives in early childhood education[5] focus on promoting play and robotics education in government day care centers run by the National System or Integral Family Development centers (DIF) and low-income schools, respectively. By using our methodologies of innovation and educational practices, we guided collaborative exercises with key stakeholders who identified concrete recommendations for improvements that continue to touch the lives of children all over the country. This collaboration also led to innovations with two other national educational initiatives supported and carried out by the foundation.

Developing Markets with SDG8 for Decent Work and Economic Growth with Social Development Citibanamex

To support small coffee producers, we designed a social enterprise business and distribution model for the *Majomut* coffee cooperative in Chiapas.[6] This pilot project will be carried out in Mexico City in 2018 and is one of the first collaborations of its kind for an organization that once focused simply on grants.

Establishing Initiatives for SDG 11 for Sustainable Cities and Communities with Bonafont, Mexico

By conducting research and mapping the value chain of waste products in Mexico City, we are designing an intervention system and running a pilot of a socially responsible and sustainable recycled polyethylene terephthalate (rPET) supply chain.

HOW TO MANAGE AND CARE FOR YOUR VISION INTERNALLY

Our productivity is highest when we feel connected and understood; it develops and deepens alongside our evolutionary process to create meaningful and positive impact. We incorporate six basic steps to facilitate human productivity in alignment with our SDGs:

- **Step 1: Require congruent behaviors and actions of team leaders.** Question how you can act with more transparency and always be open to questions and comments.

- **Step 2: Start by listening to your group's experiences with "business as usual" leadership and operations.** Write and identify the limiting behaviors that you did not like, and then share.

- **Step 3: Choose three "business as usual" beliefs that undercut the leadership and vision of the company and reflect on what supports them.** Choose to move away from these three beliefs. Instead, create beliefs and values that inspire and support your vision and work.

- **Step 4: Collectively test ways to insulate your culture from external pressures.** Don't bend to old habits.

- **Step 5: Create a weekly "safe place" in the office or online where everyone can open up and connect with three purposes:** a) questioning and disagreeing; b) purposeful resolution; and c) action.

- **Step 6: Be an interaction-conscious and contribution-conscious team.** Every member ("big picture" thinkers, designers, educators, entrepreneurs) are given ownership over their jobs and must craft its meaning and impact.

To accomplish our vision and the collective potential of our work, we must consider and invest in our team's strengths; not only our own abilities. We know that some strategies will raise doubts and fears, and that we are even going to fail at times. Still, we must show up, even if imperfectly and even when beaten down. It is in the hard times that our beliefs become our strengths. The transparency, trust, and commitment of the individual members of our company and teams remain key, allowing us to persist, stay engaged, and press forward (see Figure 6).

CONCLUSION

The world is in need of collective action aligned with the Sustainable Development Goals (UN, 2015). The Team Alignment Tool applies human-centered design principles and social innovation methodologies to help a team align their diverse skills and interests with the most relevant SDG(s). By

**Fig. 6. A Team of Successful Collaborators Can Drive One Collective
Vision.**

sharing how our company evolved from simply wanting to create positive
social change to identifying the need for focus and depth, we hope to show
other organizations:

(1) how to analyze the essential aspects of your team and company's DNA
    to identify your diverse skills and interests;

(2) how to gather relevant local and global ecosystem action and trends to
    identify needs, collaborators and other opportunities;

(3) how to synthesize all of this information to best align your organization's efforts with the most relevant SDG(s);

(4) how to leverage your SDG alignment to collaborate with other organizations and efforts; and

(5) how to create and retain enthusiasm and value alignment congruent with your chosen SDGs at all levels of your organization.

Cirklo dreams of a day when everyone lives in an economic system that depends on social inclusion and sustainable solutions to thrive. We are setting this dream in motion by sharing our Team Alignment Tool so that all organizations can align internally and with each other to collectively achieve the vision of the SDGs.

NOTES

1. Additional information on the organization Ojos que Sienten can be found in www.ojosquesienten.com

2. Additional information on AMEXCID can be found on their website www.gob.mx/amexcid

3. Additional information on GIZ can be found on their website www.giz.de

4. Additional information on GIZ can be found on their website https://bmw-foundation.org/

5. Additional information on GIZ can be found on their website http://www.lego-foundation.com/es-mx/

6. Additional information on Majomut coffee can be found on http://mycoffeebox.com/cafe-organico-majomut/

REFERENCES

Acosta, C. (2017, October 24). Las 100 empresas más responsables de 2017 [The top 100 most responsible companies of 2017]. *Expok*. Retrieved from https://www.expoknews.com/las-empresas-mas-responsables-de-2017

Anzilotti, E. (2017, September 18). The end of capitalism is already starting—If you know where to look. *Fast Company*. Retrieved from https://www.fastcompany.com/

Cirklo impulsando empresas con propósito [Cirklo, driving companies with purpose]. (2018, April). *Milenio Digital*. Retrieved from http://www.milenio.com/negocios/emprender-en-mexico/empresa-b-cirklo-proposito-disenos-ecosistema-emprendedor-economia_0_1154884760.html

Duckworth, A. (2016). *Grit: The power of passion and perseverance*. New York, NY: Scribner.

Elmansy, R. (2016, August). Decision matrix: How to make the right decision. *Designorate*. Retrieved from http://www.designorate.com/decision-matrix-decision-making

Ideo, org. (2015). *Human-centered design toolkit: The field guide to human-centered design*. Retrieved from http://www.designkit.org/resources/1

Laloux, F. (2014). *Reinventing organizations: A guide to creating organizations inspired by the next stage of human consciousness*. Brussels: Nelson Parker.

Las 10 empresas más responsables en México [The 10 most responsible companies in Mexico]. (2014, December 23). Expansion. Retrieved from https://expansion.mx/negocios/2014/12/16/las-10-empresas-mas-responsables-en-mexico

Lee, H., & Bonk, C. J. (2014). Collaborative learning in the workplace: Practical Issues and Concerns. *International Journal of Advanced Corporate Learning*, 7(2), 10–17. doi:10.3991/ijac.v7i2.3850

Liedtka, J., & Ogilvie, T. (2011). *Designing for growth: A design thinking tool kit for managers*. Chichester: Columbia Business School Publishing.

National Council for the Evaluation of Social Development Policy. (2012, November). *Evaluation report on social development policy in Mexico*. Retrieved from https://www.coneval.org.mx/Informes/Coordinacion/INFORMES_Y _PUBLICACIONES_PDF/Info_Eval_Pol_Des_Soc_2012sbiblio.pdf

Ries, E. (2013). *The Lean Startup: How Today's Entrepreneurs Use Continuous Innovation to Create Radically Successful Businesses*. New York, NY: Crown Business.

Secretariat of Foreign Affairs. (2016, July). *Implementing the 2030 agenda and the sustainable development goals in Mexico*. Retrieved from https://mision.sre.gob.mx /onu/images/discursos2016/BruchureODSeng2.pdf

Sharratt, L., & Planche, B. (2016). *Leading collaborative learning, Empowering excellence*. Thousand Oaks, CA: Corwin.

Snowden, D. (1999). *Cynefin framework introduction*. Retrieved from http://cognitive-edge.com/videos/cynefin-framework-introduction

United Nations. (2015). *Sustainable development goals*. Retrieved from https://sustainabledevelopment.un.org/?menu=1300

World Bank. (2017). *The world bank in Mexico*. Retrieved from http://www.worldbank.org/en/country/mexico

8

PERSPECTIVES AND POSSIBILITIES: ALIGNING FOR SOCIAL CHANGE

Karen Cvitkovich

INTRODUCTION

We are in the midst of urgent social change. I have spent the last 20 years as a cross-cultural consultant, studying how the various perspectives of culturally diverse teams influence how we get things done and how we collaborate with those who are different from us. Looking at current social movements, I find myself less concerned with opposing perspectives than with the lack of alignment within "causes," and the impact this has on their effectiveness. Within a "cause" we often assume that we are all moving in the same direction for the same reason. What I have found, however, is that our alignments are often fragmented. I believe that too much focus has been placed on the people "not like us" in social change. To achieve real change, we need to have better systems to ensure internal alignment within groups that are all working toward the same change – perhaps employing different perspectives, priorities, and cultural lenses in doing so.

Based on this, I pursue two questions:

- How are we different from each other, even if we are working on the same side of a social issue?

- How can we create a process that leverages our differences (within a social movement) as an asset to create sustainable social change?

Even when on the same side of a social issue, we have different perspectives and priorities. This is our strength! When leveraged strategically, differences can lead to more sustainable change. How to do this, and what obstructs this, is my focus in this chapter. Indeed, it is through this knowledge and process that we are able to bring out the best of our diverse humanity to ensure a sustainable future. This chapter aligns closest with Sustainability Development Goal #16: to promote peaceful and inclusive societies for sustainable development; provide access to justice for all; and build effective, accountable, and inclusive institutions at all levels. Progress in social change initiatives can best be made when diverse groups of people with various perspectives unite around a social issue and use their various perspectives to further strengthen the efforts toward change. This is not easy, however, as the multiple perspectives of people on the same side of a social issue often cause conflict that results in a fragmented and ineffective change initiative. It is through understanding differences and leveraging diversity as an asset that sustainable change can be achieved.

To gather this data, I interviewed twenty people from various non-governmental organizations (NGOs) including the Local Indigenous Network Collective (LINC), Peace Corp, Care, Oxfam, the Multicultural AIDS Coalition, Vermont Public Interest Research Group (VPIRG); environmentalists working at the town and state levels; as well as religious leaders and refugee organizations. I combined this data with my previous global leadership research, interviewing over a hundred global leaders on best practices in diverse teams.

SURPRISING INSIGHTS IN THE COLD

In January 2017, I traveled with my son, Matt, to Standing Rock, North Dakota, to join a group of activists working to stop the construction of the Dakota Access Pipeline (DAPL) by Energy Transfer Partners. The Dakota Access pipeline runs 1,100 miles across much of the Great Plains, connecting the Bakken oil formation in North Dakota to a refinery and second pipeline in Illinois (R Meyers, 2017). This pipeline would move half a million barrels of oil a day beneath the Missouri River, the main source of drinking water for the Standing Rock Sioux Reservation (Elbein, 2017).

The action began when members of the Hunkpapa Lakota, Sihasapa Lakota, and Yanktonai Dakota tribes rallied to protect their homes. The first to gather was a group of Native American teenagers, known as the "One Mind Youth," who established a tiny "prayer camp" just off the Dakota Access route, on the north end of the Standing Rock Sioux Reservation (Elbein, 2017). In the months after that initial Native American-led action, thousands of other Native and non-Native activists converged on Standing Rock in an effort to prevent the building of the pipeline. This amazing experience taught me lessons about the challenge of working for social change when those with very different cultures and beliefs attempt to stand together.

This prompts the question: How do we bring out the best of our diverse humanity to ensure a sustainable future? My experience tells me that it is by leveraging these diverse perspectives as an asset that we can advance change. The challenge of achieving Sustainability Development Goal #16 is enormous. It is best achieved by creating common ground among individuals with diverse backgrounds, needs, and perspectives and uniting them for a common goal.

I must admit, however, that many of these more philosophical thoughts left me when I first arrived at Standing Rock – I was more concerned with trying to keep warm. With subzero temperatures outside, a hodgepodge of people from different backgrounds huddled around the wood stove in the communal dinner tent; eating, talking, and warily getting to know each other. My son had been at Standing Rock for earlier protests in November, and he inspired me to join the camp. It was a scary time for us both. I had seen pictures of the violence that had broken out between those working against the pipeline and the police at the camp. My son had been there when it happened, cutting frozen coats off of members of the camp and trying to keep the fellow members of the camp safe. The images of individuals opposing the pipline being maced, of rubber bullets, and attack dogs spread anger across the country and moved increasing numbers of people to action – including me. Inspired by my son's passion to effect change, I wanted to support his efforts and hoped to contribute at a time when it seemed that the world had been turned upside down. We made the decision to travel to Standing Rock to set up a Volunteer Tent and encourage others to come and support the effort and clean up the camp.

When we arrived, the Sacred Fire – burning since September and symbolizing unity in the camp – had just been extinguished. This signified that the camp was undergoing a transition. After talk of moving the camp to higher ground, out of the flood zone, the Tribal Elders officially announced that the camp had to move. Talk of moving was fueled by the fact that tribes typically relocate every year when certain areas experience seasonal flooding; as well as by the belief that the camp had "bad energy" due to the violence, alcohol, and drugs – despite efforts to keep them out of the camp. Many wanted to remain in place, due to a variety of reasons. This included Native Americans known as "Water Protectors," who told me that they would die to prevent the pipeline and thus protect the water. "Water is life," they emphasized in passionately explaining why they could not leave. Others reticent to leave were Veterans and people I thought of as "community seekers": those who had found something special in the camp, a kind of community they seemed afraid of leaving. We were caught in the middle, while we tried to set up the volunteer tent. I was struck by the conflicting thoughts on how to address the difference of opinions regarding the camp's location. I found myself feeling confused and disappointed when I talked to one of the Native American camp members – who had been there since September – as he admitted that during his entire time there, he had not felt listened to or respected by any of the white people at the camp.

> *I begin telling them stories of my family, of a crisis or challenge we have been through. I am telling them things that are important to me. But when I mention, for example, that the story took place in Washington State, they do not express concern for my family or listen to my story. Instead they start talking about themselves. For example, they comment that they once took a vacation to Washington and begin telling me about it! It is clear they do not care about my story. And now the Tribal Elders have said we need to move the camp and many of the White people here say they do not want to go. It is as though you had guests at your summerhouse and when the summer was over and you were ready to go home, they said they wanted to stay. Don't they see none of this is right? They do not listen. They do not respect what the Tribal Elders have asked of us.*

> *They do not think of what is best for all of us – they think of*
> *themselves. They do not respect our needs. (personal*
> *communication, January 12, 2017)*

I suspected that the people he was talking about would be very surprised to hear that he did not feel respected or listened to, since many of them felt they were there in support of the Native Americans. Yet, I was also certain that he was correct. Indeed, as I watched my fellow white activists and the manner in which they interacted with Native Americans, I noticed they were not really listening – not in the deep contemplative way I experienced with the Native American camp member. When he listened to me, he leaned forward, made consistent eye contact, never interrupted; and I felt as though I was the only person he was focusing on, despite the tent being extremely crowded on that cold night. This has a direct connection with how we can "bring out the best of our diverse humanity" and ensure all voices are heard in co-creating solutions.

My dinner tent companion also expressed disappointment that many members of the camp were not listening to the Tribal Elders. This is an example of how the "decision-making authority" was unclear with different perspectives being expressed. According to many of the Native Americans with whom I spoke in the dinner tent and at the prayer circles, the final word belonged to the Tribal Elders, who solicited the opinions of others in making their decisions for the best of the community. For veterans, students, and environmentalists, however, there was far less clarity on who had the authority to make decisions; thus, questioning the decisions of the Elders seemed acceptable.

SEEKING CLARITY IN CONFUSION

It seemed that all of us at this camp were on "the same side." We saw those who supported the pipeline as our common adversaries. However, many of the people around me seemed to feel not only unheard and disrespected by others in the camp but also confused about the next steps and how to make decisions as a group. Nonetheless, many important things were accomplished through the actions at Standing Rock in the months that followed – an Army Corps engineer ruling in favor of the tribes was an indicator of this. In June 2017, James Boasberg – who sits on the DC district court — found that the U.S. Army Corps of Engineers had failed to perform an adequate study of the pipeline's environmental consequences when it first approved its construction (R. Meyer, 2017). In January 2017, however, the future seemed unclear. While miscommunication in the camp frustrated me, I was inspired to further understand how differences in perspective could fuel or hurt the cause of social change — thus prompting my journey to explore this question.

HOW ARE WE DIFFERENT?

At Standing Rock, I observed that people at the camp had three key differences: their political beliefs, cultural/ethnic background, and view of their roles in the social change they sought. In their research on the impact of diversity on teams, Jehn, Northcraft, and Neale (1999) found that differences in information, such as those of political perspectives and social categories or cultures, when understood and leveraged, could help performance, while differences in view of roles or motivation could have a negative impact on performance. This research seemed to echo my own experiences and the experiences of those whom I interviewed.

Different Political Beliefs

Different political beliefs can assist in advancing a social change initiative in two main ways:

- by providing access to a wider variety of stakeholders to assist in change; and

- by improving dialog and problem-solving.

Neale found that placing people with different beliefs and information together generates constructive conflict and/or debate about the task at hand. People deliberate about the best course of action. Indeed, she argues, "This is the type of conflict that absolutely should be engendered in organizations" (Jehn et al., 1999).

I experienced this first hand at Standing Rock. The combination of Native Americans, veterans, environmentalists, and others created a rich dialogue of ideas and perspectives as well as a greater potential for impact, as each had different constituent groups they could influence. For example, when the veterans joined Standing Rock to support the blocking of the Pipeline, they brought with them a large group of allies who might not have supported the effort otherwise.

A leader at a major human rights NGO explained that her organization intentionally connects people who would not normally work together – she discussed the difficult alliance between religious conservatives and feminists to create change in the area of human trafficking. "By putting the [the religious conservatives and feminists] together," she noted, "We had a distinct advantage in that they had access to different constituent groups. With all their stakeholders working toward the same goals, we had more power and influence to pass important legislation" (Personal communication, December 17, 2017).

While feminist organizations were active on this issue in the 1990s, they received little support from the US government (Graham, 2015). President George W. Bush established the Office of Faith-Based and Community Initiatives in 2001, granting religious organizations new access to federal funds for social causes, including anti-trafficking work.

Despite disagreeing in many areas, the two groups accomplished more together than they ever could apart. Combined, feminists and religious conservatives moved the issue forward more quickly – their alliance giving them deeper and broader access to funding and governmental support, which allowed them to get more work done faster (Berstein, 2010).

Different Ethnic/Cultural Backgrounds

Standing Rock also brought together people of different cultural backgrounds. The most obvious difference was between Native Americans and European Americans; nevertheless, individuals from many different cultures were together in the camp. I observed that although these differences created conflicts, they also resulted in an increase of perspectives and ideas. When acknowledged and mediated, cultural differences within a team can lead to their being far more effective than homogeneous ones. Katherine Phillips (2014) cites various examples of this, ranging from a Columbia University and Credit Suisse study that found a direct correlation between leadership teams that were diverse and better financial performance in organizations; to a University of Texas study linked racial diversity to higher levels of innovation and financial performance (Phillips, 2014). Research has shown that diverse teams can be less productive; however, if their internal differences go unacknowledged and/or no systems are implemented to help team members work through these differences (Adler & Gundersen, 2008). Cultural diversity provides the greatest benefit for teams involved in complex tasks that require innovation and creativity – two skills that are instrumental in solving social change issues (Adler & Gundersen, 2008). One of the positive benefits is that it reduces "group-think" – prompting people to question assumptions, thereby generating better outcomes (Adler & Gundersen, 2008).

But these same cultural differences can also lead to misunderstandings, if not identified and addressed. In all of the cultures that I have studied, people want the same three things:

- They want to be *listened to*.

- They want to be *understood*.

- They want to be *respected*.

The challenge is that the behaviors people seek to feel listened to, understood, and respected vary based on the cultural background in which they grew up (Gundling, Hogan, & Cvitkovich, 2011).

In *The Culture Map* (2014), Erin Meyer outlines the key areas in which cultures tend to be similar and different. The intercultural research of Myers and others indicates that the lack of listening and respect that many of the Native Americans felt from the "white activists" at Standing Rock, stemmed from both the cultural differences between European and Native Americans, and the long history of colonialism. According to Meyer, Native Americans are more comfortable with silence in conversations. Indeed, the "rapid fire" exchanges between European Americans may be seen as "not listening" by many Native Americans (E. Meyer, 2014). When people do not listen carefully, they can easily make inaccurate assumptions (Crockett, 2011). Consequently, a European American may unknowingly offend a Native American during a conversation.

These dynamics contributed to the miscommunication I observed at Standing Rock. While both Native Americans and white activists were on the same side in protesting the pipeline, the way in which they communicated their individual or group's needs resulted in miscommunication and conflict – such as that relayed to me in the dinner tent.

Differences in Motivation

Neal identifies differences in our motivation for the work and our view of our role as a third area of difference and explains that this area, contrary to the first two areas, has the potential to significantly impede groups from accomplishing their goals (Jehn et al., 1999). My interviews confirmed Neale's findings.

If those participating in a social change initiative are not from the communities being directly impacted by the issue, they need to be especially sensitive to these differences. Joseph Grady, the founder of LINC, emphasized this problematic difference. He explained that some come into an indigenous culture with the attitude of "We are here to help you – to save you;" whereas others come in saying, "You know what your issues are – how can I be of service?" The latter approach is deemed far more respectful and effective in creating real change. Reflecting on his time at the Multicultural AIDS coalition, Rene Milet agreed that a "I am here to save you" mentality is especially problematic when the individuals working for social change come from a "majority" group that has more power and influence than those they are helping. He emphasized important questions, such as "Who has power and who does not have the power? How do you decide who speaks for these groups?" (R. Milet, personal communication, December 17, 2017).

A former member of the Peace Corp and recently returned from working with immigrants and refugees in Samos, Greece, Laurette Bennhold-Samaan has also observed these differences. "Some volunteers came feeling like they know better, they are the 'saving grace' – there is a sense of arrogance," Bennhold-Samaan notes, "Some came to teach, feeling their knowledge was superior. But the most effective [volunteers] were the ones who came to partner" (Bennhold-Samaan, personal communication, January 8, 2018).

As such, these leaders emphasized the need to promote peaceful and inclusive societies in a respectful way, work with a goal of "service," and maintain an awareness of who has power and influence in a change initiative. To do our best work and bring out the best in both ourselves and others, it is critical to have an attitude of "service to" rather than "saving" others.

WHAT OBSTRUCTS THE LEVERAGING OF OUR DIFFERENCES?

The research cited above confirms that diversity within teams can be leveraged to create better results; however, three main themes have emerged as challenges to be aware of.

(1) minimizing the differences based on the assumption that we were all on the same side;

(2) a lack of openness to others' ideas because of a passion and need to "be right" when there is conflict; and

(3) lack of working agreements; for example, how decisions are going to be made.

Minimizing Differences between People on the Same Side of a Social Issue

Adler and Gundersen's (2008) research on diverse teams indicates that differences can only be leveraged as an asset if they are brought to the surface and dealt with openly. Neuroscience, the study of how our brain works, shows that our brain is wired to make snap judgments in order to keep us safe, as well as to simplify the overwhelming amount of data we process every day. This results in our not always seeing others accurately. When we consider someone to be "like" us, we may actually assume them to be far more like us than they actually are (Rock, Grant, & Grey, 2016). Consequently, we tend to focus on the differences between us and those on the other side of an issue and minimize the differences within our own group. While people may seek to gloss over differences with others in the same group in the interest of harmony, differences should be taken seriously and examined (Rock et al., 2016). Indeed, awareness of dissimilarities within teams and groups is critical to prompting discussions, identifying the variations in perspective, and finding collaborative approaches. Broader thinking on issues occurs by acknowledging differences in perspectives.

Are You Listening?

In addition to cultural differences, the data also suggested that the passion of those working for social change can sometimes contribute to them not really listening to other perspectives. Based on his experience as a part of the Multicultural AIDS Coalition, Milet encapsulated this problem.

> *In these settings people are really invested in being "right" and "being a good person." This isn't Wall Street. In Wall Street people do not typically put as much value in being "good" and "right" but in these settings, feeling good about yourself is really important to people. People get very defensive (R. Milet, personal communication, December 17, 2017).*

This is important to note because, as we explore ways to bridge differences, vulnerability and defensiveness can be a barrier. My own experiences provide an example of this. When I joined the Standing Rock initiative, I went with grand ambitions of making an impact, and wanted to help others come to the camp and assist with the clean-up. Essentially, I felt that I was doing a good thing. When I arrived, however, it soon became clear that the Native Americans at the camp may not have wanted others like me to come. This made me feel sad, disappointed, and, admittedly, unappreciated. I truly wanted to believe that the arrival of additional volunteers would help the efforts to prevent the pipeline. Subsequently, when some told me that no more outside volunteers were wanted because the camp was moving, I became defensive of my actions. Upon reflection, I realize that – as Milet said – I wanted to be right in such a way that I was less open to the views of others.

Several of the people I interviewed brought up the same point: when people volunteer time for a cause they are committed to, their need to be "right" inevitably increases. I had not anticipated this theme, and the consistency with which it was mentioned was both surprising and interesting. Passion creates change, but it can also create an environment of resistance. Given how much is at stake and the degree of emotion involved, we need to unearth differences carefully.

Working Agreements: Alignment and Decision-making

An additional area that was challenging in Standing Rock was having a clear decision-making process. In our research around successful global teams, we found that as the diversity increased, the need for concrete working agreements also increased (Gundling et al., 2011). As I explored other social

change initiatives, one stood out as a best practice in this area: The
Blackfoot Challenge.

The Blackfoot Challenge has brought together ranchers, environmentalists, and others from various backgrounds, to better manage the land in the
best interests of all involved in land management. With such important
resources at risk, the US Fish and Wildlife Service wanted to be involved in
resolving resource problems in the Blackfoot.

Indeed, the Challenge is a great example of a best practice in decision-
making for diverse groups. They attribute their success, in part, to a working
agreement they call the "80/20 rule": a commitment to focusing on the
eighty percent (of issues) they agreed on, and leave out the twenty percent
that led to disagreement. This consensus-based approach is effective because
everyone is at the table, voicing their concerns and listening to those of
others. While this is a time-intensive process, this deliberate approach
ensures that everyone is invited to participate, thus accomplishing more
(Bisson, 2012). In this second example, working agreements around
decision-making were integral to leveraging different perspectives. They have
been cited as one of the most successful land management collaborations in
the US. "It's so easy for people to get caught up in their own world and not
think about other groups. We connect people to people and people to place
[…] I think that's so important" (Madison, 2014). This is a perfect example
of leveraging diverse perspectives for a sustainable future!

WHAT HELPS BRIDGE THE DIFFERENCES IN PERSPECTIVES ON ISSUES?

In reflecting on the process of facilitating diverse groups to find common
ground, I see several consistent themes. In many ways, these themes correspond with our research for "Third Way Solutions" in a previous publication, *What's Different About Global Leadership?* (Gundling et al., 2011).
Composed of five steps, the following model/process is informed by both
current and previous research.

(1) **Listen.** The first step in collaborating across different perspectives is to
     set aside your point of view for a moment and listen!

     As Matt Cvitkovich reflected on his experiences as an activist at
     Standing Rock,

So, when you talk about what blocked progress, it was the fact that we all had different motivations—we were doing it for different reasons, sovereignty issue vs. hardcore environmentalists—and nobody listened to each other. We were all trying to stop a pipeline but doing it for different reasons. So when you are talking about what works and what does not—this lack of listening impeded progress in this situation. We needed to listen (M. Cvitkovich, personal communication, January 8, 2017).

(2) **Relate.** This refers to the connection that the people in the discussion feel for one other. Does everyone involved in this process know one other? How can we develop a foundation of personal trust and mutual understanding across cultural differences?

John Hudson, a minister and writer, spoke of his collaboration with churches of different backgrounds and denominations for initiatives like Black Lives Matter, and emphasized the power of sharing a common context and viewing one other as people.

We were different from each other. But when we all sat around a table and talked about a time we felt excluded—it created a common bond that carried us through the difficult times. The willingness to be vulnerable and to talk about what was real to each of us: that made all the difference. (J. Hudson, personal communication, December 10, 2017)

(3) **Inquire.** An effective way to develop strategies and raise awareness is to discuss the differences within the group by asking questions. What do each of us not know about this situation that we should? How can we work together to find this missing information? What are the indisputable facts and what are the perspectives? Are there aspects of my style or strategic approach that I should consider changing to better support our work?

As one activist put it, "If I see that people have been marginalized in a situation, I will specifically bring them into the circle, inviting others to participate in making decisions in things involving them" (personal communication, December 17, 2017).

(4) **Co-Create.** When we "co-create," we bring together the diverse perspectives and ideas of all the individuals working on the social change initiative to produce something that could never have been achieved alone. It is the combination of all the perspectives that creates the innovative solutions. Who are likely to be key players in influencing the decision and implementing the outcome, including those who have not previously been decision-makers? How can I involve the latter in creating the solution? One global leader said,

> *Sometimes I end up with a completely different solution because*
> *I listen to all players, a solution not even related to what*
> *I originally thought. Sometimes I push through my thought process*
> *and get others to adapt [...] but generally I end up with something*
> *different. (Gundling et al., 2011)*

(5) **Commit.** Does each person who participated in the process feel that the final outcome is their own? Do they have some sense of authorship? Have we fully leveraged the different perspectives represented in the groups working toward the change?

THE JOURNEY HOME

After our time together at Standing Rock, my son dropped me off at the Bismarck airport and I boarded my flight home to Boston. As I sat in my seat and looked out the window in the sterile environment of the airplane, I became increasingly aware of the smell of campfire smoke on my clothes. While many of the questions that flooded my mind during that trip home remain, of this, I am certain: our differences are our strength, one we can use to effect change.

We live in powerful times; a period in which unified movement forward is critical to creating a change. I am confident that, as stated in the *2030 Agenda for Sustainable Development*, "The future of humanity and of our planet lies in our hands." This chapter has focused primarily on Sustainability Development Goal #16 — that is, promoting peaceful and inclusive societies for sustainable development; providing access to justice for all; and building effective, accountable, and inclusive institutions at all levels. Through researching case studies, interviewing individuals at the forefront of social change movements and in global leadership positions, as well as surveying the research on leveraging the best from diverse teams, I have made some recommendations to assist in aligning the efforts of diverse people and perspectives on the same side of a social issue.

Individuals working together should clearly ask:

- How are we different from each other, even if we are working on the same side of a social issue?

- How can we create a process that leverages our differences (within a social movement) as an asset to create sustainable social change?

Research on teams and interviews with the individuals revealed that our differences in political beliefs and culture could be used to our advantage as long as we do not overlook these differences and remain open to other perspectives. It also illustrated the need for additional working agreements, such as around decision-making, when working in diverse teams toward a social change.

SUMMARY

In short, this chapter has shown that:

- Political, cultural, and informational differences between people on the same side of a social change initiative can be a really good thing. It can mean access to more people, resources, and ideas.

- Differences are positive when they are brought to the surface and addressed. Our brain's attempt to oversimplify the anomalies, and our ego's need to "defend" us when we feel we are "right," can impede honest and productive alignment discussions.

- The discussion and clarification of these differences can facilitate change.

Leveraging our differences can be achieved through a structured and careful process of understanding one another and focusing more on where we agree rather than where we disagree. This process includes:

- **listening** to those who have a different perspective;

- **relating** and connecting to them on a personal level;

- **inquiring** and asking questions, while reserving judgment;

- **co-creating** solutions together; and

- **committing** to the change together.

So, let us make change happen. After all, we are stronger together because of our differences, not in spite of them.

REFERENCES

Adler, N. J., & Gundersen, A. (2008). *International Dimensions of Organizational Behavior* (pp. 138–143). Mason, OH: Thomson Higher Education.

Bernstein, E. (2010). Militarized humanitarianism meets carceral feminism: The politics of sex, rights, and freedom in contemporary antitrafficking campaigns. *Signs: Journal of Women in Culture and Society*, 36(1), 45–71.

Bisson, H. (2012, September 15). Blackfoot challenge: Public lands foundation. Retrieved from https://publicland.org/awards/blackfoot-challenge

Crockett, R. O. (2011, March 14). Listening is critical in today's multicultural workplace. *Harvard Business Review*. Retrieved from https://hbr.org/2011/03/shhh-listening-is-critical-in

Elbein, S. (2017, January 31). The youth group that launched a movement at standing rock. *The New York Times*. Retrieved from https://www.nytimes.com/2017/01/31/magazine/the-youth-group-that-launched-a-movement-at-standing-rock.html?mcubz=3

Graham, R. (2015, March 5). How sex trafficking became a Christian cause. Retrieved from http://www.slate.com/articles/double_x/faithbased/2015/03/christians_and_sex_trafficking_how_evangelicals_made_it_a_cause_celebre.html

Gundling, E., Hogan, T., & Cvitkovich, K. (2011). *What is global leadership? 10 key behaviors that define great global leaders*. Boston, MA: Nicholas Brealey Publishing.

Jehn, K. A., Northcraft, G. B., & Neale, M. A. (1999). Why differences make a difference: A field study of diversity, conflict, and performance in workgroups. *Administrative Science Quarterly, 44*(4), 741–763.

Madison, E. (2014, October 14). Blackfoot challenge celebrates 20 years of conservation. *Great Falls Tribune*. Retrieved from https://www.greatfallstribune.com/story/outdoors/2014/10/01/blackfoot-challenge-celebrates-years-conservation/16565635

Meyer, E. (2014). *The culture map: Breaking through the invisible boundaries of global business*. New York, NY: Public Affairs.

Meyer, R. (2017, June 14). The standing rock Sioux claim "Victory and Vindication" in Court. *The Atlantic*. Retrieved from https://www.theatlantic.com/science/archive/2017/06/dakota-access-standing-rock-sioux-victory-court/530427

Phillips, K. (2014, October 1). How diversity makes us smarter. *Scientific American*. Retrieved from https://www.scientificamerican.com/article/how-diversity-makes-us-smarter

Rock, D., Grant, H., & Grey, J. (2016, September 22). Diverse teams feel less comfortable—and that's why they perform better. *Harvard Business Review*. Retrieved from https://hbr.org/2016/09/diverse-teams-feel-less-comfortable-and-thats-why-they-perform-better

PART III

RELATIONSHIPS AND THE HEART OF OUR SHARED HUMANITY

9

RELATIONAL LEADERSHIP AND *LAUDATO SI'*: POPE FRANCIS' CALL TO CARE FOR OUR COMMON HOME

Dung Q. Tran and Michael R. Carey

INTRODUCTION

These are turbulent times for earth and its nearly eight billion inhabitants (Poole, Gharib, & Sofia, 2017). Technological advancements, economic globalization, and a mentality of excessive consumption, among other factors, have contributed to the extraction of our planet's natural resources at an unprecedented rate and magnitude (Chappell, 2017; Peppard, 2014; Steffen, Broadgate, Deutsch, Gaffney, & Ludwig, 2015; United Nations General Assembly, 2015). However, in an "important sign of hope" (Francis, 2015c, para. 10), the 70th session of the United Nations General Assembly (2015) adopted a resolution titled, *Transforming Our World: The 2030 Agenda for Sustainable Development*, a non-binding international action plan with 17 Sustainable Development Goals (SDGs). These goals are "aspirational and global, with each Government setting its own national targets guided by the global level of ambition but taking into account national circumstances" (p. 13).

While the commitments and contributions of concerned governments, politicians, scientists, economists, and business leaders are necessary and important in bringing out the best of our diverse humanity to ensure a sustainable future, "merely tinkering with institutional reform is insufficient because it fails to strike at the deeper root of the problem" (Eggemeier, 2014, p. 63). In an address to the General Assembly of the United Nations, Pope Francis (2015c) alerted world leaders to the danger of "declarationist nominalism" (para. 10), the practice of assuaging consciences with agreeable declarations. Rather than resting on the laurels of a long list of good proposals, the pontiff urged international community leaders to move beyond the notion that, "a single theoretical and aprioristic solution will provide an answer to all the challenges" (para. 11), and to remember that, "above and beyond our plans and programmes, we are dealing with real men and women who live, struggle and suffer, and are often forced to live in great poverty, deprived of all rights" (para. 11).

As the activity of leadership practitioners like Pope Francis, and the theoretical reflections of relational leadership scholars like Mary Uhl-Bien (2006) both suggest, leaders and followers are relational beings who are engaged in a dynamic and emerging process of human relationship. In his book, *Relational Being*, Kenneth Gergen (2011) asserted that "a relational process [that] stands at the center of all intelligible action" is a vital framework for human self-understanding, which includes the following revelation: "that our future viability on this planet depends on the care devoted to relational process" (p. 281).

For Uhl-Bien (2006), important to the investigation of relational leadership is a sensitivity to the integrative processes that suggest not only the quality and type of relationship but also "the social dynamics by which leadership relationships form and evolve" (p. 672). More recently, Ospina and Uhl-Bien (2012) concluded that the way forward in developing relational leadership theory is through the interplay of multi-paradigmatic perspectives, where practitioners and scholars of relational leadership "share the assumptions, designs, and insights of multiple perspectives without trying to eliminate what makes each unique" (p. xliv). The creation of a life-affirming dialogical space, where all perspectives and people are welcome, offers the greatest potential for bringing out the best of our diverse humanity to enlarge the conversation about both relational leadership and its role in ensuring a sustainable future.

In his groundbreaking 2015 encyclical, *Laudato Si'*, Francis broadened the dialogue about earth's environmental crisis by framing the conversation as a "spiritual and moral concern, and not just a matter of politics, science, and economics" (Goodstein & Gillis, 2015, para. 1). While unafraid of engaging scientists in a scholarly dialogue about environmental issues, much of the encyclical's focus is on the "social, moral, educational, and theological dimensions of the present global ecological crisis" (Briliute, 2017, p. 101). As both *Laudato Si'* and *Transforming Our World: The 2030 Agenda for Sustainable Development* underscore, the world's poor suffer the most from the planetary crisis because, "they are cast off by society, forced to live off what is discarded, and suffer unjustly from the abuse of the environment" (Francis, 2015c, para. 8).

To that end, the purpose of this chapter is to highlight Pope Francis' theological reflections on the interconnectedness of creation and explore how they can enhance our relational leadership theory and practice (Northouse, 2018). Consequently, this chapter attempts to answer the following questions:

(1) Who is Pope Francis?

(2) Why did he write *Laudato Si'*?

(3) How does *Laudato Si'*'s grounding of human life as a series of interconnected relationships — with the transcendent, with one's neighbor, and the earth itself — broaden the dialogue about ecological degradation and align with the Sustainable Development Goals from the *2030 Agenda for Sustainable Development* of the United Nations General Assembly?

(4) How might *Laudato Si'*'s spiritual understanding of interconnectedness enrich relational leadership theory and practice as we collectively inspire our diverse humanity to evolve our leadership to ensure a more just, humane, and sustainable future?

WHO IS POPE FRANCIS?

As Cardinal Archbishop of Buenos Aires, Jorge Mario Bergoglio was beloved for his availability, austere lifestyle, and closeness to the poor. For instance, he lived in a simple apartment, cooked his own meals, and even established a direct phone line exclusively for priests to reach him (Lowney, 2013, p. 73). The future Pope Francis would spend his days traveling by bus to celebrate Mass in shantytowns, assist in soup kitchens, and visit those afflicted by AIDS (Moynihan, 2013, pp. 150–151). Francis' closeness to the poor was especially embodied in his practice of washing the feet of marginalized people from Buenos Aires each year on Holy Thursday, a tradition he has carried into his papacy.

Through word and gesture, Pope Francis has disrupted traditional narratives through relational leadership – leveraging his position as Vatican head of state and universal leader of 1.2 billion Catholics to socially influence others to evolve their attitudes (Uhl-Bien, 2006) about the poor, the planet, the refugee, and the lesbian, gay, bisexual, transgender, and queer community (Tran & Carey, 2017). Despite some warranted criticism about his overall handling of the sexual abuse scandal (Allen, 2018), since his election on March 13, 2013, Pope Francis has moved millions with his relational, man-of-the-people manner (Levs & Pearson, 2013), masterful preaching (Heille, 2015), passion for "discernment with special consideration of the poor" (Sedmak, 2016, p. ix), inspirational acts of mercy and inclusive leadership (Tran & Carey, 2017), and concern for the global ecological crisis (Irwin, 2016).

WHY DID POPE FRANCIS WRITE *LAUDATO SI'*?

Prior to Francis' pontificate, the primary lacunae in Catholic social thought was the "paltry attention given to the environment" (Massaro, 2015, p. 174). However, from the onset of his papacy, Francis signaled an interest in advancing the doctrinal discourse on the environment. On March 16, 2013, just three days after his election, he shared with journalists the inspiration for his new leadership identity and concern for creation: "For me, [Francis of Assisi] is the man of poverty, the man of peace, the man who loves and protects creation; these days we do not have a very good relationship with creation" (Francis, 2013b, para. 7). In choosing to align his papal leadership with Francis of Assisi, the pontiff was signaling a desire to lead in a way that would bring him into a closer relationship with nature and the poor, as many artistic depictions of Francis of Assisi as a beggar and lover of animals show.

Three days later, in his papal inauguration homily, Francis reflected on humanity's shared vocation of being a protector, highlighting the relationship between protecting both people and the environment. For Francis

(2013c), serving as a protector involves protecting, "the beauty of the created world... respecting the environment in which we live. It means protecting people, showing loving concern for each and every person, especially children, the elderly, those in need, who are often the last we think about" (para. 6). He concluded that "In the end, everything has been entrusted to our protection, and all of us are responsible for it" (para. 6). In Dorr's (2016) estimation, Francis was broadening the definition of the term "solidarity" — inviting all people of good will to, "not merely to be in solidarity with excluded and fragile humans, but also with nonhuman creatures and the whole of the fragile ecosystem" (p. 411). Through his invitational and relational rhetoric, Francis was leveraging his inauguration, an event with international media coverage, to socially influence people throughout the world to revisit, rethink, and renew their relationship with all creatures.

Invigorated by Pope Francis' emerging eco-leadership, Schaefer (2013) wondered: "Can we also hope for the first encyclical dedicated to the climate crisis and related ecological issues of which there are many?" (p. xxxi). While the Catholic Church is not known for its rapid response rates (Faggioli, 2015), Francis replied to this query within the first two years of his papacy. Building on the work of regional Bishops' Conferences and his predecessors (Benedict XVI, 2009; John Paul II, 1979, 1981, 1987, 1991, 1995, 2003; Paul VI, 1971), Francis promulgated *Laudato Si'*, the Catholic Church's "first Papal document dedicated entirely to ecology" (Marengo, 2017, p. 42) on June 18, 2015.

One day prior to its publication, Francis (2015b) provided a preview to the assembled crowd in Saint Peter's Square:

> *Tomorrow, as you know, the Encyclical on the care of "our*
> *common home," which is creation, will be released. This "home"*
> *of ours is deteriorating and this harms everyone, especially the*
> *poorest. Mine is therefore a call to responsibility, based on the task*
> *God gave to human beings in creation: "to till and keep" the*
> *"garden" in which he placed him (cf. Gen 2:15). I invite all people*
> *to accept with an open heart this Document, which is in line with*
> *the Social Teaching of the Church. (para. 7)*

In the encyclical itself, Pope Francis (2015a) suggested that since the health of our planet effects every person on earth, what is necessary is an inclusive dialogue that can contribute to conversion in how we understand the causes and effects of the environmental challenges we are facing (para. 14). Francis' call for a social influence process of dialogue and discernment regarding the ecological crisis was another example of how relational leaders encourage people to "work together to define their relationships in a way that generates leadership influence and structure" (Uhl-Bien, 2006, p. 668).

HOW DOES LAUDATO SI'S EMPHASIS ON INTERCONNECTED RELATIONSHIPS BROADEN THE DIALOGUE AND ALIGN WITH THE SUSTAINABLE DEVELOPMENT GOALS OF THE UNITED NATIONS' 2030 AGENDA?

According to Vigini (2016), *Laudato Si'* is a,

> *...true compendium of Christian social doctrine, which sets out the priorities for an "ecological conversion" and a genuinely "integral ecology": unity against any partial, separate, or exclusively scientific-technical perspective; dialogue and collaboration between states and governments against any form of ideological conflict or the temptation to make unilateral decisions; constant effort to renew links between individuals and nations against any withdrawal into a "private and particular" scenario. (pp. xiv-xv)*

As Kelly (2016) concluded, this comprehensive agenda makes this encyclical, "quite a 'game-changer,' in terms of Catholic teaching and its dialogue with science, and in the field of ecumenical and even interreligious collaboration and communication" (p. 1).

For example, encyclicals are usually addressed to a particular group within Catholicism, e.g., all Roman Catholics and/or ordained Catholic clergy. Instead, *Laudato Si'* opened with an invitation for every person living on the planet to share in his "broad perspective on the role of humans in care for the Earth and all its inhabitants" (Dorr, 2016, p. 416). Since planet earth is our common home and this home is the dwelling place of the human family, "all the members of the family have relation with one another" (Alva, 2016, p. 177), nature, the self, and God (Sachs, 2017). Francis' relational and inclusive perspective on the planetary crisis creates a welcoming space for all concerned persons of good will, underscoring a fundamental assumption of relational leadership: "that social reality lies in the context of relationships" (Uhl-Bien, 2006, p. 661).

Naturally, Francis began his encyclical by relating to and recalling what his predecessors had written regarding ecology, underscoring their concern for the misuse of the natural environment. Francis also drew upon the ecological insights published by Conferences of Bishops throughout the world, demonstrating a "respect for and a reliance on the wisdom" (Irwin, 2016, p. 37) of "Church leaders who have been addressing real-life justice and ecological problems 'on the ground' in their particular regions" (Dorr, 2016, p. 417). He went on to see common cause in the statements of scientists, philosophers, theologians, and civic groups who had also expressed concern. Francis quoted Ecumenical Patriarch Bartholomew, who noted that all must acknowledge "our contribution, smaller or greater, to the disfigurement and destruction of creation" (Francis, 2015a, para. 8). Francis' "highly unusual" (Dorr, 2016, p. 417) decision to highlight the contributions of Patriarch Bartholomew and the Orthodox Church on the environment was significant for at least two reasons. First, it concretized Francis' commitment to bring about unity among Christian Churches. Second, it demonstrated that the debate about the relationship between science and religion is a common concern and that Catholicism has much to learn from other wisdom traditions (Irwin, 2016, p. 60). In fact, one of Francis' footnotes included the work of ninth-century Sufi mystic, Ali al-Khawas (Francis, 2015a, para. 233). For Dorr (2016), this underscored Francis' "respect for other religions and his belief that religious people of all persuasions need to work together on issues of ecology and justice" (p. 417).

Francis (2015a) also described his namesake, Francis of Assisi, as "the example par excellence of care for the vulnerable and of an integral ecology lived out joyfully and authentically" (para. 10). In Irwin's (2016) view, the pontiff's decision to open *Laudato Si'* by quoting Francis of Assisi's *Canticle of the Creatures* was rhetorically strategic: "It lays the foundation for the encyclical's explicit and implicit understanding that all created beings are just that, beings in relationship with one another" (p. 101).

Finally, Francis (2015a) concluded the encyclical's preface by articulating his purpose: "I urgently appeal, then, for a new dialogue about how we are shaping the future of our planet. We need a conversation which includes everyone, since the environmental challenge we are undergoing, and its human roots, concern and affects us all" (para. 14). As Irwin (2016) concluded, from the beginning of the encyclical Francis "invites us to view the earth as our common home through a wide-angle lens to include all created reality" (p. 96).

Before articulating a "biblical ecological spirituality, and before spelling out what is involved in an ecological conversion, he invites us first to reflect on the sinful way we are despoiling and neglecting our world" (Dorr, 2016, p. 417). In the first of six chapters, Francis (2015a) contrasted the naturally slow pace of biological evolution with what he called "rapidification" – that is, the speed with which human activity has developed. Describing the terrible consequences of pollution – "The earth our home is beginning to look more and more like an immense pile of filth" (Francis, 2015a, para. 21) – he laid the root cause at the feet of a "throwaway culture which affects the excluded just as it quickly reduces things to rubbish" (para. 22). Climate change is related to this culture of consumerism, and Francis identified developing countries that would be most impacted by the effects of climate change in the coming decades. The encyclical also examined the pollution of water supplies and asserted that "access to safe drinkable water is a basic and universal human right since it is essential to human survival and, as such, is a condition for the exercise of other human rights" (para. 30).

Francis' deep concerns about water scarcity, the plundering of the planet and their impact on the poor resonates with many of the United Nations' (2015) SDGs. Most obvious are the following: Goal 1 – the global eradication of poverty in all forms (p. 15) – and Goal 6 – "to ensure availability and sustainable management of water and sanitation for all" (p. 18).

Additionally, given the encyclical's compelling narrative and stylish rhetoric (Sachs, 2017), *Laudato Si'* aligns with Goal 13, which is to "take urgent action to combat climate change and its impacts" (United Nations General Assembly, 2015, p. 23), and Goal 15, to "protect, restore and promote sustainable use of terrestrial ecosystems, sustainably manage forests, combat desertification, and halt and reverse land degradation and halt biodiversity loss" (p. 24). For example, the second chapter of the encyclical – "The Gospel of Creation" – addressed these same goals by an examination of what the Biblical tradition had to offer to a reflection on the planet. Drawing on the accounts of creation from Genesis, the pope suggested that human life is rooted in three relationships: with God, with a neighbor, and with the earth itself. Francis (2015a) said that in the Genesis story, these relationships are ruptured, which distorted the mandate to "'have dominion' over the earth (cf. Gen 1:28), to 'till it and keep it' (Gen 2:15)" (para. 66). Going further, he argued that the biblical granting of dominion to humankind had been misinterpreted allowing the unbridled exploitation of nature: "When nature is viewed solely as a source of profit and gain, this has serious consequences for society" (para. 82). For Letellier (2017), transforming the mentality of domination to stewardship is a hermeneutical key to understanding "the whole intention of the Encyclical" (p. 142).

In the third chapter, "The Human Roots of the Ecological Crisis," Francis assessed the strengths and shortcomings of both technology and globalization, "in terms of what they contribute to the good of society and how they can also be harmful" (Irwin, 2016, p. 101). In a globalized and technologically advanced society, Francis (2015a) asserted that "We have to accept that technological products are not neutral, for they create a framework which ends up conditioning lifestyles and shaping social possibilities along the lines dictated by the interests of certain powerful groups" (para. 107). At its best, scientific research ought to be pursued with a sense of discernment towards the good of both the people and the planet. In Francis' view, "Decisions which may seem purely instrumental are in reality decisions about the kind of society we want to build" (para. 107). The pontiff's concern for the common good and consequent invitation to the rich to discern more efficient and inclusive ways of resource consumption can be tied to Goal 12, ensuring "sustainable consumption and production patterns" (United Nations General Assembly, 2015, p. 22).

The fourth chapter explored the concept of integral ecology, which extended the work of previous popes, yet departed from the "anthropocentric thrust of Catholic social teaching during the period from Vatican II up to the coming of Pope Francis in 2013" (Dorr, 2016, p. 422). Francis (2015a) insisted that all living beings have intrinsic value and not just instrumental value, reflecting an inclusive perspective on creation: "A good part of our genetic code is shared by many living beings.... Nature cannot be regarded as something separate from ourselves or as a mere setting in which we live. We are part of nature, included in it" (paras. 138–139). Given that every living being is connected and interconnected (Francis, 2015a, paras. 70, 91), humans have a responsibility for every facet of our lives – "political, social, economic, and cultural – and with particular reference to how our actions and whole way of life affects the Earth" (Dorr, 2016, pp. 422–423). Francis' urgent appeal for action on behalf of the poor and the planet is in accordance with Goal 13, which calls for "urgent action to combat climate change and its impacts" (United Nations General Assembly, 2015, p. 23).

After outlining the environmental and social challenges of our time, Francis (2015a) contended in the fifth chapter – "Lines of Approach and Action" – that a more creative and healthier sense of "politics is sorely needed, capable of reforming and coordinating institutions, promoting best practices and overcoming undue pressure and bureaucratic inertia" (para. 181). He invited all members of the global community to engage in debate and discernment, "which can help us escape the spiral of self-destruction which currently engulfs us" (para. 163). While the "Church does not presume to settle scientific questions or to replace politics," Francis is primarily interested in encouraging substantive dialogue "so that particular interests or ideologies will not prejudice the common good" (para. 188). Ultimately, "The gravity of the ecological crisis demands that we all look to the common good, embarking on a path of dialogue which demands patience, self-discipline, and generosity, always keeping in mind that 'realities are greater than ideas'" (para. 201). All this supports the same concern of Goal 17, which is to "strengthen the means of implementation and revitalize the Global Partnership for Sustainable Development" (United Nations General Assembly, 2015, p. 26).

In the sixth and final chapter – "Ecological Education and Spirituality" – Francis asserted that positive change in global ecology is impossible "without a change in each person's heart" (Briliute, 2017, p. 101). Similar to the issue addressed by Goal 12 – to "ensure sustainable consumption and production patterns" (United Nations General Assembly, 2015, p. 22) – Francis (2015a) is concerned that humans have completely adopted a consumerist and techno-economic paradigm: "Since the market tends to promote extreme consumerism in an effort to sell its products, people can easily get caught up in a whirlwind of needless buying and spending" (para. 203). This can lead people "to believe that they are free as long as they have the supposed freedom to consume" (para. 203). However, in his view, the only ones free "are the minority who wield economic and financial power" (para. 203).

Despite this challenging situation, "...all is not lost. Human beings, while capable of the worst, are also capable of rising above themselves, choosing again what is good, and making a new start, despite their mental and social conditioning" (Francis, 2015a, para. 205). He posited that the paradigms of techno-economic consumption and consumerism cannot "completely suppress our openness to what is good, true and beautiful" since, "We are able to take an honest look at ourselves, to acknowledge our deep dissatisfaction, and to embark on new paths to authentic freedom" (para. 205).

Pope Francis (2015a) concluded the encyclical by offering two prayers that recapitulate the important themes of *Laudato Si'*. In prayer for the earth, he asked, "that we may protect the world and not prey on it" and "to discover the worth of each thing, to be filled with awe and contemplation, to recognize that we are profoundly united with every creature" (para. 246). In the second prayer, Francis addressed God as understood by Christians to "accompany creation as it groans in travail" and to "Enlighten those who possess power and money that they may avoid the sin of indifference, that they may love the common good, advance the weak, and care for this world in which we live" (para. 246).

Francis' lengthy meditation on the interconnection of every living creature broadened the discourse on ecological decay by emphatically linking the notions of justice and ecology, and the "concern for the fragile earth with concern for fragile people" (Dorr, 2016, p. 448). Furthermore, Francis explored the ecological dimensions of various fields not often understood together: "morality, economics, science, spirituality, theology, liturgy, and the sacraments" (Irwin, 2016, p. 102).

How Might *Laudato Si's* Understanding of Interconnectedness Enrich Relational Leadership?

Pope Francis' invitation to "bring to flower new relationships" (Marengo, 2017, p. 46) between humanity and the planet, along with his challenge to "envision a future that responds to both the human and ecological crises together" (Cloutier, 2015, p. 50) suggest an integrated approach to leadership. As Bass and Bass (1974/2008) noted, one measure of effective leadership is one's "competence in both tasks and relationships" (p. 789). For relational leadership scholars such as Ospina and Uhl-Bien (2012), the interplay of multiple competencies and multidisciplinary perspectives and paradigms is useful for advancing an understanding of relational leadership that is both broad and deep. While contexts vary, "every leadership situation needs a degree of both task and relationship behaviors" (Northouse, 2018,

p. 99). The sudden resignation of Pope Benedict XVI effective February 28, 2013 was one such leadership situation that required the selection of a strong leader who was capable of integrating and optimizing the task and relational aspects of the papal leadership role.

True to the central argument of *Laudato Si'*, "which is, quite simply, that everyone and everything is related because it is all part of Creation" (Oreskes, 2015, p. viii), Pope Francis has employed an integrated approach to the task and relational dimensions of leadership since his historic 2013 election (Allen, Jr., 2015; Faggioli, 2015; Kasper, 2015; Tran & Carey, 2017). As Ospina and Uhl-Bien (2012) underscored, the interplay across a variety of dimensions allows for the "assumptions and insights from multiple perspectives to highlight connections and distinctions – identifying reso- nances as well as tensions" (p. xxxi) – and using these to advance understanding.

Francis' holistic approach to organizational reform and relationship building has unfolded across four dimensions: style, priorities, structure, and spiritual vision (Curran, 2016). From the moment Francis first appeared on the Vatican balcony, there was a palpable sense that this papacy was going to be characterized by a simpler, more humble style. By taking the name Francis, a first, the new pontiff aligned his pontificate with the beloved medi- eval Italian saint from Assisi who is revered for his humility, simplicity, and concern for the poor (Armstrong & Brady, 1982). Francis' emphasis on humility was immediately evident in his wardrobe. Instead of donning the ermine-trimmed, elbow-length velvet cape intended for the occasion, Francis opted for a less formal white cassock instead. He also chose to keep his exist- ing silver pectoral cross, declining the offered gold one. After leading the people in prayers for his predecessor, Francis then bowed his head, asking for the people's prayers prior to imparting his first official blessing. In Ivereigh's (2014) estimation, this "gesture of great humility" was also a "touching gesture of mutuality" that signaled a relational approach to lead- ership that was "bent on implementing collegiality" (p. 365).

Perhaps the best sign of Francis' reform of style was his decision to decline the spacious, yet isolating, confines of the apostolic palace and live in a guesthouse, which is regularly inhabited by Vatican officials and other visi- tors. He dines in the common downstairs cafeteria and often presides at the morning Mass for Vatican employees in the guesthouse's chapel. In other leadership practices, such as washing the feet of prisoners, embracing the physically disfigured, adopting Muslim refugees, and hosting homeless persons for dinner at the Vatican Museum and a private tour of the Sistine Chapel (Springer, 2015), Francis has demonstrated an abiding awareness of attending to the task of reforming Catholicism's priorities *and* taking an interest in others by, "valuing their uniqueness, and giving special attention to their personal needs" (Northouse, 2018, p. 105). Francis (2014) has emphasized in both word and deed that "A simple lifestyle is good for us, helping us to better share with those in need" (para. 1).

As mentioned earlier, Goal 1 of the 2030 Agenda of the General Assembly of the United Nations (2015) is to "end poverty in all its forms everywhere" (p. 15). By making the poor the core social concern of his leadership agenda (Francis, 2013b), Francis is reforming the hierarchical priorities of Catholicism. Rooted in his emphasis on the virtue of mercy as the paradigmatic logic that undergirds Catholicism's standard operating procedures and processes, Francis has asserted that,

> *We cannot insist only on issues related to abortion, gay marriage and the use of contraceptive methods… when we speak about these issues, we have to talk about them in a context. The teaching of the church, for that matter, is clear and I am a son of the church, but it is not necessary to talk about these issues all the time.*
>
> *Source*: As cited in Spadaro (2013, para. 59)

As evidenced in his writings, Francis has consistently critiqued humanity's consumerist mentality and idolatry of market economies, which often serves those wielding economic power rather than those on the peripheries. Time and time again, Francis has urged all people of good will to consider "a change of heart and attitudes as well as a change of structures" (Curran, 2016, p. 267). This is consistent with Goal 12 of the *2030 Agenda* of the General Assembly of the United Nations (2015), which include commitments to "substantially reduce waste generation through prevention, reduction, recycling and reuse"; encourage companies, especially large and transnational companies, to adopt sustainable practices and to integrate sustainability information into their reporting cycle"; and "ensure that people everywhere have the relevant information and awareness for sustainable development and lifestyles in harmony with nature" (pp. 22–23).

Exactly one month after his election, Francis matched his rhetoric of structural reform by creating a committee of eight (now nine) non-Vatican

cardinals from all continents (only two from Europe) to advise him on organizational change. According to Faggioli (2015), "it was an unprecedented
step in the history of attempts to reform the central government of the
Church as it was created in the late sixteenth century" (p. 33). Additionally,
during his first year, Francis hired consultants from McKinsey and KPMG to
bring Vatican communications and finances in line with contemporary practice (Moloney, 2013). Despite some missteps with the clergy abuse scandal
(Hale, 2018), Francis created a papal commission for the protection of min-
ors, which initially included a survivor of clerical sexual abuse, to advise him
on child protection policies, processes, and procedures. In line with his vision
to be more in touch with the global peripheries, Francis has appointed 41%
of the 120 cardinals who will elect his successor. Represented among the 49
Francis-appointed cardinals are 15 countries that had never had one before,
including Bangladesh, Cape Verde, Myanmar, Laos, Tonga, and the Central
African Republic (Allen, Jr. & San Martin, 2018).

For Francis (2015a), the Vatican's disconnection from the Church's international realities and the ecological deterioration of the planet are both due
to the deterioration of human relationship:

> *Human beings and material objects no longer extend a friendly*
> *hand to one another; the relationship has become confrontational.*
> *This has made it easy to accept the idea of infinite or unlimited*
> *growth, which proves so attractive to economists, financiers and*
> *experts in technology. It is based on the lie that there is an infinite*
> *supply of the earth's goods, and this leads to the planet being*
> *squeezed dry beyond every limit. (para. 106)*

In Francis' view, this reality has harmed the quality of both the environment
and human life itself, and "there is a breakdown in the moral order that
alone can guarantee fairness in the use of natural resources, peaceful co-
existence between human beings, and the physical and spiritual well-being of
all" (Vigini, 2016, pp. xii–xiii).

Consequently, by advancing a reconsideration of human relationship that
is inextricably linked to the environmental choices humanity must make in
order to achieve a more meaningful and life-affirming sense of human rela-
tionality, Francis (2015a) articulated a worldview that he called an "integral
ecology" (para. 11). For Francis,

A sense of deep communion with the rest of nature cannot be real if our hearts lack tenderness, compassion and concern for our fellow human beings. It is clearly inconsistent to combat trafficking in endangered species while remaining completely indifferent to human trafficking, unconcerned about the poor, or undertaking to destroy another human being deemed unwanted. This compromises the very meaning of our struggle for the sake of the environment.... Everything is connected. Concern for the environment thus needs to be joined to a sincere love for our fellow human beings and an unwavering commitment to resolving the problems of society. (para. 91)

From this perspective emerged the pontiff's "fundamental basis for human dignity and for our obligation to care for one another, the planet, and the diverse creatures on it" (Oreskes, 2015, p. viii). If everyone and everything is interconnected, the crises of our time are all part of "one complex crisis which is both social and environmental" (Francis, 2015a, para. 139). Therefore, all people and information from all branches of knowledge ought to be "integrated into a broader vision of reality" (para. 138). In Francis' view, this expansive vision of reality will avail an "integrated approach to combating poverty, restoring dignity to the excluded, and at the same time protecting nature" (para. 139). Ultimately, Pope Francis has articulated "a global vision of humanity and the world, with multiple relationships and responsibilities enabling us to live together in our common home" (Vigini, 2016, p. xi).

CONCLUSION

As evidenced in the aforementioned presentation of *Laudato Si'* and the reforms of style, priorities, structures, and spiritual vision embodied and enacted by Pope Francis, an integrated leadership approach optimizing both task and relationship behaviors is critical. The case of Francis affirms the research of leader-member exchange (LMX) theorists who found a "link between relational quality and personal and organizational effectiveness" (Johnson & Hackman, 2018, p. 96). Through his holistic approach, Francis is "doing what all good leaders do, jostling our imaginations when we become too complacent and stripping away the veneer of the familiar to expose the raw feel of a challenging truth" (Lowney, 2013, p. 43). Given his hunger for human relationship and his passion for the interrelated plight of the poor and the planet, Pope Francis understands leadership as "a shared experience, a voyage through time" (Hollander, 1995, p. 55), in which a significant portion of human relating is one's perception of self-relative to others, the planet, and the divine. The pontiff points to his namesake, Saint Francis of Assisi, who "shows us just how inseparable the bond is between concern for nature, justice for the poor, commitment to society, and interior peace" (Francis, 2015a, para. 11). Through his groundbreaking encyclical, Francis contributed to the development of relational leadership by encouraging others to (re)examine the "interactive dynamics that contribute to emergence or direction of social order and action" (Uhl-Bien, 2006, p. 2006) by dialogically discerning "a new way of thinking about human beings, life, society and our relationship with nature" (Francis, 2015a, para. 215). Otherwise, without an interior change that will bring out the best in our diverse humanity to ignite a global change in sustainable development for the common good, "the paradigm of consumerism will continue to advance, with the help of the media and the highly effective workings of the market" (para. 215).

REFERENCES

Allen, E. (2018, January 20). Cardinal O'Malley speaks out against pope's comment to sex abuse victims in Chile. *Boston Globe*. Retrieved from https://www.bostonglobe.com/metro/2018/01/20/cardinal-malley-speaks-out-against-pope-comment-sex-abuse-victims-chile/QoT3LunUSDUUgFQvrp2UjL/story.html

Allen, Jr., J. L. (2015). *The Francis miracle: Inside the transformation of the pope and the Church*. New York, NY: Time Books.

Allen, Jr., J. L., & San Martin, I. (2018, February 21). As cardinals age, looking ahead to Pope Francis's next consistory. *Crux*. Retrieved from https://cruxnow.com/vatican/2018/02/21/cardinals-age-looking-ahead-pope-franciss-next-consistory.

Alva, R. (2016). Sustainable development in the light of the teachings of the encyclical Laudato Si. *European Journal of Sustainable Development, 5*(4), 177–186.

Armstrong, R. J., & Brady, I. C. (Eds.). (1982). *Francis and Claire: The complete works.* New York, NY: Paulist Press.

Bass, B. M., with Bass, R. (2008). *The Bass handbook of leadership: Theory, research, and managerial applications* (4th ed.). New York, NY: Free Press. (Original work published 1974).

Benedict XVI. (2009). *Caritas in Veritate.* Retrieved from http://w2.vatican.va/content/benedict-xvi/en/encyclicals/documents/hf_ben-xvi_enc_20090629_caritas-in-veritate.html.

Briliute, B. (2017). The Catechism of the Catholic Church and *Laudato Si'*. In M. Mills, J. A. Orr, & H. Schnitker (Eds.), *Reflections on Pope Francis's encyclical Laudato si'* (pp. 100–116). Newcastle upon Tyne: Cambridge Scholars Publishing.

Chappell, K. (2017). An ecologist's perspective on *Laudato Si'*. In M. Mills, J. A. Orr, & H. Schnitker (Eds.), *Reflections on Pope Francis's encyclical Laudato si'* (pp. 6–17). Newcastle upon Tyne: Cambridge Scholars Publishing.

Cloutier, D. (2015). *Reading, praying, living Pope Francis's Laudato Si: A faith formation guide.* Collegeville, MN: Liturgical Press.

Curran, C. (2016). *Tradition and church reform: Perspectives on Catholic moral teaching.* Maryknoll, NY: Orbis.

Dorr, D. (2016). *Option for the poor & for the earth: From Leo XIII to Pope Francis* (Rev. ed.). Maryknoll, NY: Orbis.

Eggemeier, M. T. (2014). *A sacramental-prophetic vision: Christian spirituality in a suffering world.* Maryknoll, NY: Orbis.

Faggioli, M. (2015). *Pope Francis: Tradition in transition.* Mahwah, NJ: Paulist Press.

Francis. (2013b, March 16). *Address to representatives of the communications media.* Retrieved from https://w2.vatican.va/content/francesco/en/speeches/2013/march/documents/papa-francesco_20130316_rappresentanti-media.html.

Francis. (2013c, March 19). *Homily of Pope Francis.* Retrieved from https://w2.vatican.va/content/francesco/en/homilies/2013/documents/papa-francesco_20130319_omelia-inizio-pontificato.html.

Francis. [Pontifex]. (2014, April 24). A simple lifestyle is good for us, helping us to better share with those in need [Tweet]. Retrieved from https://twitter.com/pontifex/status/459246483930218497?lang=en.

Francis. (2015a, May 24). *Encyclical letter: Laudato si' of the Holy Father Francis: On care for our common home.* Retrieved from http://w2.vatican.va/content/francesco/en/encyclicals/documents/papa-francesco_20150524_enciclica-laudato-si.html.

Francis. (2015b, June 17). *General audience.* Retrieved from https://w2.vatican.va/content/francesco/en/audiences/2015/documents/papa-francesco_20150617_udienza-generale.html.

Francis. (2015c, September 25). *Meeting with the members of the General Assembly of the United Nations Organization: Address of the Holy Father.* Retrieved from http://w2.vatican.va/content/francesco/en/speeches/2015/september/documents/papa-francesco_20150925_onu-visita.html.

Gergen, K. J. (2011). Relational being: A brief introduction. *Journal of Constructivist Psychology, 24,* 280–282.

Goodstein, L., & Gillis, J. (2015, June 18). On planet in distress, a papal call to action. *The New York Times.* Retrieved from https://www.nytimes.com/interactive/2015/06/18/world/europe/encyclical-laudato-si.html?_r=0.

Hale, C. J. (2018, February 6). Pope Francis' failure to address abuse allegations jeopardizes his papacy. *Time.* Retrieved from http://time.com/5135338/pope-francis-sex-abuse

Heille, G. (2015). *The preaching of Pope Francis: Missionary discipleship and the ministry of the word.* Collegeville, MN: Liturgical.

Hollander, E. P. (1995). Ethical challenges in the leader-follower relationship. *Business Ethics Quarterly, 5*(1), 55–65.

Irwin, K. W. (2016). *A commentary on Laudato Si': Examining the background, contributions, implementation, and future of Pope Francis's encyclical.* Mahwah, NJ: Paulist.

Ivereigh, A. (2014). *The great reformer: Francis and the making of a radical pope.* New York, NY: Henry Holt.

John Paul II. (1979). *Redemptor Hominis.* Retrieved from http://w2.vatican.va/content/john-paul-ii/en/encyclicals/documents/hf_jp-ii_enc_04031979_redemptor-hominis.html.

John Paul II. (1981). *Laborem Exercens.* Retrieved from http://w2.vatican.va/content/john-paul-ii/en/encyclicals/documents/hf_jp-ii_enc_14091981_laborem-exercens.html.

John Paul II. (1987). *Sollicitudo Rei Socialis.* Retrieved from http://w2.vatican.va/content/john-paul-ii/en/encyclicals/documents/hf_jp-ii_enc_30121987_sollicitudo-rei-socialis.html.

John Paul II. (1991). *Centesimus Annus.* Retrieved from http://w2.vatican.va/content/john-paul-ii/en/encyclicals/documents/hf_jp-ii_enc_01051991_centesimus-annus.html.

John Paul II. (1995). *Evangelium Vitae.* Retrieved from http://w2.vatican.va/content/john-paul-ii/en/encyclicals/documents/hf_jp-ii_enc_25031995_evangelium-vitae.html.

John Paul II. (2003). *Ecclesia de Eucharistia.* Retrieved from http://www.vatican.va/holy_father/special_features/encyclicals/documents/hf_jp-ii_enc_20030417_ecclesia_eucharistia_en.html.

Johnson, C. E., & Hackman, M. Z. (2018). *Leadership: A communication perspective* (7th ed.). Long Grove, IL: Waveland Press.

Kasper, W. (2015). *Pope Francis' revolution of tenderness and love.* Mahwah, NJ: Paulist Press.

Kelly, A. J. (2016). *Laudato Si': An integral ecology and the Catholic vision.* Hindmarsh, SA: ATF Press Publishing.

Letellier, R. (2017). The scriptural roots of *Laudato Si'*. In M. Mills, J. A. Orr, & H. Schnitker (Eds.), *Reflections on Pope Francis's encyclical Laudato si'* (pp. 139–163). Newcastle upon Tyne: Cambridge Scholars Publishing.

Levs, J., & Pearson, M. (2013, December 11). Pope Francis named *Time* Person of the Year 2013. *CNN.* Retrieved from http://www.cnn.com/2013/12/11/living/time-person-of-the-year

Lowney, C. (2013). *Pope Francis: Why he leads the way he leads*. Chicago, IL: Loyola Press.

Marengo, G. (2017). The anthropological questions and the care of our common home. In M. Mills, J. A. Orr, & H. Schnitker (Eds.), *Reflections on Pope Francis's encyclical Laudato si'* (pp. 42–50). Newcastle upon Tyne: Cambridge Scholars Publishing.

Massaro, T. (2015). *Living justice: Catholic Social Teaching in action* (3rd ed.). Lanham, MD: Rowman & Littlefield.

Moloney, L. (2013, December 19). Vatican hires global firms to modernize communications, accounting. *The Wall Street Journal*. Retrieved from https://www.wsj.com/articles/vatican-hires-us-firms-to-modernize-communications-accounting-1387469598.

Moynihan, R. (2013). *Pray for me: The life and spiritual vision of Pope Francis, first pope from the Americas*. New York, NY: Image.

Northouse, P. G. (2018). *Introduction to leadership: Concepts and practice* (4th ed.). Thousand Oaks, CA: Sage Publications.

Oreskes, N. (2015). Introduction. In P. Francis (Ed.), *Encyclical on climate change & inequality: On care for our common home* (pp. vii–xxiv). Brooklyn, NY: Melville.

Ospina, S. M., & Uhl-Bien, M. (2012). Introduction – mapping the terrain: Convergence and divergence around relational leadership. In M. Uhl-Bien & S. M. Ospina (Eds.), *Advancing relational leadership research: A dialogue among perspectives* (pp. xix–xlvi). Charlotte, NC: Information Age.

Paul VI. (1971). *Octogesima Adveniens: Apostolic letter of Pope Paul VI*. Retrieved from http://w2.vatican.va/content/paul-vi/en/apost_letters/documents/hf_p-vi_apl_19710514_octogesima-adveniens.html.

Peppard, C. Z. (2014). *Just water: Theology, ethics, and the global water crisis*. Maryknoll, NY: Orbis.

Poole, J., Gharib, M., & Sofia, M. K. (2017, June 23). Future humans: How many of us will there be? *NPR*. Retrieved from https://www.npr.org/sections/goatsandsoda/2017/06/23/533549231/future-humans-how-many-of-us-will-there-be.

Sachs, W. (2017). The sustainable development goals and Laudato si': Varieties of post-development? *Third World Quarterly, 38*(12), 2573–2587.

Schaefer, J. (2013). Introduction: Celebrating and advancing magisterial discourse on the ecological crisis. In J. Schaefer & T. Winright (Eds.), *Environmental justice and climate change: Assessing Pope Benedict XVI's ecological vision for the Catholic Church in the United States* (pp. xix–xxxiii). Lanham, MD: Lexington.

Sedmak, C. (2016). *A church of the poor: Pope Francis and the transformation of orthodoxy.* Maryknoll, NY: Orbis.

Spadaro, A. (2013, September 30). A big heart open to God: An interview with Pope Francis. *America Magazine.* Retrieved from http://americamagazine.org/pope-interview.

Springer, A. (2015, March 26). Vatican tour. *ABC News.* Retrieved from http://abcnews.go.com/International/pope-francis-surprises-homeless-vistors-private-vatican-tour/story?id=29923638.

Steffen, W., Broadgate, W., Deutsch, L., Gaffney, O., & Ludwig, C. (2015). The trajectory of the anthropocene: The great acceleration. *The Anthropocene Review, 2*(1), 81–98.

Tran, D. Q., & Carey, M. R. (2017). Mercy within mercy: The heart of Pope Francis' inclusive leadership in a broken world. In A. Boitano, R. Lagomarsino, & H. E. Schockman, (Eds.), *Breaking the zero-sum game: Transforming societies through inclusive leadership* (pp. 231–248). Bingley: Emerald Publishing.

Uhl-Bien, M. (2006). Relational leadership theory: Exploring the social processes of leadership and organizing. *Leadership Quarterly, 17*(6), 654–676.

United Nations General Assembly. (2015). *Transforming our world: The 2030 agenda for sustainable development.* Retrieved from https://sustainabledevelopment.un.org/post2015/transformingourworld/publication.

Vigini, G. (2016). Introduction. In G. Vigini (Ed.), *Care for creation: A call for ecological conversion* (pp. ix–xv). Maryknoll, NY: Orbis.

10

THRIVING AS ONE GLOBAL FAMILY: LEADERSHIP BEYOND THE NATION STATE

Ejaj Ahmad and Hugh O'Doherty

INTRODUCTION

In January 2018, at a UN Security Council meeting on building regional partnerships in Afghanistan and Central Asia, Secretary-General Guterres stated that "Only by addressing the root causes of crisis, including inequality, exclusion and discrimination, will we build peaceful societies resilient to terrorism and violent extremism" (Gutteres, A, January 2018). When making this comment, the Secretary-General probably had in mind Goal 16 of the United Nations' Sustainable Development Goals. Goal 16 aspires to "promote peaceful and inclusive societies for sustainable development, provide access to justice for all and build effective, accountable and inclusive institutions at all levels" (United Nations Sustainable Development Goals).

Goal 16 is, of course, a noble aspiration. However, getting there presents profound challenges to ethnic groups and nation states everywhere. What aspects of identity, what cultural values, what "truths" might have to be sacrificed in the interest of creating an inclusive, cooperative future for the whole human family — a future that we can't clearly envisage in this moment because we have no models, and that we don't know where to begin as we have no road map? Engaging the human family in addressing these questions will require a different understanding of leadership than the present one that, ironically, has colluded in creating the violent and desperate global situation we find ourselves in.

Based on our 40 years of collective experience of teaching leadership to transcend boundaries and resolve conflict, we propose two ideas in this chapter that we hope will stimulate fresh thinking about the concept of leadership. Our first proposition involves the need to breaking away from tribalism to understand the motives of others and to create a new future based on the principle of the prior unity of all human beings, rather than the idea that we are separated by ethnicity and nationality. The second proposition is about the need for humanity to take ownership of problems without depending on the authority to provide solutions.

CURRENT REALITY

The UN Refugee Agency's annual Global Trends study found that 65.6 million people were forcibly displaced worldwide at the end of 2016. On average, 20 people were driven from their homes every minute, or one every three seconds. According to the latest IDMC report, "some of the worst ever levels of violence and displacement were recorded in 2017, driven by political instability and conflict, complex humanitarian emergencies, failed peace agreements, urban warfare and disasters." The number of new displacements almost doubled, "from 6.9 million in 2017 to 11.8 million in 2017." Syria, DRC, and Iraq together accounted for more than half of the global figures. A total of 40 million people remained "internally displaced" as of the end of 2017 (GRID, May 2018).

The conflict in Syria, now in its seventh year, was the world's biggest producer of refugees (5.5 million). The disastrous break-off of peace efforts in July 2016 in South Sudan contributed to an outflow of 737,400 people by the end of the year. In Sudan, between 1983 and 2002, some estimates suggest that as many as 2 million people were killed in the war between the north and south (UNHCR Global Trends, 2016).

The continent of Africa tells a similar desperate story of genocide and displacement. In Angola, between 1975 and 2002, there were an estimated 1.5 million war-related deaths. In Rwanda, an estimated 800,000 were killed in the 1994 genocide, in only 100 days. The death toll in eastern Congo between 1998 and 2004 is estimated to be nearly 4 million. In the

Democratic Republic of the Congo, as many as 2,166,000 new displacements were recorded during 2017, second only to Syria, and there were about 4.5 million IDPs in the country as of the end of 2017 (GRID, 2018) In the mid-2000s, Darfur was recognized as the first genocide of the twenty-first century (Reeves, Eric, NYT, 2016).

Of course, the violence taking place in Syria and Yemen is utterly heartbreaking. Most of us turn away because it is so painful and we feel so incompetent and hopeless. The last comprehensive number widely accepted internationally — 470,000 dead — was issued by the Syrian Center for Policy Research in 2016. Based on that estimate, which takes into account both civilian and combatant deaths, around 2.33 percent of Syria's prewar population of 22 million has been killed (Specia, Meghan, NYT, April 13, 2018). In Yemen, according to Save the Children, more than 50,000 children are expected to die by the end of the year as a result of disease and starvation caused by the stalemated war in the country. Seven million people are on the brink of famine in the country, which is in the grips of the largest cholera outbreak in modern history (Save the Children: Yemen Report, 2018).

PEACEMAKING IN A GLOBAL WORLD

Collectively, these facts underscore one of our most urgent global needs: a new model for understanding what peace is, and a better understanding of the leadership required to establish peace and make it last. Our world is changing so rapidly that the models for interaction that we've developed over thousands of years of civilization are no longer helpful — in fact, they can cloud our perception of what is needed *now*. The human population continues to mushroom. Technology has put these increasing numbers of people in previously unimaginable close communication with one another, allowing us to cross cultural boundaries as never before. At the same time, the power of nation-states is being eroded and replaced by the influence exerted by multinational mega-corporations. Simply put, more people are rubbing elbows with one another than ever before in history — and it's happening everywhere, all around the globe.

While this trend to globalization can be positive in many ways, it also means that the demarcations by which we've defined the societies and groups we live in are changing rapidly. As populations swell, communication proliferates, and economic and environmental factors make us increasingly enmeshed, social groups are coming into contact with one another with unprecedented frequency. As this happens, the way we define who we are and our place in the world is challenged. As value systems collide and clash, our sense of identity — national, cultural, personal — can seem deeply threatened, and in turn, deeply threatening. In the new global world we now live in, fears about the loss of local identity are greatly heightened. As the Internet shrinks the size of the world, providing easy access and almost unavoidable exposure to different value systems, people can feel as though they no longer know who they are; they can feel that their value system is in danger; they wonder if they have control of any piece of the world any more. In the face of these fears, a powerful urge to re-exert the sense of local, national, or even cultural identity is born. Unfortunately, this renewed assertion of local identity often takes the form of conflict with other groups who are similarly trying to re-exert their own local identity.

Obviously, this is a formula for disaster and has led directly to the situation of pervasive global tension we're in today. Our very survival as a species relies on our ability to understand our new global situation and make peace with one another in it. When it comes to brokering peace, however, if we don't understand the nature of what is actually required, we invariably approach the task in a misguided way.

HUNKER DOWN OR RECALIBRATE?

In this time of uncertainty, we have two options. We can treat the current moment as a one-time crisis that we need to overcome, or as a signal that the sands are permanently shifting and that all our assumptions need to be dredged up, examined, and recalibrated. The temptation to "keep calm and carry on" is understandable — hibernate like a bear, and hope that when we wake up, all will be better. Recalibrating, however, will demand that we rethink leadership.

P1: Leadership will require mobilizing people to transcend tribalism.

Out beyond ideas of wrongdoing and rightdoing, there is a field. I'll meet you there.

Source: Rumi (2010)

As we write, Bangladesh is faced with a humanitarian crisis on an unprecedented scale. Over the past several months, more than 500,000 Rohingya refugees, currently stranded in makeshift camps in Cox's Bazar, Bangladesh, have fled the Rakhine state in neighboring Myanmar, where the military has launched a systematic attack on them, burning villages, and butchering ordinary people (Solomon, 2017). Myanmar's 1.1 million Rohingya Muslims have been living as outcasts for decades. While they assert themselves as an ethnic minority of Myanmar, with their history reaching back centuries in the state of Rakhine, they are not recognized as citizens of Bangladesh (Mohdin, 2017). They are deprived from access to public services such as healthcare, education, and employment opportunities in civil service as Myanmar's 1982 nationality law does not recognize them among Burmese ethnic groups. The Rohingya have been coming into Bangladesh since Myanmar's independence in 1942 because of growing tensions, and the numbers keep growing (Mohdin, 2017). The recent exodus spurred by attacks described by the United Nations as a "textbook example of ethnic cleansing" (Safi, 2017).

Citizens of Myanmar do not admit to a shared history with the Rohingya. Instead, they believe that the Rohingya are illegal immigrants from Bangladesh. There is an aggressive campaign by extremist Buddhist monks who believe that Muslims are out to destroy Myanmar's traditional Buddhist identity, take over their population by having large families, and establish an Islamic caliphate (Callahan, M., 2017). The situation is made more complex by the emergence of Rohingya militant groups who have launched attacks on security checkpoints and police (Callahan, M., 2017). Both sides use the argument of self-defense.

The Myanmar government's position on the current crisis is that only Rohingya with "verifiable ties" to Myanmar will be allowed to return to their homeland (Homes, 2017). However, the systematic disempowerment of the Rohingya and the pervading anti-Islam narrative makes it improbable that most will meet that requirement. The process demands that the Rohingya identify as Bengalis, which would deny them their cultural identity and history.

The solution to the Rohingya refugee crisis cannot be solved by a single nation. It will require cooperation between Myanmar and its bordering countries, as well as the international community. This is recognized in Sustainable Development Goal (SDG) 17 which states that "a stronger commitment to partnership and cooperation is needed to achieve the SDGs. That effort will require coherent policies, an enabling environment for sustainable development at all levels and by all actors and a reinvigorated Global Partnership for Sustainable Development" (United Nations Sustainable Development Goals).

While Britain, France, and Australia have urged Myanmar's *de facto* authority figure, Aung San Suu Kyi, to push for an end to military violence against the Rohingya Muslims, India and China have taken a more nuanced position, supporting Myanmar, because of geopolitical interests.

Again, at an espoused level, the UN's call for partnership is noble and inspiring. However, to date, the human family has no form of global governance that can address global challenges like the conflict between the Myanmar government and the Rohingya. The League of Nations, established in 1920 to maintain world peace, failed; the United Nations is failing presently with each nation competing for its share of the pie (Ross, March 2016; Trueman, 2015). Even humanity's most promising cooperative experiment, the European Union, is starting to crack with Britain voting to withdraw from membership.

Indeed, nation states are a relatively new form of governance (Hauss, 1996). Most of the new nations are postcolonial creations with artificial boundaries drawn by colonial powers for their own convenience, frequently with little rationale. Borders have routinely lumped together many heterogeneous tribal and religious groups that don't want to be together (Fisher, 2012). At the same time, unified groups in places like Iraq, Afghanistan, and Somalia have been divided across artificial boundaries (Waduge, 2018).

The result of this chaos is a world in which people feel their identities are threatened and look to a new generation of populists who, "Claiming to speak for 'the people', ... treat rights as an impediment to their conception of the majority will, a needless obstacle to defending the nation from perceived threats and evils" (Roth, K., World Report 2017).

THE TRIBAL MIND

In his book, *Us and Them*, David Berreby explains how and why people are wedded to the notion that they belong to different categories like races, ethnic groups, nations, religions, and castes. The result is that none of us are free of what we refer to as a *tribal mindset*. We are all plugged in. We are saturated in the specific thought forms of various groups, defining ourselves as separate and different from one another. Our individual energy goes into maintaining the life force of the tribe (or tribes) to which we belong or identify with. This involves an implicit agreement to think like the tribe thinks, evaluate situations and people as the tribe does, and believe in right and wrong according to tribal values. As long as the tribal mentality remains unexamined and opaque to our awareness, we unwittingly subject others to our tribal prejudices. Children, born into the hatred and intolerance of their parents and ancestors, quickly internalize a tribal mentality that differentiates itself from all "outsiders." People grow up hating and demonizing other people – people they have never seen – based purely on tribal identity and group affiliation. This is the shadow side of the tribe (Berreby, 2005).

The first step beyond this demonizing is to become aware of our own tribal thinking. However, this "runs deeply against the grain. It's counterintuitive. It's emotionally unpleasant. It fights against our very DNA. Compared with bathing in the affirming balm of a tribe, it's deeply unsatisfying" (Sullivan, 2017).

NEPAL CASE STUDY

While working in Nepal in 2010, Hugh faced this dilemma. On November 21, 2006, the government and the Maoist rebels in Nepal signed a Comprehensive Peace Accord that gave birth to the Federal Democratic Republic of Nepal, thus ending centuries of monarchy. As part of establishing the Republic of Nepal, the major parties created a 601-member constitutional assembly with the challenge of producing a new constitution by May 2010. The intention was to design a decision-making process that would be nation-wide, engaging all stakeholders in building a new democratic republic.

However, progress was immediately hindered due to severe inter-party mistrust, leading the UN Security Council to warn in January 2010 that "The brinkmanship and confrontation between the Maoists and the government, accompanied by a sharp and dangerous hardening of positions, is making a negotiated solution significantly more difficult" (Article II. 10, United Nations Security Council, 2010).

Negotiations between the major parties reached stalemate, and the US State Department asked The Karuna Center for Peacebuilding, a nonprofit organization that offers nonviolent solutions in troubled or war-torn countries, and its Nepali partner, the Institute for Conflict Management, Peace, and Development, to partner in designing a program to help Nepali political leaders complete the design of a new, inclusive, constitution. Based on his expertise with the adaptive leadership model and his experience in peacebuilding in Northern Ireland conflict, Cyprus, and other parts of the world, the Karuna group invited Hugh to participate.

Federal restructuring of the state and how to treat the 19,000 former Maoist combatants emerged as major demands of ethnic and regional activists in Nepal. However, many in the Nepali government were nervous about the strong influence of the Maoists and questioned the Maoist's commitment to a democratic process. For their part, the Maoists, who comprised a full third of the constitutional assembly and a clear majority, were suspicious that the mainstream parties were trying to wipe them out by casting them as dangerous extremists. Solutions to this adaptive challenge were nowhere in sight.

While each party fiercely held onto the position that their view was "the truth" and the other's view was "the problem," the underlying adaptive challenge required that each group acknowledge the legitimacy of interpretations other than their own and begin to recognize their own role in maintaining the conflict. The various groups would have to give up their paranoid attachment to ways of seeing themselves as good and right and the other groups as some variety of bad and wrong.

The Karuna team did this by inviting each of the parties to experiment with stepping into "other's" shoes. The first step in this process introduced the parties to the difference between a "position" and an "interest" (Fisher & Ury, 1991). We then asked them to address each of the issues, guided by the following questions: (1) From your point of view, what do you think the other parties want? (2) What do they need? (3) Why do they fear you? Step two involved each party sharing its thinking with the other groups so that their views could be confirmed or disconfirmed.

The National Congress members shared with the Maoists their perception that they thought that the Maoists wanted to establish a communist regime. They feared that even though the Maoists espoused a multi-party state when given an opportunity, they would impose a single-party communist government. For their part, the Maoists responded that they, in fact, did not want a communist regime but that they didn't want pluralism because to them pluralism left open the possibility for the monarchy to return, which in their opinion was unthinkable.

The result of this process of inquiry, of standing in the other's shoes, is that each party was able to test its view of reality and to move from argumentation and debate to inquiry and dialogue. They were able to acknowledge that they understood the rationale behind the other's fear — how they each represented an existential threat to each other. They could then move to the next stage of the process that involved joint work on options that took into account the interests and fears of each party.

In psychodynamic language, the parties were able to "take back" their projections and recognize them as parts of themselves over which they had control. The exercise provided a mirror so that each group had an opportunity to view their own projections and notice their desire to deny to that which their projections: the impulse to dominate and manipulate that fear engenders.

> P2: Leadership in today's complex world will require people to break the longstanding addiction of looking to authority figures for solutions.

On the campaign trail, Donald Trump informed the American public that "Politicians have used you and stolen your votes. They have given you nothing. I will give you everything. I will give you what you've been looking for 50 years. I'm the only one" (Johnson, 2016). He promised that voting for him would "make possible every dream you've ever dreamed (Bump, 2016)."

During his acceptance speech at the Republican National Convention, having described America as a nation in crisis, suffering from "poverty and violence at home," "war and destruction abroad," and "international humiliation," Trump boasted, "Nobody knows the system better than me, which is why I alone can fix it.... I am your voice (Appelbaum, 2016)."

What we see in Trump's comments is the classic strategy of the populist authority figure. Notice we don't say "leader."

In our work as leadership educators, we've seen firsthand how people confuse leadership with authority. They grant someone an authority role and begin referring to him/her as the "leader." A powerful example of this is the frequently heard mantra that the President of the United States is the "leader of the free world." The problem with attaching the label "leader" to someone in a position of authority is that the term "leader" does not tell us anything about the activity of leadership. There is no guarantee that simply because someone has the role of President that he/she inevitably exercises leadership.

Leadership is best understood as an activity – the capacity to mobilize people to address not any old problems, but the *adaptive* ones (Heifetz & Linsky, 2002). Unlike technical problems that have a clear definition and a clear strategy for a solution and so don't require systemic change, adaptive problems arise when there is a gap between an organization's or a community's aspirations and its current state and the organization or community doesn't have the knowledge and skills required to close the gap (Heifetz & Linsky, 2002). To solve adaptive challenges, responsibility for problem-solving must shift from the authority within an organization to all of the stakeholders who own the problems. Simply occupying a position of authority is no guarantee of leadership.

However, human beings are hardwired to look to senior authorities, whether the President, the Prime Minister, the CEO, the Executive Director, or Mom and Dad, to create stability and security and clarity for us (Heifetz & Linsky, 2002). We want direction, protection, and order – tell us where we're going, keep us safe on the journey, and keep the ship clean and orderly. We learn quickly from the day we're born to depend on authority to provide those services. And as long as they do, we will reward them with whatever is the coin of the realm: loyalty, votes, money, or more responsibility.

BANGLADESH CASE STUDY

We've seen in our work how leadership, when recognized as an activity opposed to a position or title, can empower ordinary citizens to step up, take ownership of their own collective problems, and make progress on it. Ejaj has been running the Bangladesh Youth Leadership Center (BYLC) for the past 10 years in Bangladesh. The mission of BYLC is to unite youth from diverse backgrounds, equip them with leadership skills, and engage them in active citizenship. Since 2008, Ejaj and his team have trained more than

3500 high school, college, and university students, who have logged more than 35,000 hours of service in the community and have launched more than 100 community initiatives.

One such community initiative in Bangladesh, which can help illustrate the value of perceiving leadership as an activity as opposed to a position of authority, is the Campaign RED Project.

Led by four graduates of BYLC's Building Bridges through Leadership Training (BBLT) program, the Campaign Red project worked to raise awareness on menstrual health and hygiene, and break the misinformation and stigma surrounding the issue in the remote area of Ukhia in Cox's Bazar. Their research found that a large number of girls in the area drop out of school when they begin menstruation (personal communication, October 15, 2017). Despite much progress being made on a number of different sectors in Bangladesh, access to appropriate sanitation facilities remains a challenge, especially in the rural parts of Bangladesh. The lack of facilities, coupled with almost no orientation to students on safe menstrual hygiene management, is believed to be related to the sense of shame and resulting silence surrounding menstrual hygiene, which is also evident in many other countries across the region. The consequence of dropping out from school leads to multiple social challenges such as loss of a human resource for the economy, increased income inequality, child marriage, and severe health complications.

Campaign RED uses a holistic approach to work on the issue by engaging university students as volunteers, to work collectively for one common goal – an inclusive society. The team trained 63 volunteers to conduct sessions every week, teaching school-going children, both boys and girls, about the natural processes of puberty and menstruation. They wanted to include boys in the process because they believed young men play an integral role in ensuring equality between genders and that an inclusive society could only be realized if social barriers between them were confronted.

The group is made of three girls who studied in Bengali medium schools (where the primary language of instruction is Bengali) and two boys who studied in Madrassas. Coming from different backgrounds, they worked together in a group during the BBLT program where they received training on adaptive leadership over two months. A core part of their training focuses on building the skills required to exercise leadership without formal authority. There are several assumptions surrounding boys from Madrassa backgrounds that their religious education denounces free mixing between genders and that they don't believe in the equal participation of women in society. However, the active engagement of these two young men on this particular issue contests those assumptions.

Their work faced the greatest resistance from the principals and administrators of the schools. Puberty and menstruation are not taught as part of biology curricula in schools, and in Madrassas, menstruation is spoken about as a female issue. Students are taught that during menstruation girls cannot fully participate in public life because of biological constraints. When they eventually allowed Campaign RED into their schools, they fought the idea that boys too needed to learn about menstruation, arguing that it was only something that affected girls. They resisted losing a part of their cultural identity which held that women and men are inherently different and have specific roles in society. In a culture where discussing puberty and sex is a taboo, the idea that boys along with girls would learn about menstruation as a natural phenomenon with the intent to further empower girls was an assault to their tradition and belief system. Accepting the adaptive challenge of disregarding a notion that they had held true for so long was uncomfortable to them.

Campaign RED members had to have several meetings to reassure and convince the principals of the long-term benefits. They ensured that the classes would be segregated and led by volunteers of their own gender; male volunteers would conduct sessions with boys and female volunteers would conduct sessions with girls. Over time, Campaign RED gained the trust of the principals, who eventually began to see the positive impact on the school children. They even invited the group back for refresher sessions and allowed Campaign RED to train peer educators who would continue to work on the issue on their campuses. Some have gone on to create separate bathrooms for girls and boys and provided bins. With new funding provided by BYLC, the group is now planning to register as a nonprofit to scale up their efforts.

CONCLUSION

What the situations in Bangladesh and Nepal illustrate, painfully, is that as long as humans stay trapped in tribal identities, and as long as we keep looking to authority figures to solve problems, we will remain alienated from one another and from ourselves. Our aspirations for love and freedom will continually evade us. What the planet needs is a new kind of leadership that depolarizes and helps human beings realize that none of us, when identified as one family, is "other" or "enemy."

We have arrived at a "tipping point" — a moment in history when we need to acknowledge that we're lost and afraid — a moment when we need to be willing to lose face and acknowledge that we've all colluded in creating the mess we find ourselves in. In a world of rapid global change where national borders are increasingly eroded and identities are in a state of continuous flux, we, the human family, find ourselves confronting a series of challenges never before encountered. We are now faced with the need to seek — in vain, it seems — local solutions to globally produced problems. We have to choose to act, or not act, under conditions of pervasive uncertainty.

We propose that leadership for the collective future of humankind will require finding ways to support humans everywhere to transcend the tribal mindsets that keep us separated, ignoring our unity as one human family, and avoiding coming together as one human family to address the problems that are beyond any single nation-state to solve. This leadership will be "morally enlightened" in that those in positions of authority will be able to "leave their flags at the door" and act on behalf of the whole human family, not their respective national communities. They will be able to hold spaces for parties in conflict to transcend their tribal mindset as they risk a true engagement with the enemy "other," distinguishing what's precious in each of their cultures that they wish to preserve, from what's expendable, what they need to give up for unity and peace.

REFERENCES

Appelbaum, Y. (July 21, 2016). I alone can fix it. *The Atlantic*. Retrieved from https://www.theatlantic.com/politics/archive/2016/07/trump-rnc-speech-alone-fix-it/492557/. Accessed on November 1, 2017.

Berreby, D. (2005). *Us and Them: Understanding Your Tribal Mind*. New York, NY: Little, Brown & Co.

Bump, P. (September 28, 2016). Donald Trump pledges to make every dream possible, which seems ambitious. *Washington Post*. Retrieved from https://www.washingtonpost.com/news/the-fix/wp/2016/09/28/donald-trump-pledges-to-make-every-dream-possible-which-seems-ambitious/?utm_term=.5aea61373964. Accessed on November 12, 2017.

Callahan, M. (October 12, 2017). Myanmar's enemy within and the making of anti-Muslim Rage. *Time*. Retrieved from http://time.com/4964592/myanmar-rohingya-muslims-francis-wade/. Accessed on October 30, 2017.

Fisher, M. (September 10, 2012). The dividing of a continent: Africa's separatist problem. *The Atlantic*. Retrieved from https://www.theatlantic.com/international/archive/2012/09/the-dividing-of-a-continent-africas-separatist-problem/262171/. Accessed on November 2, 2017.

Fisher, R., & Ury, W. L. (1991). *Getting to Yes: Negotiating Agreement Without Giving In*. New York, NY: Penguin Books.

GRID. (2018). *Global report on internal displacement*. Geneva: Internal Displacement Monitoring Center (IDMC). Retrieved from http://www.internal-displacement.org/global-report/grid2018/

Guterres, A. (2018, January 19). Remarks to the Security Council on Building Regional Partnership In Afghanistan and Central Asia, to Link Security and Development. Retrieved from https://www.un.org/sg/en/content/sg/speeches/2018-01-19/building-regional-partnership-afghanistan-and-central-asia-remarks

Hauss, C. (1996). *Beyond confrontation: transforming the new world order*. Westport, CT: Greenwood Publishing Group.

Heifetz, R., & Linsky, M. (2002). *Leadership on the Line: Staying Alive Through the Dangers of Change*. Cambridge, MA: Harvard Business Review Press.

Homes, O. (September 20, 2017). Fact check: Aung San Kyi's speech on the Rohingya crisis. Retrieved from https://www.theguardian.com/world/2017/sep/20/fact-check-aung-san-suu-kyi-rohingya-crisis-speech-myanmar. Accessed on November 3, 2017.

Johnson, J. (May 29, 2016). Even in victory, Donald Trump can't stop airing his grievances. *Washington Post*. Retrieved from https://www.washingtonpost.com/politics/even-in-victory-donald-trump-cant-stop-airing-his-grievances/2016/05/29/a5f7a566-2526-11e6-8690-f14ca9de2972_story. html?noredirect=on&utm_term=.c1616791ec05. Accessed on November 2, 2017.

Mohdin, A. (October 2, 2017). A brief history of the word "Rohingya" at the heart of a humanitarian crisis. *Quartz*. Retrieved from https://qz.com/ 1092313/a-brief-history-of-the-word-rohingya-at-the-heart-of-a-humanitarian-crisis/. Accessed on November 3, 2017.

Reeves, E. (2016, February 11). Don't Forget Darfur. *The New York Times*.

Rumi. Translated by Coleman Barks. (2010). "A Great Wagon." *The Essential Rumi*. New York, NY: Harper Collins.

Roth, K. (2017). *The dangerous rise of populism: Global attacks on human rights values*. World Report 2017. New York, NY: Human Rights Watch. Retrieved from https://www.hrw.org/world-report/2017

Safi, M. (September 11, 2017). Myanmar treatment of Rohingya looks like 'text book ethnic cleaning', says UN. *The Guardian*. Retrieved from https:// www.theguardian.com/world/2017/sep/11/un-myanmars-treatment-of-rohingya-textbook-example-of-ethnic-cleansing. Accessed on October 29, 2017.

Save The Children, *Yemen Report*, 2018.

Solomon, B. C. (September 29, 2017). In grim camps, Rohingya suffer on 'scale that we couldn't imagine. *The New York Times*. Retrieve from https:// www.nytimes.com/2017/09/29/world/asia/rohingya-refugees-myanmar-bangladesh.html. Accessed on November 1, 2017.

Specia, M. (2018, April 13). How Syria's Death Toll Is Lost in the Fog of War. *The New York Times*.

Sullivan, A. (2017). America wasn't built for humans. *New York Magazine*. Retrieved from http://nymag.com/daily/intelligencer/2017/09/can-democracy-survive-tribalism.html

Trueman, C. N. (2015, March 17). League of Nations Failures. *The History Learning Site*.

UNHCR Global Trends: Forced Displacement in 2016. Retrieved from http://www.unhcr.org/afr/news/stories/2017/6/5941561f4/forced-displacement-worldwide-its-highest-decades.html.

United Nations Security Council. (January 7, 2010). Report of the Secretary-General on the request of Nepal for United Nations assistance in support of its peace process. Retrieved from http://www.un.org/en/ga/search/view_doc.asp?symbol=S/2010/17. Accessed on November 2, 2017.

United Nations Sustainable Development Goals. Retrieved from https://www.un.org/sustainabledevelopment/

Waduge, S. D. (2018). Present day conflicts: The result of "artificial borders" and colonial "divide and rule". Global Research — Centre for Research on Globalization. Retrieved from https://www.globalresearch.ca/present-day-conflicts-the-result-of-artificial-borders-and-colonial-divide-and-rule-policies/5626775

11

HOW TO NEGOTIATE FOR SUSTAINABLE RELATIONSHIPS AND PROSPERITY

Mehrad Nazari

As we address the issue of the sustainability of our ecosystems, it is essential to recognize that human interactions and human behaviors are part of our ecosystems. The laws of nature (Mumford, 2004) apply to our interactions and relationships (Heywood, 1995).

The main focuses as outlined by the United Nation's Sustainable Developmental Goals (SDG) 2030 Agenda include *People*, *Prosperity*, and *Partnership* (United Nations, 2015). In order to effectively apply these principles as defined in the SDGs, people need conscious negotiation skills, especially to "strengthen the means of implementation and revitalize the global partnership for sustainable development," as outlined in SDG 17. Proper negotiation skills enhance life on a personal and professional level and empower people to connect, communicate, and support evolved leadership for sustainable and long-lasting prosperity.

The Enlightened Negotiation approach elevates human interactions and maximizes the collective gain for all by drawing on integrative negotiation, emotional intelligence, neuroscience, behavioral sciences, wisdom traditions, and mindfulness practices. It is a practical method of negotiation in which parties transcend the myopic vision of self-interest by harnessing the innate desire of the human spirit to connect, communicate, and co-create optimum results that fulfill the desires of all participants (Fishbane, 2007). Parties thrive in a mindset fueled by enlightened self-interest. The notion of survival of the fittest is replaced by survival of the wisest.

In the following chapter, you will find a practical guide to Enlightened Negotiation – an essential skill needed to implement evolved leadership's philosophy on both global and local levels. You will learn some of the eight Laws (principles) of Enlightened Negotiation: Intention, Trust, Communication, Strength, Flexibility, Mindfulness, Manifestation, and Reflection. These principles empower anyone to capitalize on inner wisdom in their interactions to establish trust, cultivate creativity, and collaborate; all of which are important factors to promote inclusive, sustainable economic growth, full and productive employment, and decent work for all.

Proper negotiation reduces the potential of conflict and can be applied as a preventative approach to our collective decision making. As such, the following laws or principles are universally applicable to many, if not all, negotiations that aim to prevent conflict and ensure peace and security, a cornerstone of the SDG 2030 Agenda (United Nations, 2015).

In the world short of both hope and time, we need to practice Raymond Williams's truth that "To be truly radical is to make the hope possible, not despair convincing. Hope becomes possible, practical – even profitable – when advanced resource efficiency turns scarcity into an abundance. The glass, then, is neither half empty nor half full; it has a 100 percent design margin, expendable by efficiency" (Lovins, 2011, p. 1).

The following case of two sibling farmers, Carlos and Carolina, will be referred to throughout this chapter to demonstrate the practical application of Enlightened Negotiation. While this case refers to two individuals, the same principles are easily applied to entities of any kind: corporations, NGOs, independent entities, or governments. Also, the subject of negotiation, which in this case is a division of a physical inheritance, can be replaced by other resources or services.

Carlos and Carolina were two young siblings in their 20s, living in a village in El Salvador. When their father died, they were forced to deal with the division of their inheritance – a classic negotiation that generally would cause friction among heirs. Land is considered a limited resource, where if one side gets more, the other side gets less. The obvious option was to split the farm into two equal shares between the siblings. It was a fair and equitable negotiation by some standards, but not a resource-efficient negotiation that could maximize the collective gain.

Instead of rushing to a conclusion and dividing the land, the siblings decided to apply the principles of Enlightened Negotiation. They decided to walk the land side by side to discover each party's needs. They talked about their goals, dreams, passions, families, community, and life purpose.

Carolina was passionate about becoming economically independent. Her goal was making blue corn tortillas. She knew they were in short supply in the village, and she knew she could make enough to support the demand.

Carlos had a much grander entrepreneurial spirit. He had learned there was a huge demand for the soy beans in the nearby city and knew that he could export them for a great price.

After three weeks of discussion, Carlos and Carolina decided not to divide the land. They agreed to farm the entire land together at the same time: Carolina growing corn and Carlos growing soy beans in a process called *intercropping*. As a result of this agreement, they individually had twice the land to farm, and both increased their productions substantially. Not only did they create a thriving farming business, but also their relationship became much stronger, setting an example for sustainable agriculture and family relationships within their community.

A negotiation is a noble act of cocreation. Carlos and Carolina paused and embraced an opportunity to create something noble instead of rushing to a conclusion with their self-interest and dividing the land. They were eager to elevate their interactions and approached this opportunity with *enlightened self-interest*. They methodically applied the laws of Enlightened Negotiation by carefully considering each other's needs and aspirations, as well as the outside needs of the village and land. Only by revealing everyone's needs and by Enlightened Negotiation did they create something noble, sustainable, and economical.

Ultimately the success of the SDGs on a global and local scale requires a collaborative mindset that is driven by enlightened self-interest. Many different industries, policy-makers, government agencies, and cultures need to cocreate with efficiency to sustain themselves socially, economically, and ecologically. We as human beings need to learn the science and art of mindful negotiating and collaboration for a better future.

THE LAW OF TRUST

Trust is the foundation of any relationship or any agreement (Firestone, 2015). Confidence that the other party will keep its commitments provides both parties with the assurance necessary to keep moving forward productively, even though many issues may remain to be worked out.

What is trust? In the broadest terms, it is assured reliance on the character, ability, strength, or truth of someone or something (Trust, 2018). The practical definition of trust in the process of negotiation is a mutual perception of congruity of words and actions (Gordon, 2003).

Though the trust was already established by bloodline in the case of Carlos and Carolina, they further reinforced their bond by removing any doubts of performance. Walking side by side the siblings discussed what they could and could not reasonably cocreate with the farmland they were given. They emphasized their interdependent relationship and their aspirations to do the most with the land to further deepen their trust.

In many cultures and societies, trust forms the connecting threads in a web of relationships (Fairholm, 1994). Members of a group sharing a bond of trust can trade and negotiate efficiently on the basis of reliable underlying assumptions. Trust also allows us to connect with members outside of the organization, community, or culture (Kramer, 2006).

A sense of trust is critical in shaping an environment of positivity and mutual support that helps the parties aspire toward excellence and endure frustrations along the path to an agreement (Fredrickson, 2004). The broaden-and-build theory of positive emotions states that a positive environment promotes bonding and creativity, which leads to productivity and more creativity; it is an upward spiral (Fredrickson, 2004).

It was this environment of positivity that promoted creativity and allowed Carlos and Carolina to think outside of the box. The result proved much more productive than the traditional alternative of splitting the land.

How to Establish Trust

Establishing trust takes time, and in many negotiations, time can be limited. If trust needs to be established quickly, negotiators can use these four elements for creating trust (Program on Negotiation, 2017):

1. Authenticity is the foundation upon which you can build trust. Be truthful to yourself and others.

2. Understand and speak the nuances of the other party's language, slang, terminology, and jargon. That means knowing their culture.

3. Emphasize the importance of your relationship with the other party and the interdependent nature of your relationship.

4. Offer a concession before asked AND emphasize the value and importance of it.

THE LAW OF COMMUNICATION

Again, as we focus on the implementation of the SDGs, we must refer back to SDG 17 and the resolve to strengthen bonds "between multi-stakeholder partnerships that mobilize and share knowledge" (United Nations, 2015). Sharing knowledge and successful negotiation between partners requires effective and clear communication. Communication is one of the central pillars of any negotiation or, indeed, any relationship between people (Mahajan, 2015). The act of communication requires a sender, a message, and a receiver. In the act of communicating, you constantly switch roles between sender and receiver. A good negotiator should take responsibility for coherent communication regardless of whether they are the sender or receiver.

Elements of Communication

- *Tonality.* Verbal or written tonality plays a significant role and conveys the emotions. Make sure your tonality is aligned with your intent.

- *Active Listening.* The best way to understand people and be understood is by active listening (Johnson & Bechler, 1998). Active listening is when a listener is actively engaged to ensure proper communication.

- *Proper Use of Questions: Open-ended.* Open-ended questions require or invite more than a one-word reply. They are useful to solicit information and learn more about a counterpart's feelings and motives: for example,

How can I help you? What are your concerns? What are the objectives you are trying to satisfy?

- *Proper Use of Questions: Closed-ended.* Closed-ended questions require shorter answers: for example, Can I help you? Does this timetable work for you? Would you prefer Wednesday or Thursday?

Carlos and Carolina's communication had a tonality of excitement and collaboration. They had made a commitment to make sure they were actively listening, using open-ended question for more information.

Framing the Message

In delivering a message, perhaps one of the most effective and least used skills is framing, meaning to plan precisely how you will present your case. A "framing effect" is usually said to occur when equivalent descriptions of a decision problem lead to systematically different decisions (Shafir & LeBoeuf, 2002). For example, the popular term for the worldwide climate effects caused by human activity was at first *global warming*. However, the term fell out of favor because of its divisiveness. *Climate change*, the new preferred term, is intentionally neutral and open-ended, inviting an explanation.

THE LAW OF STRENGTH

You need strength to protect your own interests and the leverage to move the other side toward a mutually beneficial outcome in any negotiation (Segal & Smith, 2014).

We negotiate because we *need* something. *Knowledge* and *wisdom* are about the needs of each party, and the context of the exchange is the true source of strength in negotiation (Ez Jacintha, Gertrude, & Ibegbulam, 2016).

This was the primary reason for Carlos and Carolina took an extended time to increase their knowledge and have a better overall understanding of parties and potential opportunities.

The Source of Our Motivations

The life force within us drives us in one direction or another based on physical, psychological, and social aspects of our beings (Bastable, Gramet, Jacobs, & Sopczyk, 2011). Whether we're buying equipment or applying for a new job, our situation is shaped by specific needs that are the source of our motivations.

On a different scale, the needs at the root of organization policies and boardroom decisions are what brings a company to the negotiating table. In the case of the SDGs, the need to implement sustainable development in order to build a better, more sustainable planet for all is our motivator. Needs bring all players in all situations – diplomats in international negotiations, community activists, or volunteers with charitable organizations – into a negotiation.

Whoever the opposing party in your negotiation is, they are also there, just like you, because of the life force that has compelled them at this point to come to the table. Whatever your differences, it is important to note you share a starting point.

The Hierarchy of Needs

Abraham Maslow's Hierarchy of Needs describing human's basic need structure is best pictured as a pyramid ranging from a base of direct biological needs at the bottom to spiritual aspirations at the top (Maslow, 1970).

- *Physiological.* Our need for food, sleep, and sex.

- *Safety.* Physical and psychological safety.

- *Belongingness and Love.* Our need to be part of a family or community.

- *Esteem.* The drive to cultivate a positive self-image or public image.

- *Self-actualization.* The need to be what we were born to be, our true purpose.

Needs Vs Positions

In any negotiation, the process of satisfying needs is the working-out of specific issues at stake and finding resolutions where all parties agree. Based on the need at stake, we take a specific position: An investment must be examined for X number of days of due diligence; tolerance for the fit of a product part must be no more than Y millimeters.

We have a need and to satisfy it we take a specific position. A position-focused model brings parties to the negotiation with hardened wills. As an Enlightened Negotiator, your job at such times is to explore beyond hardened positions and discover the underlying needs that have brought the parties to the table. Once you're informed and clear about what's required to satisfy everyone's needs, you can then make wise choices that benefit everyone.

In the case of Carlos and Carolina, it was the strength of the knowledge of each other's needs that enabled them to achieve the optimum result. By understanding each other's underlying interests for their community and region, they were able to create options not seen at first.

The Knowledge of "Self"

Before you enter any negotiation, take the time to reach deep within and discover what it is that you need, where the need is coming from, and what practical issues are at stake in satisfying these needs and prioritize them.

Knowledge of "Them"

After the initial periods of ice breaking and building rapport, you can begin an information exchange by offering some information about yourself and your needs. Once you have set the tone for information sharing, you ask your counterparts about their interest. If the other side is reluctant to respond to direct questions, you could ask "Why not?" or "What is wrong with doing it this way?"

The Knowledge of Context

All negotiations are to some extent influenced by their environments — "Situational awareness," as jet pilots call it.

- *Time.* The relevance of time is obvious, as things constantly change.

- *Place.* Honor the norm and condition of the location and place.

- *Market Conditions.* Factual market information and statistics are essential.

- *Competition.* Are you the only one offering what the other party wants, or are there others who perhaps are willing to offer a sweeter deal?

- *Industry Standards, Laws, and Regulations.* It is important to know what steps both parties have to take to satisfy the requirements of institutions outside the negotiation. In the case of SDGs, sometimes the standards, laws, and regulations may be what you are negotiating.

There is strength in the knowledge of all negotiating parties and the world around us.

THE LAW OF FLEXIBILITY

Many negotiations fail due to a lack of flexibility (Druckman & Mitchell, 1995). Flexibility in negotiation is the capacity to embrace alternatives without compromising on principles or core values. One of the characteristics of successful negotiators is a capacity for flexing against pressures that might otherwise cause a breakdown in forward progress. The key to a successful negotiation is to focus on the goal, not a specific path to it. The core of mental flexibility is the ability to see things from several different perspectives, to be able to handle a situation in different ways, and to solve problems with fresh ideas.

In behavioral science, mental flexibility is not simply a state of mind or a personality trait; it's a set of behaviors that can be modified or developed. What enables flexibility is creativity.

Creativity

The *process* of creativity is the act of setting aside established ideas and visualizing something different and new.

For Carlos and Carolina, it was this act of conscious determination for being creative that they set aside the traditional and most obvious of dividing the farm in two. Instead of looking at the land as a limited resource, they embraced it as a new opportunity with unlimited possibilities.

Brainstorming

Brainstorming is the part of the negotiation process when you harvest the fruits of your flexibility and creativity. When roadblocks arise, you are able to draw on your natural wellspring of creativity and work flexibly with your counterparts to cocreate mutually beneficial solutions.

The cardinal rule of brainstorming exploration is to separate the creating time from the evaluating time. First, put all ideas on the board and *then* start evaluating and choosing. Separating the processes creates a nurturing environment for creativity before judgment is passed.

THE LAW OF MANIFESTATION

Manifestation is the transformation of thoughts into a new reality. The Theory of Aspiration asserts that participants with high levels of aspiration achieve higher end results for both themselves *and* the other side of the negotiation (Siegal, 1957). By having high expectations for yourself, you motivate yourself to excel. In addition, having high expectations about the negotiation also has a positive influence on the behavior of the other side, driving them toward achieving higher goals.

As you take the first step on the path to manifesting your intention, you can capitalize on Aspiration Theory by setting optimistic goals for both sides.

According to another long-standing model of negotiation, Dual Concern Theory, negotiators with a higher level of *assertiveness* and *empathy* achieve higher results (Pruitt, 1986). In addition, a negotiator who has high concern for themselves and high concern for the other party will reach more constructive outcomes. Therefore, enthusiasm will be manifested through assertiveness and empathy.

Avoiding Common Pitfalls

Two common reasons why most negotiations fail:

(1) Parties come to the table with a zero-sum assumption (Wilkins, 2015).
   In order for me to gain, you have to lose is rarely true; there are almost always opportunities for co-creation and collaboration that would

benefit *both* parties if we enlarge the scope of vision and open ourselves to new possibilities.

(2) Parties come to the table with fixed positions. For instance, they come with a specific salary (though non-monetary benefits might be worth even more.) A fixed position represents only one option to our goal and therefore limits our chances of success.

Embracing Common Expectations

When people come to the negotiation table, the very least they expect is:

- *To be treated fairly.*
- *To be treated with respect.*

As you evolve your consciousness toward Enlightened Negotiation, you should already be perceiving the world, instead, as an open field of *inexhaustible* possibilities. The SDGs support the notion of "permitting the full realization of human potential and contributing to shared prosperity," which may only be achieved by openness and inclusiveness that bridges the gap of gender, race, culture, and economic status (United Nations, 2015). As evolving human beings, however short of perfection, we all have within us a divine touch that deserves awe and respect.

BATNA

Know your Best Alternative to a Negotiated Agreement (BATNA) before engaging in a negotiation (Fisher & Ury, 1991). What if you don't reach an agreement here? What do you do? What *second* choice would you be happy with?

Knowing your BATNA requires deliberation and research, an exploration of all your alternatives and analysis to prioritize needs. A strong BATNA gives you the confidence to know when to talk and when to walk. What are *their* other alternatives, and are those viable? When changing a law or regulation to improve SDGs comes to an impasse, are there ways to work within the existing laws and regulations to achieve similar results?

Establishing the Objective Criteria

An important guideline in cocreating an agreement is to assemble your supporting materials — the facts, statistics, case law, cultural background, and objective criteria for measuring the results (Fisher & Ury, 1991). Where there is not a clear standard for evaluation and comparison, if possible, it would be very constructive to cocreate a set of guidelines.

Understanding Human Biases

It is useful to appreciate general human tendencies that affect everyone's decision-making behavior and judgment, even in the most rational negotiations. One all-too-human failing is the tendency toward a heuristic approach to problem-solving and decision-making (De Martino, Kumaran, Seymour, & Dolan, 2006). In negotiations with important issues at stake, we must remain vigilant against the human tendency to trust limited personal experience, "everyone says" information or unexamined assumptions as the basis for wise and safe results.

The Anchoring Phenomenon

An anchor is a value that serves as an initial reference point. What's useful to our purposes is that, when put forth with confidence, an anchor can establish a *cognitive bias* that actualizes the human tendency to strongly favor a known quantity over an abstract possibility when making decisions (Kahneman, 2013).

The Power of Priming

Another unconscious influence on our decision-making process is the *priming* effect, which occurs when exposure to one cognitive category unconsciously triggers a reference to related categories of knowledge (Forgas, 1998). Just mentioning words such as "fairness," "equity," and "mutual benefit" at the outset of a negotiation exchange, even if the words are used in an unrelated context, can set the momentum of the process toward collaboration (McGinn & Noth, 2012).

Negotiating with the Right Person

If the outcome of the negotiation is to be manifested, make sure from the outset that you are dealing with people who have the authority to turn words into actions. For example, should the other side need outside approval, make it clear you can commit to a *tentative* deal.

Establishing Rapport

Ultimately people are the ones with whom we have to make a deal (Nadler, 2003). In any negotiation, establishing rapport with your counterparts is far more than an "ice-breaking" social nicety; it can mean the difference between impasse and going the extra inch to bridge an unresolvable gap on the basis of personal trust. On a global scale, just as with trust, establishing rapport means understanding cultural differences and needs.

It's the Package, Not the Pieces

Although we dissect and discuss issues one by one, the goal is the *totality* of the agreement. It's useful for both parties to make clear at the beginning of the process that there is no deal until *all* issues have been addressed and agreed to.

Avoid Traps

There are many ancient ploys and tricks that some people are not above using to tip a negotiation to their advantage unfairly. These include deliberately supplying false information, or using psychological pressure tactics such as stonewalling or unreasonable delays. In order to avoid these common traps, first, you must recognize them and then bring them out into the open. A ploy recognized is a ploy disarmed.

Do Not Burn Your Bridges

Not all negotiations result in an agreement. You are not guaranteed to walk away with everything you want simply because you are a skillful negotiator.

The best message is to say, "this does not seem to be a good time to work together, but I look forward to other opportunities in the future." It is best to neutralize personal issues by pointing to external economic or physical issues that do not make agreement practical.

THE LAW OF MINDFULNESS

A human being is a part of the whole, called by us 'Universe,' a part limited in time and space. He experiences himself, his thoughts and feelings as something separate from the rest—a kind of optical delusion of his consciousness.

Source: Albert Einstein (Calaprice, 2005)

Mindfulness in Enlightened Negotiation is about mindfulness of Self (our true essence, our authentic self, or our higher self), mindfulness of others, mindfulness of our environment, and mindfulness of the creative process. Mindfulness for a sustainable future requires awareness of each of the UN's SDGs. Full implementation cannot take effect unless we are mindful of the relations of each SDG to the broader goals of the 2030 Agenda.

Negotiation requires the convergence of two or more parties toward a collectively satisfactory agreement. Regardless of how you master all other elements and follow the other principles of negotiation, the ultimate test of your success is how you deal with *people*.

Understanding People

People will forget what you said. People will forget what you did. But people will never forget how you made them feel.

Source: Maya Angelou (Kelly, 2003)

Mindfulness in any negotiation involves an awareness that behind any name, face, voice, title, or signature; there is a unique human being, a self. We must have a clear vision in order to understand others.

Along the process of understanding, we observe other human beings through various filters; all human interactions are influenced by some degree of distortion or lack of information. Among the many filters that veil the truth, the most prominent fall into three categories: perceptions, emotions, and cultures.

Carlos and Carolina had to deal with the filter of both the traditional way in which people in their village related to inheritance and the filter of their already established bond as brother and sister.

Perception

In a sense, there is no fixed physical reality; there are only individuals' interpretations of it. Therefore, in any negotiation, it is imperative that we compare people's perception of the situation and examine how they arrived at their conclusions.

Culture

Another "veil" that quite often colors our perception of a situation is cultural conditioning. The diversity of our distinct cultures adds much beauty, color, and nuance to our understanding of facts and events, but cultural differences can also generate ambiguity, unfamiliarity, and uncertainty (Brett & Crotty, 2008).

The code of conduct and fundamental beliefs of a society, community, or organization, or of an ethnic, racial, socioeconomic, or religious group are "givens," expected behaviors of the group's members as they interact with one another. Since cultural behaviors represent longstanding traditions as well as shortcuts for smoothing the way forward, they are expected to be honored not only by the society's members but also by outsiders seeking acceptance. A very simple and genuine desire to learn about other cultures will go a long way, whether in Paris, Mumbai, or the Bronx.

The Power of Emotions

When dealing with people, remember you are not dealing with creatures of logic, but creatures of emotion.

Source: Carnegie (1981)

Drawing upon positive emotions cultivates more cooperative frames of mind in the parties to a negotiation, facilitating agreement, and a satisfying arrangement. On the other hand, negative emotions owing from distrust or an expectation of unfairness slow down the process by requiring increased levels of persuasion, explanation, and clarification for every step forward (Druckman & Olekalns, 2008).

THE LAW OF REFLECTION

> *By three methods we may learn wisdom: first, by reflection, which is the noblest; second, by imitation, which is the easiest; and third, by experience, which is the most bitter.*
>
> *Source*: Confucius (Woods, 2012)

Reflection is necessary for sustainable negotiation skills and fulfilling SDG 17. After we reach the completion of negotiation, as enlightened negotiators we should feel a duty to reflect on how the process unfolded and what progress has been made. We can only know if the SDGs are making their intended progress by examining what we have already accomplished in our attempts to implement the UN's Agenda. We must reflect on what brings out the best of our diverse humanity to ensure a sustainable future. We should be able to answer the following questions satisfactorily:

- Are you better off?

- Is the other side better off?

- Have you made a positive contribution to the world around you?

- Could you have done this more intelligently?

- Have you maximized your resources?

- Are your relationships stronger?

Whatever measurements you use, take time to reflect.

The following are some suggested types of reflections:

Prosperity. The outcome of negotiation should be measured by the enrichment of our overall purposes and principles.

Infinity. When you look back over your performance, you should also take in a broad perspective that includes how the environment is now changed and the ripple effect of your actions on events in the future.

Karma. Karma in simplest terms is the law of cause and effect, both from an esoteric view and from a scientific perspective. It is the Newtonian law of motion that states that every action creates a reaction. Essentially, in our lives and our social interactions, *karma* means that our deeds, good or bad, will be reflected to us at some point in the future.

Love. In Enlightened Negotiation, mindfulness of the state of oneness enables you to feel connected and secure, not threatened. It establishes a framework for cooperation, opens you to new opportunities for mutual benefit, increases the efficiency of the process, and expands your relationships. Love has the power to motivate people, build bridges of understanding, and melt unyielding positions.

CONCLUSION

Effective organizational skills including leadership skills require personal *interactions, communication, conflict management,* and *negotiation.* No matter what skills we want to bring to our organization, these are the threads that create the fabric of the culture of our organization or community.

By adhering to laws of Enlightened Negotiation, we reduce stalemates and conflict and are able to channel that conserved energy toward creativity, productivity, and prosperity. Treating human interactions as a resource that needs to be sustainable and efficient leads us to build a future where partnerships and collaboration are maximized. Remembering SDG 17 and the UN tenants of *People, Prosperity,* and *Partnership* allows us to bridge the gaps between the other SDGs for a coherent front to our Global Aspirations.

REFERENCES

Bastable, S., Gramet, P., Jacobs, K., & Sopczyk, D. (2011). *Health professional as educator: principles of teaching and learning.* Sudbury, MA: Joans & Bartlett Learning, LLC.

Brett, J., & Crotty, S. (2008). Culture and negotiation. In P. B. Smith, M. F. Peterson, & D. C. Thomas (Eds.), *Handbook of cross-cultural management research* (pp. 269–283). Thousand Oaks, CA: Sage.

Calaprice, A. (2005). *The New Quotable Einstein*. Princeton, NJ: Princeton University Press.

Carnegie, D. (1981). *How to Win Friends and Influence People*. New York, NY: Simon and Schuster.

Cohen, R. (2001). Language and negotiation: A middle eastern lexicon. Retrieved from https://www.diplomacy.edu/resources/general/language-and-negotiation-middle-east-lexicon

De Martino, B., Kumaran, D., Seymour, B., & Dolan, R. J. (2006). Frames, biases, and rational decision-making in the Human brain. *Science (New York, N.Y.), 313*(5787), 684–687. doi:10.1126/science.1128356

Druckman, D., & Mitchell, C. (1995). Flexibility in negotiation and mediation. *The ANNALS of the American Academy of Political and Social Science, 542*(1), 10–23. doi:10.1177/0002716295542001002

Druckman, D., & Olekalns. (2008). Emotions in negotiation. *Group Decision and Negotiation, 17*(1), 1–11. doi:10.1007/s10726-007-9091-9

Fairholm, G. (1994). *Leadership and the Culture of Trust*. Westport, CN: Greewood Publishing Group.

Firestone, L. (2015, June 29). 5 Ways to Build Trust and Honesty in Your Relationship. Retrieved from https://www.psychologytoday.com/blog/compassion-matters/201506/5-ways-build-trust-and-honesty-in-your-relationship.

Fishbane, M. D. (2007, August). Wired to connect: Neuroscience, relationships and therapy. *Family Process, 46*(3), 395–412. doi:10.1111/j.1545-5300.2007.00219.x

Fisher, R., & Ury, B. (1991). *Getting to Yes*. New York, NY: Penguin Publishing.

Forgas, J. P. (1998). On feeling good and getting your way: Mood effects on negotiator cognition and bargaining strategies. *Journal of Personality and Social Psychology*. doi:10.1037//0022-3514.74.3.565

Fredrickson, B. L. (2004). The broaden-and-build theory of positive emotions. *Philosophical Transactions of the Royal Society B: Biological Sciences*, 359(1449), 1367–1378. doi:10.1098/rstb.2004.1512

Gordon, J. (2003). *Successful leadership development tools*. San Francisco, CA: John Wiley & Sons.

Heywood, J. (1995). Human interactions and natural environments: Implications for ecosystem management. In H. Ken Cordell (Ed.), *Integrating Social Science and Ecosystem Management: A National Challenge* (pp. 3–7). Athens, GA: USDA Forest Services.

Jacintha, E., Gertrude, U., & Ibegbulam, I. (2016). The use of information, awareness and communication in conflict resolution: Role of libraries in South-East Nigeria. *International Journal of Library and Information Science*, 8(4), 27–35. doi:10.5897/IJLIS2015.0579

Johnson, S. D., & Bechler, C. (1998). Examining the relationship between listening effectiveness and leadership emergence: Perceptions, behaviors, and recall. *Small Group Research*, 29, 452–471.

Kahneman, D. (2013). *Thinking, Fast and Slow*. New York, NY: Farrar, Straus and Giroux.

Kelly, B. (2003). *Worth Repeating: More than 5,000 Classic and Contemporary Quotes*. Grand Rapids, MI: Kregel.

Kramer, R. (2006). *Organizational Trust: A Reader*. Oxford: Oxford University Press.

Lovins, A. (2011). *Applied Hope: Commencement remarks to the Natural Science School University of California at Berkeley*. [PDF] Retrieved from https://d231jw5ce53gcq.cloudfront.net/wp-content/uploads/2017/04/OCS_Applied_Hope_2011.pdf. Accessed on May 29, 2018.

Mahajan, R. (2015, December). The key role of communication skills in the life of professionals. *IOSR Journal of Humanities and Social Science*, 20(12), 36–39.

Maslow, A. (1970). *Motivation and personality: A theory of Human motivation*. New York, NY: Harper & Row.

McGinn, K., & Noth, K. (2012). Communicating Frames in Negotiation. Retrieved from http://www.hbs.edu/faculty/Publication%20Files/12-109_5c4e3b09-d49d-4452-955d-6983f6dc7b66.pdf

Mumford, S. (2004). *Laws in Nature*. New York, NY: Routledge.

Nadler, J. (2003). Rapport in Negotiation and Conflict Resolution. Retrieved from http://heinonline.org/HOL/LandingPage?handle=hein.journals/marqlr87&div=52&id=&page=

Program on Negotiation. (2017). How to build trust at the bargaining table. Retrieved from https://www.pon.harvard.edu/daily/negotiation-skills-daily/six-strategies-for-building-trust-in-negotiations.

Segal, J., & Smith, M. (2014). Conflict resolution skills: Building the skills that can turn conflicts into opportunities. Retrieved from http://www.helpguide.org/articles/relationships/conflict-resolution-skills.

Shafir, E., & LeBoeuf, R. A. (2002). Rationality. *Annual Review of Psychology, 53*, 491–517.

Siegal, S. (1957). Level of aspiration and decision making. *Psychological Review, 64*(4), 253–262.

Trust. (2018). In *Merriam-Webster.com*. Retrieved from https://www.merriam-webster.com/dictionary/trust. Accessed on May 29, 2018.

United Nations. (2015). *Transforming our world: The 2030 agenda for sustainable development*. New York, NY: United Nations Publications.

Wilkins, C. (2015). You can win but I can't lose: Bias against high-status groups increases their zero-sum beliefs about discrimination. *Journal of Experimental Social Psychology, 57*, 1–14. doi:10.1016/j.jesp.2014.10.008

Wood, Rev. J. (2012). *Dictionary of Quotations*. London: Frederick Warne & Co.

PART IV

THE MORAL AND ETHICAL IMPERATIVE OF AN INCLUSIVE ECONOMY

12

THE LIVING COMPANY: A SYSTEMS APPROACH

Jennifer M. Chirico and Anette M. Nystrom

INTRODUCTION

We live on a finite planet, a closed system, yet with all the means necessary to live in abundance and in harmony — with each other, with nature and wildlife. Life has been thriving and evolving on earth, while nature has intuitively invented and developed solutions for survival for an estimated 3.8 billion years (Harman, 2014). The fruits of these developments are the intelligent life systems we witness in abundance everywhere we look in nature — untouched nature, which has become a rarity today.

> The Anthropocene, the geological epoch of humans, teaches us
> about the impacts we have on virtually every earth system. Human
> societies have seldom adopted anything but short-term
> considerations, something that is largely reflected in the current
> capitalistic society of most of the world. This is witnessed in our
> current government and business models, approaches to nature,
> and even in our individual models of health and well-being
> (Heinberg, 2014).

Recent research points to a new way of understanding the world and how we can coexist peacefully with the earth and other humans, while also remaining economically viable. The new paradigm shift is about incorporating conscious business models and using a systems approach to create more sustainable societies that support life on earth. This chapter explores the concept of systems thinking models as they relate to the United Nations Sustainable Development Goals (UNSDGs) of environmental protection, social inclusion, and economic development. It discusses new business models and how adopting an integrative systems perspective can help to better understand the current resource and humanitarian crisis, and lead to greater equality, better human rights, a healthier earth, happier people, and more long-term financial success that ultimately affects the world in which we live.

THE IMPACT BUSINESS AS WE KNOW IT

Businesses, big and small, are largely dictating the current and future state of our planet. A fundamental problem lies in our system's inherent design. We will not be able to meet our common challenges without having businesses on board and creating new ways of thinking that acknowledge our interconnectedness with the planet and with each other.

In line with new technologies that paved the way for mass production, the pursuit of self-interest through the acquisition of private property was regarded as an inherent attribute of human nature. A biologically driven urge to satisfy physical or psychological needs or desires led to the concept of "the more the merrier." The new capitalist world promised improved welfare and unlimited progress. This "new" world has been ripe with abundance for some but sorely lacking for many. Today, we witness increasing poverty, growing inequalities, and a global energy and resource crisis.

A growing body of evidence shows that we are close to reaching the end of growth, using resources and emitting pollution faster than ecosystems can handle. Several planetary boundaries have been surpassed, including climate change, biodiversity losses, and the nitrogen cycle that have reached devastating states, while the phosphorus cycle, ozone depletion, ocean acidification, freshwater use, and land use change are all under great pressure. Although the concept of sustainable development was first put on the global agenda over 25 years ago at the Rio Earth Summit, we keep discovering new phenomena and growing awareness to understand the complex systems with which we actively interact. Learning about the dynamics between human and natural systems throughout history challenges the common perception that negative anthropogenic impact is a relatively recent occurrence.

One of the key outcomes of the UNSDGs is to reduce global inequalities by 2030. Apart from transforming the environmental landscape, foundations of inequality are also tightly linked to the various labor systems that emerged in line with natural resource exploitation – resources that are still being drained today. The exploitation of people in an effort to extract minerals, precious metals, and forests for profit has, in turn, placed greater pressure on oil reserves, natural gas, coal, and freshwater as the world population grows by over 220,000 people every day (Worldometers, 2018).

> *Historical events help contextualize sustainable development and acknowledge the multiple causes and systemic effects. Learning about the fate of past societies is perhaps our greatest asset. Today, it is no longer a matter of gathering more knowledge or data, as we have for a long time possessed enough evidence to justify radical action. A great transition in human history is the fundamental change that the exploitation of fossil fuels had on human societies, which was generally treated as inexhaustible. As a result, societies and cities were created on the premise of high energy use, a dependence that still characterizes modern society. We are progressively rendering the earth unrecognizable in the last several centuries (Wright, 2004).*

For example, we have now lost half of the planet's original forest cover, mostly in the past 30 years. It is disturbing considering the importance of forests for the sustainability of the earth and its people, such as regulating temperatures and weather patterns, sustaining wildlife, containing yet-to-be-discovered medicines, and maintaining supplies of fresh drinking water that are paramount to our survival.

Up until now, doing more of the same has been the answer to virtually every problem in our current economy. In order to keep the ball rolling, we need ever more people to consume ever more stuff. Business endeavors take from the earth but rarely give back as extractive and exploitative practices have become the norm under the mantra of exponential growth. The linear take-make-waste design of our industrial system was created in an environmentally unaware era where considerations for externalities were left out of the equation. As a result, we have up until today been shifting the burden to nature to take the toll of our pollution, waste, and destruction. Failing to acknowledge (or ignoring) that infinite growth cannot be sustained on a finite planet, companies typically apply symptomatic solutions (i.e., short-term quick fixes to environmental externalities), often considering them to be "someone else's problems" (Senge, Smith, Kruschwitz, Laur, & Schley, 2008). This creates a dependency on the quick fixes that temper the symptoms, yet simultaneously undermine more fundamental action and even exacerbate the problems in the long run (Stroh, 2015).

This is certainly the case for the environmental degradation we all witness. Our relentless pursuit of growth is founded upon the premise of limitless resources. The irony is that the resources we have become so heavily dependent upon are largely non-renewable. From the perspective of "market cornucopians" economic growth is the solution to our sustainability problems through facilitating technological innovation and identifying solutions to natural resource scarcity. Waiting for the turning point of the Environmental Kuznets Curve[1] may not be the optimal solution (Speth, 2008). Although this potential might be present, this view is naively optimistic. Much stronger forces are needed to find true solutions that move humanity away from devastating exploitation and irreversible damage to the planet and people, and towards a benign presence that is mutually beneficial.

NEW WAYS OF THINKING

How we choose to make these changes requires an overall shift in our perspective. This shift is captured in Aldo Leopold's essay, "Thinking Like a Mountain." He illustrates how one poor decision that does not take into account a holistic perspective can affect the systemic natural relationships, leading to further destruction and harm. In his essay, the wolves "on the mountain" were killing the farmers' livestock, and so the decision was made to kill all of the wolves. This process revealed that the elimination of the wolves led to a near elimination of vegetation, a proliferation of starving deer, and erosion that depleted the ecosystem and left the mountain a wasteland, which leads to more problems in the long term. The mountain, and all of the parts that made up its ecosystem, were not taken into account when they decided to eliminate the wolves. Thus, *Thinking Like a Mountain* means adopting a systems thinking model that transverses spatial and temporal boundaries. It means having a profound appreciation for our inter-connectedness within the ecosystem(s) of life on earth.

This concept has become a model for understanding and implementing healthy, balanced ecosystems. For example, in Yellowstone National Park, wolves were eliminated at the turn of the twentieth century. In the 1990s, they started reintegrating wolves back into the ecosystem of the Park, and over time, saw an enhancement of the ecosystem with an increase in vegeta-tion, aspen trees, and beaver populations.[2]

Mother Nature, as it turns out, is a brilliant systems thinker. Nature serves as a mentor and blueprint for solving most of our economic, social, and environmental problems. For example, nature operates on a completely different timescale with no quick fixes, and similarly, our solutions ought to be of an evolving nature that can adapt to changing circumstances over time. Additionally, everything in nature is dynamic and fluid, constantly moving, yet determined and confident in its progress.

Systems thinking has taught us that if we identify a high leverage point, it may produce effective, large-scale and long-lasting effects. Contrastingly, one poor decision that does not take into account a holistic perspective can affect the systemic natural relationships, leading to further destruction and harm. A relatively small change down the line can produce boundless ripple effects. And since today we are all networked together, literally and figura-tively, what we do, and the decisions that we make, can have a ripple effect throughout the network of our lives that affects the whole. When our sense of place is understood from this holistic perspective, we can better use our actions as individuals, communities, businesses, and countries to positively affect the rest of the world as we take care of the whole system and not only the parts.

REDEFINING WEALTH

Throughout history, humans have created new environments (farming com-munities, permanent settlements, and cities) and economies that have had a profound impact on public health, manifested in new "diseases of affluence" (Ponting, 2007). Today, this burden is ever present due to unprecedented and rapid population growth. Many governments and businesses are still holding on to the belief that ever-increasing and preferably rapid economic growth is the only blueprint for success and vital to moving society forward (Speth, 2008). The foundation of this belief system is that the only way to endure, and to live a more comfortable life, is to climb higher up the corporate ladder, with the sole focus on generating more profit and more power in order to continue the pursuit of exponential growth, often at the expense of people and the earth. While prosperity has been achieved by some, it has come with large-scale environmental and social costs. Markets were systematically created that faied to consider these costs.

Many businesses continue to pursue growth and profits, while the environment continues to deteriorate. It is a vicious cycle of increasing demand and decreasing resources. A classic example is that of a forest; the way our economic system is designed today, a forest is attributed value only when it is being cut down and turned into the timber and raw materials to be sold in the market. Nobody is paying for the ecosystem services that nature provides such as food, habitats, medical discoveries, oxygen production and many more. A forest is rather viewed as a business externality to be exploited. Perhaps we have been conditioned to believe that there is no alternative to our current system, as all its facets are well ingrained in our society; from the indicators by which we measure success (i.e., GDP for nations, and sales and profits for companies), to the way we educate the young who will soon become our future leaders (Korten, 2010). One can ponder whether the world simply has become too complex for anyone to claim responsibility.

The environmental deterioration driven by economic growth and human activities has, as of recent, accelerated immensely. The potential for additional deterioration of environmental and social capital is enormous. We have a profound commitment to profit, which will continue to enhance as long as the environmental and social costs of economic activities are kept off the books of companies (i.e., externalities). Externalization of costs not only sustains profitability, but also keeps the market prices of the goods we buy, and the services that we use, artificially low, particularly for activities that are highly destructive. From a holistic point of view, these prices are not reflective of the real costs of goods.

The lone measure that increases our pursuit of profit is the gross domestic product (GDP), not the quality of life of populations, not happiness, not equality, and not the health of our environment (Ponting, 2007; Speth, 2008). In no way can we make sustainable progress possible, whether social, environmental or economic, if we do not deviate from the present norm of believing that profit is the only path to a better quality of life. It is important to note that a post-growth society does not mean a no-growth one. There is great potential in radically transforming the values underpinning the current system, in order to guide market forces in the right direction. Even using the economic argument, it is much cheaper to prevent environmental and social decline than trying to cure it (Speth, 2008).

Collectively, we are redefining what true wealth means and identifying new ways to measure its growth. We are beginning to see businesses, organizations, and communities around the world that are prospering in line with nature's principles while respecting the earth, local communities, and cultures. Businesses are increasingly experiencing that working towards economic *and* social *and* environmental sustainability produce the most rigid bottom line in the long term. These groups are utilizing conscious business models that regard wealth as *being one with the environment and community*.

Recognizing our common purpose and working towards a shared vision of values can serve as a solid foundation for sustainable progress. By acknowledging that all human and natural systems are interconnected, we understand that what one does affects us all. If the goal of our economic activities that are focused on increasing GDP shifts to increasing quality of life and well-being – for all life forms – we will see a profound change. One can describe it as a great shift from our current industrial growth society to a life-sustaining society, which inherently means to redefine wealth as we know it.

SYSTEMS MEASURES

New research and a growing number of people are learning that material abundance does not equal happiness and satisfaction in life. Instead, when we view things through a holistic lens, we can see the whole picture of health (of a business, individual, or society), rather than only addressing one part that might achieve short-term economic gains. Even in healthcare, a significant shift has occurred over the last two decades with the integration of Eastern and Western medicine. People are increasingly seeking more holistic health treatment rather than the traditional reductionist approaches of allopathic medical treatment.

The last decade has seen a monumental shift in economics and finance. New market indices are offering comprehensive alternatives to only profit as a measure of success and welfare that seek to address real human and environmental issues that affect overall success and happiness. Real growth is facilitated and monitored by measures that reflect a broad scope of true human values – healthy environments, caring communities, and a good society – directly and thoughtfully, and especially for the least fortunate. At the company level, measures that strengthen long-term resilience are also "real growth" measures that address environmental and social performance, in addition to economic performance. Investors and Wallstreet are now analyzing environmental and social metrics as a more accurate measure of company performance and future outlook. Generally, one finds a positive relationship between environmental and social performance and economic performance. In other words, *a company largely benefits economically if it also operates responsibly and adopts principles within ecology and social well-being.*

One of the most pivotal areas for this shift is from leaders, especially within business, to illustrate the new sustainable blueprint for success. Businesses are already proving that by investing in sustainability – adopting triple bottom line models that focus on creating positive environmental, societal, and economic impacts – they simultaneously increase their profits. Eccles, Ioannis, and Serafeim (2014) observed that companies investing in sustainability versus companies that did not make 4.8% higher profits overall over an eighteen year period. By institutionalizing sustainability within their models, they had happier employees, less turnover, and did not exploit or harm the environment in their business dealings. When they focused on a long-term vision rather than short-term profits, they did better overall – and they were better corporate citizens of humanity and the earth.

Materiality and Stakeholder Engagement

A precondition for effectively defining and measuring sustainability is participation across sectors and at all levels of society through cross-sectoral collaboration, public participation, and bottom-up approaches. For businesses, this means undergoing a materiality assessment. Materiality is a threshold at which certain topics or issues become significantly important to a company or organization based on what matters most to their stakeholders. A materiality assessment seeks to identify the greatest concerns of stakeholders and where the greatest impacts are as a result of a company's operations. For example, this could entail waste management and pollution in a manufacturing business, or social issues of employee equity or happiness. When specific material topics have been agreed upon, key performance indicators can be developed to guide further progress and track improvements. Materiality is a valuable process to a company and a central initial principle of most sustainability reporting (GRI, 2011).

Sustainability Values Reflected in Indicators

The fate of our planet and human life rests upon our ability to put sound and inclusive sustainability indicators at the center of measuring our development and success (Norton, 2005). Community or organizational values, based on inclusive processes involving key stakeholders, form the basis for what sustainability means in a given context, for example in relation to the field of expertise, location, sector, industry, history, and type of company. This can subsequently inform a vision for sustainable development within a company or organization and how the various operations could change or be optimized. From there, performance indicators and metrics can be developed to measure progress towards respective goals and sub-goals, which are collectively agreed upon. The overall aim of developing sustainability indicators and metrics is to provide businesses, organizations and various communities with sufficient information to track progress toward sustainable operations and help define sound and attainable goals. In order for indicators to be sensitive to that specific company or organization, the goals can be defined in a SMART format: specific, measurable, attainable, realistic, and timely. This is key for effectively managing performance, which typically involves benchmarking that compares the processes in a company to that industry's best practices from other companies. Sustainability metrics and indicators can inform evidence-based strategies and policy development that are context sensitive, provided that the development processes are inclusive, multi-stakeholder/disciplinary, and transparent. The choices of indicators in a community, organization, institution, business or non-profit reflects their collective values, vision, and mission – in other words, what is considered material, or what matters most – to them.

Sustainability Reporting

One of the primary ways that companies are investing in greater sustainability is through sustainability reporting. More than 80% of public companies are now producing annual sustainability reports. This number has increased to almost 90% in the last decade. In many countries, sustainability reporting, or rather corporate social responsibility, is required by law. In the United States, it is still voluntary, and so it is even more how many companies produce them.

These reports, while usually self-published, require companies to follow a triple bottom line framework for collecting indicators and publically reporting their progress. Today, these indicators and metrics are collected by money managers and given values based on their overall sustainability. Investors have increasingly been relying on these measures as they are better estimates of risk and assess many of the intangibles that are hard to determine from numbers alone.

Social measures that companies are starting to track largely entail the relationships and engagement with all stakeholders, whether they are employees, workers in the value chain, customers, or the local community. Examples include good, well-paying jobs, increased employee satisfaction, minimized layoffs and job insecurity, provisions for adequate retirement incomes, as well as more family-friendly policies at work, including flex time and easy access to good-quality childcare (Speth, 2008, p. 145). Environmental measures might include carbon emissions, renewable energy investments, energy efficiency, waste reduction, zero waste efforts, water reduction, green building integration, and many more. Universal frameworks with proven indicators are available for companies to use for reporting, such as the Global Reporting Initiative (GRI), Sustainability Accounting Standards Board (SASB), Integrated Reporting (IR), and Carbon Disclosure Project (CDP).

The growing demand for transparency is a major contributor to the increase in sustainability reporting. Companies that disclose and track their environmental performance with these frameworks are considered less risky to investors since they reduce potential environmental exploitation, pollution, or disasters. Recent developments in social media have presented both immense opportunities and potential risks for businesses. Every citizen has become a watchdog for social and environmental impacts by businesses, which spread rapidly through the internet and social media. Businesses have responded by becoming more proactive rather than reactive.

The Circular Economy

Living and operating sustainably does not mean compromising or limiting humans' unique ability to create. Rather the opposite is true — it has widened our outlook to recognize the interconnected systems we live in and that everything we do has environmental, social, and economic effects. Systems thinking, conscious business models, and sustainable development are not merely about problem-solving, but about creating. It is vital to foster creative thinking that is anchored in future visions about the world in which we desire to live. Creating alternatives is a key component in the development of a regenerative society, requiring aspiration, imagination, and perseverance. "We have no idea of our capacity to create the world anew" (Senge et al., 2008, p. 292). It is possible to adjust our system to be one of natural capitalism where our businesses operate based on the notion of a circular economy, where everything we extract from the earth is returned tenfold back to the earth in a thoughtful and healthy way. By changing our mental modes, we can create regenerative business models that not only sustain but regenerate resources and make things even better than we left them.

A RESPONSIBLE BUSINESS MODEL

As underlying social and environmental problems grow, the costs of doing business as usual are also increasing. Governments around the world are progressively pushing for stricter laws, regulations, and so-called green taxes to incentivize changes in business practices. Yet, how high of a lever are these instruments really? Do paying taxes and being in compliance with the law guarantee a responsible business in light of sustainability, or are they just a growing number of quick fixes?

The "radical industrialist" and founder of Interface, the world's largest carpet manufacturer, Ray Anderson, asked himself these questions. He was confronted by a customer regarding what Interface was doing for the environment, and this became the start of the sustainability journey for his company. Operating by the traditional linear factory model, dominated by petroleum-derived chemicals to make carpets, and fossil fuels for transportation and manufacturing, Anderson realized that even though Interface had not broken one environmental rule, the company was still contributing to great environmental harm (Anderson & White, 2009). In many cases it is legal for businesses to use resources inefficiently, pollute the air, and produce large amounts of waste. The entire take-make-waste linear industrial system is legal and still very much the norm in our society, built on the assumption of infinite resources, energy, and space. It is possible that being in compliance with environmental laws give companies a false impression that their practices are ethically sound, which could potentially reduce motivation (and even awareness) to create fundamental changes in business models because paying taxes is still the cheaper option (Stroh, 2015).

Systems thinking, however, uncovers the linear mental models that are underpinning current unsustainable business practices. Since the beginning of the industrial age, such beliefs and ways of seeing the world have become deeply ingrained (Senge et al., 2008). Anderson became acutely aware of this fact and decided to radically change Interface's business rationale as a result. The company shifted from being reactive to proactive, moving beyond compliance by integrating sustainability into the core vision and mission of the company (Anderson and White, 2009; Senge et al., 2008). By realizing that one is part of a greater whole, and that inaction is likely the biggest mistake, Interface decided to radically change its business practices. The new ambitious goal was zero negative impact by 2020. For his company, this meant acknowledging the company's role and influence in the larger societal and natural systems, and taking on greater responsibility; they went from linear production processes to closed loop systems, from selling carpets to servicizing, from fossil fuels to renewable energy, from petroleum-derived materials to recycled ones, from traditional mental models of design to biomimicry. He led a bold and complete redesign of virtually every area of operation. Further, Anderson co-created and consistently communicated the new vision and mission of the company together with Interface's stakeholders, including employees, customers, investors, suppliers, design teams, and residents living near the factories. This transparent communication that facilitated understanding and engagement in sustainability efforts, made sustainability the language of the company with stakeholders playing a key role in bringing about the desired change (Anderson & White, 2009; Meadows, 2008).

What makes Interface an important case study is its size and type of business and, thus, how it has influenced other businesses and industrial processes globally. Anderson pioneered the system's approach to business, has showed leadership that acknowledges and readily addresses its social and environmental impacts and offered a blueprint for other businesses to follow. Interface's story has demonstrated that the interests of business and the interests of our planet do not collide, but rather work best in synergy. If other individual companies choose a similar business model and ethics, their additive effects can produce cumulative large-scale positive impacts (Senge et al., 2008). As much as businesses have helped pave the way towards global collapse, they also have the power to turn the ship around and steer it on a regenerative course.

A HOLISTIC FUTURE

The thoughts that we have about the world around us are what legitimizes our treatment of it, thus *changing our thinking to change the world* can be a simple yet powerful motto to live by. Nature is much more complex than linear thinking will ever ascertain. What can likely generate the greatest positive change is to take a hard look at the history of anthropogenic impacts since the beginning of the Anthropocene and re-examine the questions: are we really separate from or superior to nature, or an integral part of it? (Ponting, 2007). Using holistic, long-term, systems thinking as opposed to rational, short-term, linear thinking provides a more inclusive approach, an approach where we can create a thriving economy while also ensuring the rights and health of people and the earth, sustaining it for our future generations. There is a growing pressure on companies and organizations, public and private, in all sectors and levels of society to operate in line with the principles of sustainable development. Several means can be employed to assist businesses in that process and help them evolve towards triple bottom line business models.

The UNSDGs provide a guiding framework for leaders to make decisions that may impact the rest of the world. Many organizations are adopting the UNSDGs to help them track their own progress toward environmental resiliency, equality, and sustainable economic growth. Adopting these goals in combination with viewing all organizations from the lens of holistic systems thinking helps to understand the ripple effects decision-making can have on the rest of the world, and most importantly, it provides a roadmap that increases global collaboration in working toward the greater good of the world.

What determines an effective leverage is the level of perspective, and this is where adopting a holistic understanding becomes pivotal for success. Sustainable development and the environmental movement today are drawing on very long intellectual tradition. We might benefit from returning to those roots, not in the sense that we should return to the Stone Age way of living, but in the sense of wisdom and relationship with the earth, such as recognizing that all life on earth is interconnected, addressing human values in our efforts to create sustainable societies, creating business models that move beyond the default goal of profit and power, and actively working towards the well-being of natural and social systems.

NOTES

1. The Environmental Kuznets Curve suggests that "degradation would initially increase as a country industrialized and wealth increased, but would reach a point of inflection where matters would improve" (Bell & Morse, 2008).

2. https://www.yellowstonepark.com/things-to-do/wolf-reintroduction-changes-ecosystem

REFERENCES

Anderson, R. C., & White, R. (2009). *Confessions of a radical industrialist: Profits, people, purpose–Doing business by respecting the Earth*. New York, NY: St. Martin's Press.

Bell, S., & Morse, S. (2008). *Sustainability indicators: Measuring the immeasurable?* London: Earthscan.

Eccles, R., Ioannis, I., & Serafeim, G. (2014). The impact of corporate sustainability on organizational processes and performance. *Management Science, 60*(11), 2835–2857.

GRI. (2011). *RG Sustainability Reporting Guidelines*. Retrieved from Global Reporting Initiative. Retrieved from https://www.globalreporting.

org/resourcelibrary/G3.1-Guidelines-Incl-Technical-Protocol.pdf. Accessed on February 23, 2017.

Harman, J. (2014). *The Shark's paintbrush: Biomimicry and how nature is inspiring innovation*. Ashland, OR: White Cloud Press.

Heinberg, R. (2014). The Anthropocene: It's not all about us. *Earth Island Journal, News of the World Environment, 29*(2).

Korten, D. C. (2010). *Agenda for a new economy: From phantom wealth to real wealth*. San Francisco, CA: Berrett-Koehler Publishers.

Meadows, D. H. (2008). *Thinking in systems: A primer*. White River Junction, VT: Chelsea Green Publishing.

Norton, B. G. (2005). *Sustainability: A philosophy of adaptive ecosystem management*. Chicago, IL: University of Chicago Press.

Ponting, C. (2007). *A new green history of the world: the environment and the collapse of great civilizations*. New York, NY: Random House.

Senge, P., Smith, B., Kruschwitz, N., Laur, J., & Schley, S. (2008). *The necessary revolution*. New York, NY: Doubleday.

Speth, J. G. (2008). *The bridge at the edge of the world: Capitalism, the environment, and crossing from crisis to sustainability*. New Haven, CT: Yale University Press.

Stroh, D. P. (2015). *Systems thinking for social change: A practical guide to solving complex problems, avoiding unintended consequences, and achieving lasting results*. White River Junction, VT: Chelsea Green Publishing.

Worldometers. (2018). *Current World Population*. Retrieved from http://www.worldometers.info/world-population/. Accessed on April 11, 2018.

Wright, R. (2004). *A short history of progress*. Toronto, ON: House of Anansi.

13

GUIDING PRINCIPLES FOR CO-CREATING A SUSTAINABLE ECONOMY AND FOR LEVERAGING BLOCKCHAIN FOR COLLECTIVE WELLBEING

Shanah Trevenna

PART I: THE CURRENT LIE OF ECONOMIC INCLUSION

The world is experiencing change as a global community like never before. The infiltration of multinational companies in most countries homogenizing the global marketplace, the plight of refugees forcing diverse cultures into close quarters, the globally felt effects of climate change and catastrophes, broad access to internet and cell phones in even the most remote villages, and the rise of blockchain and cryptocurrencies are just a few of the unprecedented forces transcending borders to create an entirely new world at an accelerating pace. Yet, rather than collectively shape this emergent unknown global future in an evolutionary and beneficial direction, our current trajectory is tragically replicating the economic and political thinking that has massively degraded ecosystems, reduced the human inspiration for expression and purpose to dehumanizing low wage jobs, and concentrated wealth amongst the few. The path we are taking will ensure a small number of individuals and companies wield the power to extinct many of our species and keep much of the world's population underpaid, underutilized, and unfulfilled.

This downward spiral has much to do with the global trend of removing laws protecting citizens and our natural resources from economic interests, and replacing them with exploitive rights for corporations (Della Porta & Marchetti, 2007; Pleyers, 2010; Steger, 2009; Steger, Goodman, & Wilson 2013; Tarrow, 2001, 2005). Governments influenced by corporate contributions and promises continually change the rules of their economy in favor of corporate profits. The private sector increasingly exploits human and natural capital for their own gains, all in the name of helping struggling countries join the global trade market.

In the US, personal and business bank accounts were once protected by laws limiting what financial institutions could and could not do with citizens' money. The policy was increasingly influenced by the private sector until corporations were granted the rights of people and Wall Street was allowed to fabricate financial markets (Daly, 1996; Kelly, 2012; Rifkin, 2011; Schor, 2010). The financial economy (comprised of *claims* on real assets, such as stocks, bonds, loans, and mortgages) can be imagined as a separate economic sphere dwelling above the real economy of goods and services and drawing on its energy (Kelly, 2012, p. 68). While these spheres remained similar in size for many decades, by 2005 the gross domestic product (GDP) of the financial economy was four times that of the real economy (Kelly, 2012, p. 68). In this vast landscape of fabricated theoretical financial markets, our most trusted institutions could legally invent speculative games of chance increasingly designed for banks to capture the wealth of the American people.

In the housing market creditors used the money of citizens to gamble in financial markets, kept all the wins and passed on all the losses to home owners. The movie *The Big Short* shares that when the housing bubble burst in 2008 resulting in the financial collapse of the global economy, "5 trillion dollars in pension money, real estate value, 401k, savings, and bonds had disappeared. Eight million people lost their jobs, 6 million lost their homes. The government bailed out the banks and not the American people. And business continued as usual." This is one example of how the real wealth of ordinary people transitioned to the financial assets of only the elite. And this economic model has been continually outsourced from the US and systematically replicated across the world under the guise of the natural forces of a globalizing world.

In her book *The Shock Doctrine: The Rise of Disaster Capitalism* (2008), Naomi Klein describes disaster capitalism as "the rapid-fire corporate reengineering of societies still reeling from shock." Klein strongly argues that globalization as we know it is not the result of natural forces but rather the agenda of corporate interests. Regional leaders, often newly in power, know the political and economic systems that led to the destruction didn't work, so they are raw, vulnerable and desperate for new ideas. Corporate interests flashing the glamour of a Western lifestyle and an influx of global dollars to the region talk local leaders into making themselves attractive to the world's corporate wealth and power. Countries are convinced that devaluing their currency and removing the laws that protect their people and natural resources will hurt in the short term, maybe even decades, but will be worth it in the long term. Yes, their people will be poor and might even starve, but if they can stick out this transition period, the country will eventually get the hang of the new system and attract new investment, and everyone will flourish. Like a young girl who has been abused and abandoned and talked into prostitution, the country cheapens itself under the promise of salvation, convinced by the powers that plan to exploit it. Klein's book argues that globalization as we know it is not just natural forces that have emerged as we unify our global economy, but rather the very specific workings of the exploitive corporate-led agenda, sold as a solution for societies still reeling from trauma.

Many global thought leaders envision a more evolved economy based on the "triple bottom line" (TBL) where economic activity *simultaneously* benefits people, planet, and profits. Yet many TBL efforts try to *balance* social, environmental and economic interests as tradeoffs, which still results in winners and losers. I propose that we instead strive for *harmony*. In harmony, all parts gain as they resonate together, making the whole much stronger than the sum of its parts. By functioning as one merged system, economic activity should serve ecology as much as ecology serves it. And by participating in a truly healthy economy, we should all feel the human experience enhanced in ways it couldn't be without it. Yet, given the current state of the world, what would this really look like and how can we possibly get there? The answer lies in looking at how we got here in the first place.

PART II: LEADING TO CREATE A NEW GLOBAL ECONOMY – A GUIDING FRAMEWORK

In his book *Sapiens: A Brief History of Humankind*, historian Dr Hararir studies the history of humanity to conclude that modern humans came to dominate the world because of one unique ability of our species: we believe (Harari, 2014). We are the only animal that organizes ourselves around constructs existing purely in the mind such as religion, nations, human rights, marketing, and money. None of these mere concepts would exist as meaningful forces without all participants' willingness to hold them as real in our worlds and participate with them as if they are real. While other species need a genetic mutation to evolve, the history of human systems shows that all we need is a new vision *that we collectively participate in* as real.

Another interesting insight from Harari's research reveals that humanity has been trending towards the unification of humankind through ever-increasing political and economic interdependence. He concludes that becoming one global empire is inevitable. Yet, how we do so remains guided by what has always directed our evolution […] our shared beliefs. We have an opportunity, and some would say a human obligation, like never before to influence our collective trajectory with new beliefs, with a new guiding vision.

How then can we collectively answer one of the world's most important questions: What would a truly harmonious global unified economy look like that enhances our ecology as well as the experience of being human for all? Research from 250 thought leaders in the literature, synergized with interviews with some of the world's most conscious business leaders, revealed three agreed-upon overarching goals for such a unified economy. Seven guiding principles also emerged as a useful framework we can all use to collectively achieve the goals. If applied in our day-to-day decision-making such as when creating or critiquing programs, policies, business models, and processes, our many big and small decisions could add up to collective systemic change.

To find conscious business leaders who think beyond status quo for this research, first conscious businesses needed to be identified. B Corp was the answer as it is the global gold standard third-party verification system for such businesses. B Corp certified businesses score 25% better than other self-proclaimed sustainable businesses (B Lab, 2012, p. 29), rendering them some of the world's most measurably conscious global businesses. Their leaders, along with thought leaders in the literature, have envisioned what a sustainable unified economy could look and the consensus in their thinking is captured in the following goals and principles.

THREE OVERARCHING GOALS FOR A SUSTAINABLE UNIFIED GLOBAL ECONOMY

Goal 1: Act as an Ecosystem — Emulate and Integrate with Nature's Systems

An overarching theme in the literature recognizes the economy as a human construct embedded in and dependent on society, which is in turn embedded in and dependent on nature. Since the economy is ultimately dependent on ecology, the unified economy must evolve using two guiding axioms: (1) it must function within ecological limits (Berry, 2010; Klein, 2014; Lovins & Cohen, 2011; Meadows, Meadows, Randers, & Behrens, 1972; McKibben, 2007) and (2) it must emulate ecological processes for maximum efficiency and prosperity (Benyus, 1997; Berry, 2010; Pauli, 2010; Hawken, 1993; Lovins & Cohen, 2011; Sahtouris, 1997).

The conscious emulation of nature's genius to solve human problems is called biomimicry, as described by Janine Benyus, a forest ecologist, and biomimicry expert:

> *[Biomimicry] grows from the wisdom of the species that have lived on Earth far longer than humans. To emulate nature, we would manufacture the way animals and plants do, using sun and simple compounds to produce totally biodegradable [materials]. Our farms, modeled on prairies, would be self-fertilizing and pest-resistant. To find new drugs [...] we would consult animals and insects that have used plants for millions of years to keep themselves healthy and nourished. (Benyus, 1997, p. 3)*

Thus, we would replace the industrial revolution that was based on what we can *extract from* nature, with the biomimicry revolution based on innovations *learned from* nature (Benyus, 1997, p. 2).

Nature, as a whole, operates systematically as an ecosystem and interestingly in recent years, the global startup culture has adopted the word ecosystem for their networks. Entrepreneurship and startups have become a global uprising force as Millennials and others unhappy with or marginalized from status quo jobs look for new economic opportunities. Unprecedented technology platforms remove many of the barriers of entry for forming, operating and even funding new companies. Technology also provides scaling opportunities once available to only the wealthy, well-connected and well-funded. Hence, the UN's SDG Goal 8 targets emphasize that economic growth will happen through diversification and technological upgrading and innovation (United Nations, 2018). The targets also advocate for policies that support entrepreneurship, creativity and innovation and the growth of micro-, small-, and medium-size enterprises (United Nations, 2018). Like any ecosystem, a truly beneficial unified economy would ensure everyone and everything has its place and are symbiotically interconnected, meaning all truly benefit by belonging.

Goal 2: Include and Empower All for Collective Wellbeing

In his book *Capitalism at the Crossroads*, sustainable business strategist Stuart Hart describes how communities are increasingly forced into the global money economy, driving them into cultural disruption and poverty (Hart, 2010, p. 56). Their options are few and many fall prey to the criminal sector (Korten, 2010, p. 143, Hart, 2010, p. 57; Hawken, 1993, p. 93; Ruggie, 2013, p. 35).

Goal 8 of the UN's SDGs calls for the eradication of forced labor, modern slavery, human trafficking, and child labor, as well as the creation and protection of labor rights, especially for migrant and women migrants and those in precarious employment (United Nations, 2018). It is essential to the health of humanity that multi-nationals *participate* with local populations and cater to the real needs of local communities, building local capacity and preserving or increasing esteem of individuals and the community (Hart, 2010, p. 73; Sahtouris, 1997, p. 2). Communities should also be encouraged towards self-reliance where they create their own jobs and economies based on the skills, passion, and expertise of their people and culture (Korten, 2010, p. 125). This can be accomplished with government support, which could include the provision of a basic living wage to eradicate scarcity and poverty.

However we globalize our economy, there is a crucial need to stop the obsession with profit growth above how people and the planet are treated (Bargh, 2007, p. 11; Berry, 2010, p. 26; Dietz & O'Neill, 2013, p. 15; Jackson, 2009, p. 17; Korten, 2010, p. 17; McKibben, 2007, p. 37; Schor, 2010, p. 95; UNEP/ILO/IOE/ITUC, 2008, p. 83; United Nations, 2018). Thought leaders agree that human success relies on a shift from the measurement of *money* to *wellbeing for all* (Alperovitz, 2013; Googins, Mirvis, & Rochlin, 2007, p. 4; Ruggie, 2013; Sahtouris, 1997, p. 5; Schor, 2010; Van Gelder & Adamson, 2009). We must achieve an empowering and beneficial inclusion as we globalize into one economy and one global society.

Goal 3: Raise Global Consciousness — Improve the Experience of Being Human

Economic activity has been reduced to dehumanized transactions void of values. Values are beliefs and judgments about what objectives, and modes of behavior for achieving them, are desirable (Higgins, 2006, p. 439, 440). Currently, some of the values grown by economic activity include greed, exploitation, hording, selfishness, prioritization of work over family etc. This is the system we need to wake up from as a global society.

It took conscious leaders to envision an economic system beyond the social normalization of slavery that once underpinned all economic activity for the entire history of humanity. Something caused them to believe that, despite the world agreeing otherwise, slavery was wrong. A similar consciousness is an essential design condition for a new system if we are to collectively create something beyond the current exploitive system. Consciousness is traditionally defined as a person's awareness and perceptions. I define it as it is more currently operationalized by the global consciousness movement as the process of *contemplating inner feelings and perspectives beyond personal and societal conditioning to understand one's authentic position.*

Conscious leaders are seeing that the current economy exploits and dehumanizes. They are exploring economic activity that would deepen the enjoyment of our individual and collective human experience by creating empowering opportunities for growth and expansion, fostering fulfilling expression and contribution, providing security and abundance, and circulating human connections and even love. In this way, participating in the economy would enhance, rather than diminish, the human experience.

SEVEN GUIDING PRINCIPLES FOR A SUSTAINABLE UNIFIED GLOBAL ECONOMY

Principle 1: Collaboration over Competition

Traditional economics has trained us to think and act as though we are in competition with each other for scarce resources (Korten, 2010, p. 147; Sahtouris, 1997, p. 3). Business and economic theorists advocate for a completely different view where human rationality includes ethical deliberation and complex motivations (Badeen, 2012; Hawken, 1993; Hodgson, 2001; D. Korten, 2010; Reinert, 2012; Schor, 2010; Stiglitz, 2015). For example, 48% of US adults have made a voluntary lifestyle change that resulted in earning less money (Schor, 2010, p. 107).

Business theorist David Korten describes how from a biological standpoint, species that prosper over the longer term are not the most brutal and competitive, but rather those that find a niche in which they meet their own needs in ways that simultaneously serves the needs of the whole (Korten, 2010, p. 148). Rather than "beat out the competition," collaborative businesses identify the true needs in their industry and fill in niches that are empty or underserved. They talk with other business owners to see where they can best fit in, which fosters relationships where companies continue to support each other by tag-teaming projects, providing referrals, cross-offering products and services, growing the industry, bulk purchasing, sharing lessons and knowledge, creating favorable policy and cultivating overall ecosystem health.

Principle 2: Relationships over Transactions

Business structures must evolve to put people first. In their book *Money and the Morality of Exchange* anthropologists describe how economic relationships are viewed as inherently impersonal, transitory, amoral and calculating (Parry & Bloch, 1989, p. 8). This poem beautifully captures the spirit of a different approach:

Even after all this time, the sun never says to the Earth,
'You owe Me'.

Look what happens with a love like that, it lights the Whole Sky.

—Hafiz

Putting people first was the number one reason cited by B Corp leaders for creating their companies. Whether they wanted to distribute profits internally or within the community, create a culture of work-life balance, attract and retain the best talent by ensuring employee happiness, provide proper benefits, be of service to their communities or serve the greater good, they wanted people to be at the center of their efforts, not products or profits. For example, the forward-thinking multi-national engineering company Arup is owned by its 10,000 employees rather than shareholders and has three overarching goals: (1) do good for the world, (2) ensure employee happiness, and (3) make profits, but only to serve goals 1 and 2. Progressive companies value using profits to enhance the human experience rather than using humans to advance profits.

Principle 3: Decentralized over Hierarchical Power

A study of over 20,000 employees in 22 markets after the 2008 recession showed a large decrease in employee engagement, mostly due to a lack of confidence in managers (Baker, 2014). Another study revealed an increased desire for controlling one's own work situation (Chaleff, 2009, p. 17). It is clear that employee engagement can no longer come from the employee-boss relations inherent in hierarchies.

Flat organizational structures have only two to four layers of authority and are often championed as the solution. Yet, the dynamics of domination/suppression remains with people to please for approval and advancement. In his book, *The Courageous Follower*, executive coach Ira Chaleff advocates that ideally every individual would be able to function as leader and follower fluidly according to varying needs of a common mission (Chaleff, 2009). This differs from the hierarchy in a couple of important ways. Rather than the follower orbiting around the leader, the followers and leaders both orbit around the purpose and interchange places as needed (Chaleff, 2009, p. 12). In such a model, the manager falls away as a motivator and the purpose becomes the magnetic mobilizing force (Covey, 1991, p. 303). More diverse voices contribute to decision-making and managers no longer shoulder the burden of motivating and problem-solving. And profits often soar. In a 2010 Hewitt Associates Study, companies with higher levels of employee engagement (>65% of employees) outperformed the stock market by nearly 20%, while companies with low engagement (<40%) had shareholder returns 44% lower than the average (Baker, 2014).

Principle 4: Distributed over Concentrated Wealth

While there have always been wealthy and poor, the divide between them has been continually growing. Many point to the industrial revolution as a turning point where companies grew from mostly merchant owned and operated small personal enterprises to unprecedentedly large corporations and factories. For the first time in history, those who worked to *create* profits no longer *received* the profits across much of the economy. And over the last two hundred years, more and more of company profits have been driven to the shareholders rather than to the workers. The change needed is simple: all those working to create profits should receive some of the profits proportionate to their contribution and risk. While shareholders might balk at this idea, overall profits would likely grow from the ubiquitous alignment of worker motivation with profit making. Efficiency, productivity, fulfillment, and engagement would all increase, and all are proven to translate into higher profits.

Principle 5: Internalize Externalities

In business, externalities benefit a company but are not included in their cost of doing business (Carruthers & Mundy, 2006). Examples include the cost of pollution, worker illness and unhappiness, poor wages and work conditions, and the taking of natural resources. Many thought leaders agree that if market players did have to pay the cost of externalities (called internalizing externalities), their business models would fall apart and exploitive market capitalism as we know it wouldn't survive (Berry, 2010; Carruthers & Mundy, 2006; Dator, 2010; Korten, 2010; Lovins & Cohen, 2011; McKibben, 2007; Rezai, Foley, & Taylor, 2012; Rifkin, 2011, p. 207). Recommendations for a sustainable unified economy include eliminating corporate money in politics, restructuring taxation and mandating businesses to take into account true environmental and social costs (Berry, 2010, p. 27; Korten, 2010, p. 14; "The Future We Want" 2012, p. 42).

Principle 6: Activate Purpose and the Whole Self

We need to move beyond simply doing a job for money. Economic activity could satisfy the deep human need for purpose. This emerged in many B Corp leader interviews, as exemplified by this CEO:

> *It's so much bigger than making a paycheck. It's asking how can I actually be happy and content in my everyday life. I don't want to work a 9-5 and leave that at the door when I get home. How can I integrate a work life where I'm more fulfilled overall?*

The interviews also revealed a desire for work-life balance, which was one of the top reasons B Corp CEOs created their companies. Work-life balance counters the normalization of extreme over-working in entrepreneurship where one loses their personal identity to a work identity. Many leaders limited work hours for their employees and ensured clients understood the value of this.

Many interviewees also mentioned the desire to be happy and have fun at work and to support happy families. While it may seem that the environment would be a prime motivator to create TBL companies, it was the disdain of the experience of living a robotic, overworked life that was the prime motivator described.

Principle 7: Simultaneously Protect and Evolve What Works

The development of effective policies, successful programs and innovative business models that produce prosperity for all is no small task. What may prove even more challenging is ensuring the systemic adoption and longevity of what proves successful. For example, sustainability provided a vision for businesses to honor the planet in their practices, but this eventually resulted in "green washing," which is the dissemination of false or incomplete information by an organization to present an environmentally responsible public image (Furlow, 2009, p. 22). Such false claims result in the loss of faith of consumers in business and the market. The unified economy needs to allow those who create real, measurable impact to operate and grow and not be shadowed by those with false claims.

PART III: ENACTING THIS FRAMEWORK USING BLOCKCHAIN

What Is Blockchain and Why Does It Matter?

Blockchain is essentially a vast system of globally distributed small data storage centers linked together for nearly simultaneous communication with each other. Any transaction that occurs on the blockchain network is recorded in thousands of locations. Thus, it is often called a "distributed ledger."

Having thousands of identical, up-to-date records distributed globally and constantly reconciling their information in near real time creates an incredibly resilient and reliable system. Instead of one centralized server, the entire network holds all the data. If anyone is able to hack the network, it quickly self-corrects. The result is that all records on the blockchain remain accurate and accounted for, forever.

Another important aspect of blockchain is the unique capabilities of the systems built on it. Like apps added to your phone, entire systems of exchange can be built on the blockchain. While bitcoin is the most famous, it doesn't even scratch the surface of leveraging the powerful capabilities of a blockchain based currency, often called a Cryptocurrency. Bitcoin has essentially replicated the existing money system, still replicating the speculative, transactional, profit-focused culture of money as we know it. There is an opportunity to create a more evolved form of global currency using an important capability of blockchain called Smart Contracts not currently used to their capacity by bitcoin or most Cryptocurrencies.

Currently, all of our national currencies are simply values that get exchanged. Any rules around how these amounts get moved around are documented in policies and laws that govern money, or in culturally agreed-upon ethics. But what if the rules were built right into each transaction, like the way Paypal can limit your daily transfer amount or charge you if you send money to a business. Ensuring each transaction abides by agreed-upon ethical rules could be achieved using Smart Contracts in a properly structured Cryptocurrency.

Consider Principle 4: Distributed Over Concentrated Wealth. What if society agreed that every company were required to distribute 25% of their profits to their employees. Smart contracts could allocate 25% of profits across all employees according to their individual performance and length of employment [...] all data recorded in most current systems. This amount could be deducted from taxable income real time in the system. The algorithm could also ensure the top paid employee didn't excessively exceed the lowest paid employee, that all women were paid the same as men for equal work, that an equal number of men and women held leadership roles, etc. Each individual and company could be provided an annual basic allotment so that extreme or consistent scarcity would be minimized in the system. Each dollar in the allotment could contain rules on where the money could be spent (e.g., education or food), when it could be spent (e.g., a portion every month), or other features such as providing more money if certain conditions are met. All of these rules would be automated so that transactions ultimately end up enacting values.

Leveraging Blockchain for Democracy in the Global Political-Economy

Democracy is often positioned as the solution to distributing power. Democracy is simply defined as control of a system by the majority of its members. Yet, most agree there is not a single well-functioning democracy on earth. One reason is that most are representative democracies, meaning people participate by voting for representatives. This doesn't necessarily result in the system being controlled by the many.

A representative democracy is archaic in the face of our current technology. It was developed when entire villages couldn't travel to meet together, so representatives were sent. Now that we have internet connectivity "direct democracy" has emerged as a viable option, where citizens vote on-line directly without needing to go through a representative, much like a referendum. Yet many agree that educating everyone on each issue is not possible. For example, the day after the Brexit vote, the most googled terms were "What is Brexit" and "What is the EU." The group thinking of citizens unaware of the broad implications of a policy decision doesn't seem the best answer.

"Liquid democracy" is another solution, where any voter can give their vote to someone they trust. Yet the options remain articulated by just a few participants, the process is still exposed for key leaders to be influenced by special interests, and only a few voices are activated. Those left out of the current democratic process remain left out.

In contrast, "Deep Democracy" aims to include the wisdom of minorities and those usually left out of decision-making (Lewis, 2018). A prerequisite of deep democracy is the acceptance that there is something of value to be found in all perspectives. The best results are then achieved by combining differences. This prevents narrow-mindedness and cultivates out-of-the-box thinking and diverse engagement as participants explore how to make use of differences in needs and values.

Building on the philosophy of deep democracy I propose a new Policy Process for collectively guiding our global society forward. It's an approach that leverages current technology to harvest the collective intelligence of a region and enacts most of the guiding principles. Democracy is no longer enacted through equal access to voting, but rather *equal access to participation* in a process deeper than voting.

This model begins by creating a database of society's subject matter experts (SMEs) such as those holding PhDs, non-profit and B Corp leaders, vetted community leaders, and peer-reviewed authors. The SMEs would vote on six subject areas relevant to an issue or policy decision. Using the example of Brexit, this might include macro-economics, international relations, etc. Next, teams of twelve would be created in all sub-regions. Six SMEs would be randomly selected, one for each topic area. Six additional people would be randomly selected from the citizenry, much like jury duty. In this way, all citizens would have equal opportunity to be included. And since all are randomly selected, then none could be influenced by special interests. Teams would then spend time exploring the challenges, impacts, and opportunities by articulating their unique lenses and using processes like The Lewis Method of deep democracy, MIT's Theory U, World Café, and Non-Violent Communication to explore potential solutions.

The results of all teams would then be aggregated and analyzed, effectively harvesting more comprehensive solutions from the collective intelligence of a diverse section of the entire population. Blockchain is ideal for hosting such a distributed decision-making framework that transcends all borders, as well as harvests and aggregates the results globally.

CONCLUSION

We can all use this framework synergized from the world's thought leaders to unite our efforts towards global change that actually serves rather than exploits all people and our planet:

Three Overarching Goals

Goal 1: Act as an Ecosystem – Emulate and Fit within Natures' Systems

Goal 2: Include and Empower All for Collective Wellbeing

Goal 3: Raise Global Consciousness – Improve the Experience of Being Human

Seven Guiding Principles

Principle 1: Collaboration over Competition

Principle 2: Relationships over Transactions

Principle 3: Decentralized over Hierarchical Power

Principle 4: Distributed over Concentrated Wealth

Principle 5: Internalize Externalities

Principle 6: Activate Purpose and the Whole Self

Principle 7: Simultaneously Protect and Evolve What Works

We also have an unprecedented opportunity to use this framework to create a truly sustainable global political-economy using blockchain. With the rules of the economy built into money transactions, no longer are the political and economic spheres separate. Instead, this system would represent the foundation of a global political-economy with the values and rules enacted not through law, but through the economic activity itself. And instead of spreading representative democracy as we know it, we could instead move as a global society to create a global polity united in using deep democracy on blockchain to harvest the best of all of humanity's diverse ingenuity to co-design our future. Together we could co-create a unified global political-economy with a values-based cryptocurrency that empowers our collective wellbeing.

REFERENCES

Alperovitz, G. (2013). *What then must we do: Democratizing wealth and building a community-sustaining economy from the ground up*. White River Junction, VT: Chelsea Green Publishing.

B Lab. (2012). *2012 B Corp Annual Report*. Berwyn, PA: B Lab.

Badeen, D. (2012). Bernard Hodgson's Trojan horse critique of neoclassical economics and the second phase of the empiricist level of analysis. *Business Ethics*, *108*, 15–25.

Baker. (2014, January). "Research summary: Employee engagement trends." Retrieved from http://www.bakerbrand.com/insights/employee_engagement. html

Bargh, M. (2007). *Resistance: An indigenous response to neoliberalism*. New Zealand: Huia Publishers.

Benyus, J. (1997). *Biomimicry: Innovation inspired by nature*. New York, NY: Harper Collins.

Berry, W. (2010). *What matters? Economics for a renewed commonwealth*. Berkeley, CA: Counterpoint.

Carruthers, J., & Mundy, B. (2006). *Environmental valuation*. Farnham: Ashgate Publishing.

Chaleff, I. (2009). *The courageous follower* (3rd ed.). San Francisco, CA: Berrett-Koehler Publishers, Inc.

Covey, S. R. (1991). *Principle-centered leadership*. New York, NY: Summit Books.

Daly, H. (1996). *Beyond growth: The economics of sustainable development*. Boston, MA: Beacon Press.

Dator, J. (2010). *From leisure to work to dreams to...?* Seoul: ChosunBiz Insight Forum.

Della Porta, D., & Marchetti, R. (2007). *The global justice movement: A cross-national and transnational perspective*. Boulder, CO: Paradigm Publishers.

Dietz, R., & O'Neill, D. (2013). *Enough is enough: Building a sustainable economy in a world of finding resources*. San Francisco, CA: Berrett-Koehler Publishers, Inc.

Furlow, N. (2009). Green washing in the new millenia. *Journal of Applied Business and Economics, 10*(6), 22–25.

Googins, B., Mirvis, P., & Rochlin, S. (2007). *Beyond good company, Next generation corporate citizenship*. New York, NY: Palgrave Macmillan.

Harari, Y. N. (2014). *Sapiens: A brief history of humankind*. New York, NY: Harvill Secker.

Hart, S. (2010). *Capitalism at the crossroads*. Upper Saddle River, NJ: Pearson Education Inc.

Hawken, P. (1993). *The Ecology of commerce: A declaration of sustainability*. New York, NY: Harper Business.

Higgins, T. (2006). Value from hedonic experience and engagement. *Psychological Review, 113*(3), 439–460.

Hodgson, B. (2001). *Economics as a moral science*. New York, NY: Springer.

Jackson, T. (2009). *Prosperity without growth—economics for a finite planet*. London: Earthscan.

Kelly, M. (2012). *Owning our feature: The emerging ownership revolution*. San Francisco, CA: Berrett-Koehler Publishers, Inc.

Klein, N. (2014). *This changes everything: Capitalism vs. the climate*. New York, NY: Simon & Schuster.

Korten, D. (2010). *Agenda for a new economy*. San Francisco, CA: Berrett-Koehler.

Lewis, M. (2018). "Deep Democracy - Compassion to Lead." Retrieved from http://www.compassiontolead.net/wp-content/uploads/2016/05/Compassion_InspirationCards-03.pdf

Lovins, H., & Cohen, B. (2011). *Climate capitalism: Capitalism in the age of climate change*. New York, NY: Hill and Wang.

McKibben, B. (2007). *Deep economy-The wealth of communities and the durable future*. New York, NY: St. Martin's Griffin.

Meadows, D., Meadows, D., Randers, J., & Behrens, W. (1972). *The limits to growth*. New York, NY: Universe Books.

Parry, J., & Bloch, M. (1989). *Money and the morality of exchange*. Cambridge: Cambridge University Press.

Pauli, G. (2010). *The blue economy, report to the club of Rome*. Taos: Paradigm Publications.

Pleyers, G. (2010). *Alter-globalization: Becoming actors in the global age*. Cambridge: Polity Press.

Reinert, E. S. (2012). Neo-Classical economics: A trail of economic destruction since the 1970s. *Real-World Economics Review*, *60*.

Rezai, A., Foley, D., & Taylor, L. (2012). Global warming and economic externalities. *49*(2), 329–351.

Rifkin, J. (2011). *The third industrial revolution: How lateral power is transforming energy, the economy, and the World*. New York, NY: Palgrave Macmillan.

Ruggie, J. (2013). *Just business: Multinational corporations and human rights*. New York, NY: W.W. Norton & Company.

Sahtouris, E. (1997). The biology of globalization. *Perspectives in Business and Social Change*, *2*(3).

Schor, J. B. (2010). *Plentitude: The n ew economics of true wealth*. New York, NY: Penguin Press.

Steger, M. (2009). *Globalisms*. (3rd ed.). Lanham, MD: Rowman & Littlefield.

Steger, M., Goodman, J., & Wilson, E. (2013). *Justice globalism: Ideology, crises, policy*. London: Sage.

Stiglitz, J. (2015). Reconstructing macroeconomic theory to manage economic policy. In *Fruitful Economics*. New York, NY: Palgrave Macmillan.

Tarrow, S. (2001). Transnational politics: Contention and institutions in international politics. *Annual Review of Political Science*, 4(June), 1–20.

"The Future We Want". (2012). Conference Report A/CONF.216/L.1. RIO + 20 United Nations Conference on Sustainable Development. Rio de Janeiro, Brazil: United Nations.

UNEP/ILO/IOE/ITUC. (2008). Green jobs: Towards decent work in a sustainable, low-carbon world.

United Nations. (2018). Sustainable Development Goals. Retrieved from http://www.un.org/sustainabledevelopment/economic-growth/. Accessed on March 24, 2018.

Van Gelder, S., & Adamson, R. (2009). Age-old wisdom for the new economy." *Yes!*, July Issue.

14

GROSS NATIONAL HAPPINESS: A POWERFUL INSTRUMENT FOR POSITIVE AND SUSTAINABLE GLOBAL CHANGE

Elżbieta Jabłońska

INTRODUCTION

[...] the future cannot be what it brings to us, it must be how we want it to be. The socio-economic changes must be what we seek, not completely what the forces beyond our control compel us to accept. Visioning is a means of determining our own future. Without a vision, we are unlikely to choose the right direction and pace of development. The vision attempts to strike a balance between development and environment, modernization and tradition, values and technology, immediate and long term, individuals and society, and realism and aspirations. (Bhutan Planning Commission)

In chapter 8 of *The Limits to Growth*, Meadows and Randers position "visioning" as a first tool for the transition to a sustainable society. They write, "A sustainable world can never be fully realized until it is widely envisioned. The vision must be built up by many people before it is complete and compelling (Meadows, Randers, & Meadows, 2006, p. 273)." They explain that to challenge an established system there must be courage and clarity and only innovators can do it. This challenge was undertaken by Bhutan as one of the pioneers of sustainable growth.

The Kingdom of Bhutan has become well recognized for its vision of Gross National Happiness (GNH) articulated by the Fourth King Jigme Singye Wangchuck. GNH seeks to balance economic growth with other developmental objectives that contribute to overall national well-being.

"Happiness" has been a universally shared central concern and aspiration of all human beings since very ancient times. There is nothing new or revolutionary in the idea of seeking it. Yet, Phuntso describes what *is* unusual about aiming for happiness in the case of Bhutan: "it was visionary for a monarch to crystallize the ideas and practices which remained diffused in the society into a formal national policy in order to guide development programs. The Fourth King was farsighted and judicious enough not to lose sight of the ultimate goal in the course of the frantic process of modernization" (Phuntso, 2013, p. 596).

GNH, the Bhutanese paradigm of development, is based on Buddhist tradition, which recognizes the need for holistic development from the individual to the societal level. GNH brings spiritual, emotional, and cultural well-being into balance with material well-being by proposing a broad range of appropriate policies based on nurturing the values, wisdom, and practices of spiritual traditions to support moves toward a sustainable global society. Former Minister of Education, Mr Thakur Singh Powdyel, further explains that "the Bhutanese view on political leadership ultimately connects true public leaders with the soul of the country and its people. Responsible political leaders in Bhutan pledge that the state should provide honorable service to the people and believe in the inherent goodness of the people" (Powdyel, interview, 2016). GNH is a call to fulfill the prophecy of human excellence and the blossoming of national life. In this paradigm, responsible political leaders address the needs of the moment but are mindful of the larger interests of society and the long-term aspirations of the people. The GNH development concept is the Bhutanese version of the global concept of sustainable development.

While Bhutan is a truly unique case in political science and a challenge to current theory, its approach can provide new insights for public leadership. For example, since 2004, Bhutan and its supporters have been organizing conferences to rectify the issues and limitations of gross domestic product (GDP), provides a broader view on the concept of well-being, promote the idea of GNH, and make it an international development objective. So, while Bhutan is using GNH to guide its own sustainable development, its leaders recognize that no single country can reap the full benefit of adopting and implementing any new sustainability-based paradigm unless all of humanity acts collectively and in harmony as one community. Thus, Bhutanese leaders are striving to convince the world to radically change global politics and economics, placing emphasis on a more holistic, balanced and inclusive approach based on happiness and well-being, rather than only on economic growth.

Bhutan has brought to life the UN Sustainable Development Goals (UNSDGs) through its program of GNH. My purpose in this chapter is to explore the concept of GNH as a powerful instrument and vision for global change. Using information derived from government documents, informal and structured interviews, and observations in the field from 2008 to 2018, I will begin by expanding upon the GNH vision and concept itself. Next, I will introduce the Green School Project as a case study within one of nine domains of GNH. Then I will explain the GNH Index and method. Finally, I will provide examples from around the world and share my conclusions.

THE KINGDOM OF BHUTAN – THE SMALL STATE WITH A BIG VISION

Most persons think that a state in order to be happy ought to be large; but even if they are right, they have no idea what is a large and what is a small state. For they judge the size of the city by the number of the inhabitants; whereas they ought to regard, not their number, but their power. To the size of states there is a limit, as there is to other things: plants, animals, implements; for none of these retain their natural power when they are too large or too small, but they either wholly lose their nature, or are spoiled. (Aristotle) (Jowett, 2012)

The Kingdom of Bhutan is a tiny Himalayan country in South Asia with a population of little more than 700,000. Bhutan is a small landlocked state (Kharat, 2016) situated between the world's largest democracy, India, to the south and one of the world's most powerful economies, China, to the north. Bhutan remained isolated from the rest of the world for centuries and, unlike other countries in South Asia, never experienced British colonial aggression and instead remained a sovereign state (Phuntso, 2013).

Bhutan was relatively isolated until 1961 when comprehensive efforts toward growth began. Due to the late onset of television and Internet access, there was limited influence from external practices and values on Bhutanese culture and its environment. Those factors allowed the Bhutanese Government to lead their development process at their own pace, with the luxury of learning from the successes and failures of other countries. As a result, Bhutan is currently well positioned to take a leadership role in promoting alternative development indicators.

Despite its tiny size Bhutan takes pride in doing things that are unique. This small Himalayan monarchy has a big vision that is a conceptual challenge to the currently accepted measures of progress. Global and local initiatives would benefit from a closer look at Bhutan's concept of public good, viewed as happiness.

GROSS NATIONAL HAPPINESS – THE CONCEPT IN BHUTAN

> *Put very simply, GNH is based on the conviction that material wealth alone does not bring happiness, or ensure contentment and well-being of people; and that economic growth and 'modernization' should not be at the expense of the people's quality of life or traditional values. To achieve Gross National Happiness, several policy areas were given priority: equitable socio-economic development in which prosperity is shared by every region of the pristine environment; the preservation and promotion of Bhutan's unique cultural heritage; and providing good, responsive governance in which the people participate. These are the principles that have driven the King's policies. (Ashi Dorji Wangmo Wangchuck, 2012, p. 18)*

Fourth King Jigme Singye Wangchuck's statement, "GNH is more important than Gross National Product" has gained proverbial status and forms the locus of the entire GNH discourse in vogue today" (Phuntso, 2013, p. 595). GNH was introduced as the country's development philosophy in 1999 in a document that laid out the government's vision for the next twenty years. This perspective planning document prepared by the Planning Commission in 1999 was titled *Bhutan 2020: A Vision for Peace, Prosperity and Happiness*. It identifies GNH as the "single unifying concept of development." This does not essentially reject material progress but takes GNH as a precondition for enlarging self-reliance, opportunities, and choices (Planning Commission, 1999). GNH is seen as a bridge to connect values and development. It recognizes the need to balance the material well-being of the individual and society for holistic development, drawing its ethics from the Mahayana Buddhism principle of "interdependence." From this lens, sustainability is conceptualized as interdependent ecological, economic, social, cultural, and good governance systems.

The "happiness" of GNH is not to be understood in metaphysical terms. It is a very immediate and practical concept. Happiness in Bhutan is seen as a public good and, instead of achieving it only on an individual level, the aim is to attain collective happiness. GNH emphasizes not individual advantage but rather "GNH," which is not just an aggregate of individual happiness. As such, any attempt to measure individual happiness contradicts GNH (Mancall, 2004). Happiness still remains each individual's responsibility, but there is an important role of the State to create necessary conditions for citizens to pursue the path to happiness.

From a practical point of view, Bhutan's GNH experience is a case study showing the ability to lead economic growth and modernization in balance with culture and tradition. GNH is an example of the kind of vision that Meadows et al. feel is necessary for sustainable growth (Meadows et al., 2006). Already there are several significant examples where GNH has been turned into practice including hydropower projects, a policy goal of 100% organic agriculture, a ban on plastic bags, a goal of 60% forest cover for the country, and the reduction of rural-urban migration.

Bhutan has also used the principles of GNH to achieve most of the Millennium Development Goals and is well prepared to forge ahead with the SDGs since the set of 17 SDGs are regarded as a whole system and are thus well suited for the holistic GNH framework.

GROSS NATIONAL HAPPINESS – PILLARS, DOMAINS, AND MEASUREMENT INDEX

Created in 1972 by the then 16-year-old King, GNH was originally based on four pillars:

(1) promotion of sustainable development;

(2) preservation and promotion of cultural values;

(3) conservation of the natural environment; and

(4) establishment of good governance.

The four pillars have since been elaborated into nine domains:

(1) living standards;

(2) health;

(3) ecological diversity and resilience;

(4) community vitality;

(5) time-use;

(6) psychological well-being;

(7) good governance;

(8) cultural diversity and resilience; and

(9) education.

Bhutan's *measurement* for this framework is called the Gross National Happiness Index (GNHI). The President of the Centre for Bhutan Studies & Gross National Happiness, Dasho Karma Ura, describes that the GNHI, "provides a self-portrait of a society in flux, and offers Bhutanese the opportunity to reflect on the directions society is moving, and make wise and determined adjustments." The GNHI includes 33 indicators covering all nine domains. Indicators are further disaggregated into over 120 variables.

Bhutan is still testing its ability to measure the nation's state of happiness, so the GNHI is still evolving. So far, two rounds of national surveys conducted in 2010 and 2015 have provided valuable feedback. The national surveys were conducted in all nine domains with many inter-related factors considered including the following as articulated by Karma Ura (Karma Ura, 2008):

(1) *Living standards* – The domain of living standards covers the basic economic status of the people. These indicators assess the levels of income at the individual and household levels, the number of rooms/person, the status of house ownership, and individuals' sense of financial security.

(2) *Health* – The health indicators assess the health status of the population, the determinants of public health, and the health system itself. Diverse examples of health status indicators include a body-mass index, the number of healthy days per month, knowledge about HIV transmission, and breast-feeding practices.

(3) *Ecological diversity and resilience* – By examining the state of Bhutan's natural resources, the pressures on ecosystems, and different management responses, the domain of ecological diversity and resilience is intended to describe the impact of domestic supply and demand on Bhutan's ecosystems.

(4) *Community Vitality* – The domain of community vitality focuses on the strengths and weaknesses of relationships and interactions within communities. It examines the nature of trust, belonging, the vitality of caring relationships, the feeling of safety at home and in the community, and giving and volunteering.

(5) *Time-use* – Studying how people use their time over 24 hours as well as longer periods provides one of the most effective windows on their quality of life.

(6) *Psychological well-being* – As collective happiness is the main goal of a GNH society, psychological well-being is of primary importance in gauging the success of the state in providing appropriate policies and services.

(7) *Good governance* – The domain of good governance evaluates how people perceive various government functions in terms of their efficacy, honesty, and quality. The themes include human rights, leadership at various levels of government, government performance in service delivery, the government's ability to control inequity and corruption,

and trust levels of the people in regards to media, the judiciary system, and the police.

(8) *Cultural diversity and resilience* – Maintenance of cultural traditions has been one of Bhutan's primary policy goals, as tradition and cultural diversity contributes to identity, values, and creativity.

(9) *Education* – Education contributes to the knowledge, values, creativity, skills, and civic sensibility of citizens.

ALIGNING WITH AND APPLYING THE GNH FRAMEWORK

GNH has been criticized for not being measurable or statistically sound, as well as for being too subjective. Yet, information delivered from the GNHI by the Gross National Happiness Commission (GNHC) has successfully been used to construct public policies and to allocate resources to the most essential areas of need. Countries wanting to adopt GNH indicators need first to open a national dialogue about what progress means for them so they can then create measures that fit their social and cultural context.

In Bhutan, Five Year Plans (FYPs) are the vehicle for implementing development goals. The first was launched in 1961 and each contains significant sector-specific strategies. The GNHI provides the government a clear picture of where the development policies of each FYP are succeeding and where they are not. At the operational level, every policy and every project is planned and evaluated in terms of its contribution to the total well-being of the individual and of society. FYPs are strongly guided by the Kings vision for Bhutan to achieve "Prosperity for All."

All international and regional development goals, such as SAARC development goals, Vienna Program of Action, the Istanbul Program of Action and the UNSDGs, are included in each FYP. For example, in September 2015, Bhutan joined the global community in adopting the 2030 Agenda for SDGs. They then realized that 143 of the 169 SDGs targets were relevant to the 11th FYP. They also noticed that the GNH development concept shared a common inspiration, as well as universal values, with the Millennium Development Goals, which they had achieved far ahead of the 2015 target date.

The 12th FYP, which will be implemented by June 2019, further enhances the integration of the SDGs. Bhutan's 16 National Key Results Areas are closely related with 16 of the 17 SDGs. And while all 17 goals are important, Bhutan used the GNHI to prioritize the following three SDGs for immediate implementation: Goal 1 – No Poverty, Goal 13 – Climate Action, and Goal 15 – Life on Land.

EDUCATING FOR GROSS NATIONAL HAPPINESS – GREEN SCHOOLS

A good place to observe the principles of GNH in action is the classroom. Education is at the heart of the GNH principles since it aims to improve and change society beginning with children.

As part of its holistic happiness agenda, the Bhutanese government made an effort to create "green schools." In the article, "Educating for Gross National Happiness by nurturing the concept of Green Schools for Green Bhutan" (Jablonska, 2017), I describe the initiative that the Ministry of Education launched nationwide in 2009 – Educating for GNH. This initiative put pressure on schools to change and improve the entire school system through a GNH-infused curriculum, GNH-minded teachers, and a GNH-inspired learning environment. As a result, GNH principles and values have been infused into the school curriculum at all levels. This includes emphasis on deep critical and creative thinking, ecological literacy, practicing the country's ancient wisdom and culture, contemplative learning, holistically understanding the world, genuine care for nature and for others, competency to deal effectively with the modern world, preparation for a proper livelihood, and informed civic engagement (Hayward & Coleman, 2010).

The overall objective of school education in Bhutan is to equip students with the relevant knowledge, skills, and values needed to realize the goal of Gross National Happiness. In the words of Jigmi Yoser Thinley, "education is the glue that holds the whole enterprise together." Education is seen as the crucial tool needed to help the population understand and implement GNH principles. Each school has produced its own school policy and has adopted various approaches and practices to bring GNH into the school system. Along with this new *Educating for Gross National Happiness* initiative, schools were also expected to implement robust changes in their institutions to effectively cultivate GNH values and principles through the concept of *Green Schools for Green Bhutan* (Kelly, 2013).

Thakur Sight Powdyel subsequently came up with the concept of *Green Schools for Green Bhutan* with the emphasis upon "green" as a metaphor. Green Schools are an attempt to create GNH-based schools incorporating eight dimensions: *natural greenery* that makes children feel invited, welcome, and happy to come to school; *social greenery* that permits children from different beliefs and backgrounds to learn, grow and develop in harmony and goodwill; *cultural greenery* that promotes and preserves culture, traditions and values of fair play and cooperation; *intellectual greenery* that engages children with new ideas and knowledge, positive thinking and constructive dialogue; *academic greenery* that demands high academic standards and deeper insights; *aesthetic greenery* that develops a taste for genuine and beautiful objects; *spiritual greenery* that provides conscious awareness of other beings, mindfulness of living in mutual respect and harmony, and accepts and honors the divine in us; *moral greenery* that imparts values of making sound judgements and distinguishing between right and wrong, truth and falsehood, and good and bad. These serve as an organizational and philosophical guiding framework for schools.

In addition to those eight dimensions, there are other important elements of a green school. A green school strives to build and promote good relations with the parents and the community and encourages active involvement in the education of the children. Inclusive education is another area of focus as it ensures that all the children in the community receive equal educational opportunities and are treated fairly (Royal Education Council, 2012). Teachers and students treat each other fairly and value everyone's uniqueness and contributions towards school improvement.

Thakur Singh Powdyel, Bhutan's former Minister of Education, summarizes the results as follows: "[The concept of] green schools is not just about the environment, it is a philosophy, so we're trying to instil a sense of green minds, which are flexible and open to different types of learning [...] It's a values-led approach to education that stems from the belief that education should be more than academic attainment, it should be about expanding children's minds and teaching what it is to be human." The *Green Schools for a Green Bhutan* concept is founded upon the philosophy that education goes beyond getting good grades. It should also prepare students to become responsible citizens who would look forward to their future, as well as pass the concepts and values they have been taught onto the next generation (Kelly, 2013).

GROSS NATIONAL HAPPINESS – EXPANDING BEYOND BHUTAN

Economic resources are not all that matter in people's lives. To duly capture well-being, we have to measure the expectations and level of satisfaction of individuals, how they spend their time, their paid and unpaid work, their capabilities, the relations they have with other people, their political voice and their participation in public life. (Gurría, 2009)

GNH became a trademark of Bhutan for the outside world. In 2011, The General Assembly of the United Nations added Bhutan's model of GNH to its agenda in a non-binding resolution (No 65/309) titled "Happiness: towards a holistic approach to development." The UN called on member states to draw up their own measures of happiness based on Bhutan's GNH principles. During the Conference in Paris, the former Minister of Education said, "UNESCO's vision of the world of peace and Bhutan's goal of GNH are natural allies dedicated to building a better world for all of us and for future generations to live in. UNESCO's thrust in areas of education, science, and culture [for] sustainable development find a natural home in the four pillars that support the architecture of GNH (Powdyel, 2011)." The UN further shared its support by introducing an International Day of Happiness in 2013.

In 2004, His Royal Highness (currently the Fifth King), the Crown Prince of Bhutan shared the following in his address: "I believe that while GNH is inherently Bhutanese, its ideas may have a positive relevance to any nation, people or communities – wherever they may be. I also believe that there must be some convergence among nations on the idea of what the end objective of development and progress should be. There cannot be enduring peace, prosperity, equality, and brotherhood in this world if our aims are so separate and divergent – if we do not accept that in the end we are people, all alike, sharing the earth among ourselves and also with other sentient beings, all of whom have an equal role and stake in the state of this planet and its players" (Ura & Karma, 2004).

And indeed, there are several states that have established measures to promote more sustainable, equitable, and prosperous societies. For example, in the United Kingdom there is the Measuring National Well-Being Program, which looks at the social, personal, and environmental well-being. French President Sarkozy created a Commission on the Measurement of Economic

Performance and Social Progress, whose report inspired the pursuit of more holistic measures of well-being for guiding policy (Stiglitz, Sen, & Fitoussi, 2009). Ecuador and Bolivia introduced the Buen Vivir social philosophy and China created Village Development Programs. Thailand's government partnered with several Universities to develop the National Progress Index and Venezuela has a Minister of Supreme Happiness. Several countries are exploring new ways to integrate well-being into their policies, and there are also diverse efforts on smaller scales through a myriad of NGOs initiatives. For example, The University of Leicester in the UK released the world's first "World Map of Happiness" resulting from research based on the concept of GNH.

There are also worldwide initiatives striving to measure growth and development beyond GDP. These include the UN Human Development Index (HDI); Professor Richard Estes' Weighted Index of Social Progress (WISP); Happy Planet Index (HPI); UK Measure of Domestic Progress (MDP); US Genuine Progress Index (GPI); New Zealand's Economic Living Standard Index (ELSI), and Australia's National Well-being Index (NWI).

Those countries and initiatives are demonstrating that the Bhutanese concept of GNH and the GNH-based development approach is not limited only to this small country. The conceptual measurements centering on what really matters to society are universally applicable but must be adapted to the local context.

CONCLUSIONS: GROSS NATIONAL HAPPINESS, FROM THEORY TO PRACTICE

Bhutan has worked diligently to articulate and enact the GNH concept, as envisioned by the King of Bhutan. It offers an excellent example of political theory turned into a vision that is practical and useful, particularly if tailored to the needs of each individual society. Their holistic approach to progress that takes into consideration human beings as the center of society is one worth exploring further for its broad and global implications. Bhutan shows us that human fulfillment and viewing mankind as a complex mosaic that encompasses spirituality is the key to restoring life to our planet and ensuring the survival of humanity.

The GNH idea has worked in Bhutan because it has been put into practice at all levels of society, from the education of children to the governance of top policy makers. Bhutanese education incorporates the UN vision of education for all people and aims to facilitate learning at all levels while respecting traditional values, understanding the relationship of humanity with the environment, respecting the rights of others, creating a sense of spirituality, and producing citizens who are prepared to lead in a globalized world. Bhutan has accomplished this Goal by altering public education policies and training teachers to understand GNH objectives and comprehend how they coincide with the greater global context.

The Bhutanese homegrown GNH concept has changed as times have changed and it has been refined by trial and error. Even so, it remains a strong and powerful vision that should be analyzed in greater detail as it is applied to different and larger countries. Bhutan has transformed its vision into reality and has shown that subjective measures of progress are useful from a psychological and political point of view.

Some may question if the GNH idea is one for development or modernization of an ancient society like Bhutan. In effect, they mean the same thing. The Royal Family of Bhutan is working to bring their tiny nation into the twenty-first Century while preserving the values that their people hold as being precious and more important than materialistic well-being alone. Bhutan is a laboratory that is trying to give answers to mankind's quest for meaning and has also raised questions, especially for other countries that are struggling to survive and grow on a planet that is undergoing dramatic environmental, economic, and societal transformations based on globalization and climatic change.

Countries should consider these questions as they learn from the Bhutanese example and develop their own models for development, sustainability, and progress that center on improving human capital and social well-being in their unique contexts:

- Can a "mature" democracy implement Bhutan's unorthodox policies?

- How is "progress" defined in your country?

- What indicators need to be created to measure progress?

- How should those indicators later shape public policies?

- What does "well-being" mean in the country in terms of its worldview and inherent traditional and historical values?

- How can the indicators be used to maximize well-being at all levels?

Creating a specialized model based on the Bhutanese concept requires leadership that is visionary and courageous. It demands commitment, collaboration, and cooperation from the bottom to the top of society. One can argue that a small nation with a tiny population that is more or less homogenous is easier to change than a major world power. This is true, but the concept of creating a country where people are held in importance as individuals as well as collectively is a valid one that strives to give meaning to life amid chaos, confusion, and alienation. As Powdyel describes, "responsible political leadership goes beyond the momentary and the popular and cultivates the more sublime and the sustaining capacities of human beings" (Powdyel, 2011).

Bhutan's rulers are visionary and consistent with implementing their vision. They are aware that the short-term, narrow, survival-oriented perspectives of the human mind are key barriers to sustainability. Sustainability is a process, not an endpoint, and it is the process that is ongoing in Bhutan. The moral foundation, the idea of GNH, and the enlightened monarchy have been the factors that have determined and organized the social and political life in Bhutan. The country's way to development is undoubtedly successful and is based on hard, political and practical work, which has been ongoing for years and is still evolving. While the process of development has been largely successful, it has also not been perfect. It is necessary to note that development is a consistent and continuous long-term process, providing experiences and opportunities for reflection and course correction. The Royal Government of Bhutan and His Majesty, the King of Bhutan, continue to be guided toward the fulfillment of the GNH vision, taking both the strengths of a resilient and ancient society and the genuine virtues of Western democracies.

In the end, Bhutan may not be the Shangri La that the popular media often calls it. Even if the vision and implementation of GNH have its imperfections, it is always better to try than do nothing. We need nothing less than to rethink our globalized growth-based economy and consider a new sustainability-based economic paradigm. As such, we need to create new progress measures and new institutions. Bhutan has clearly touched the nerve of what's possible and raised global awareness around expanded thinking and acting. Using their inspiration, we have a narrow window of opportunity to try something new and revolutionary before it is too late.

REFERENCES

Dorji, G. K. (2015). 91.2% of Bhutanese are happy: GNH survey. Kuensel. Retrieved from http://www.kuenselonline.com/91-2-of-bhutanese-are-happy-gnh-survey/

Gurría, A. (2009). *Charting progress, building visions, improving life.* OECD 3rd World Forum on Statistics. Busan, Korea. Retrieved from http://www.oecd.org/newsroom/chartingprogressbuildingvisionsimprovinglife.htm

Hayward, K., & Coleman, R. (2010). *Educating for GNH*. Thimphu, Bhutan: GPI Atlantic 2010. Retrieved from http://www.gpiatlantic.org/pdf/educatingforgnh/educating_for_gnh_proceedings.pdf

Informal interview with the former Minister of Education. Thakur S Powdyel, Bhutan, Thimphu, March 2016 (Elzbieta Jablonska).

Jablonska, E. (2017). *Educating for gross national happiness by nurturing the concept of green schools for green Bhutan*. Brussels: SADF. Retrieved from https://www.sadf.eu/sadf-comment-78-educating-gross-national-happiness-nurturing-concept-green-schools-green-bhutan-elzbieta-jablonska/

Jowett, B. (translation) (2012). *The Essential: Aristotle*. New York, NY: Start Publishing LLC.

Kelly, A. (2013). *Let nature be your teacher: Bhutan takes conservation into the classroom*. The Guardian. Retrieved from https://www.theguardian.com/global-development/2013/jan/02/nature-teacher-bhutan-conservation-classroom

Kharat, R. S. (ed). (2016). *Bhutan: Contemporary Issues and perspectives*. New Delhi: Adroit Publishers.

Mancall, M. (2004). *Gross national happiness and development: An essay, proceedings of the first international conference on operationalization of gross national happiness*. Thimphu, Bhutan: Centre for Bhutan Studies & GNH.

Meadows, D. H., Randers, J., & Meadows, D. (2006). *Limits to growth: The 30-year update*. London: Earthscan.

Phuntso, K. (2013). *The history of Bhutan*. New Delhi: Random House.

Planning Commission. (1999). *Bhutan 2020: A vision for peace, prosperity and happiness*. Thimpu, Bhutan. Retrieved from http://unpan1.un.org/intradoc/groups/public/documents/APCITY/UNPAN005249.pdf

Powdyel, T. S. (2011). *Statement by Thakur S Powdyel, Minister of Education Royal Government of Bhutan Chairman, Bhutan National Commission for UNESCO during the 36th session of the General Conference*. Paris, France. Retrieved from http://www.unesco.org/new/fileadmin/MULTIMEDIA/HQ/GBS/36GC/pdfs/Speech_Bhutan_EN.pdf

Royal Education Council. (2012). The national education framework: Shaping Bhutan's future. Thimpu, Bhutan. Retrieved from http://www.ibe.unesco.org/curricula/bhutan/bt_alfw_2012_eng.pdf

Stiglitz, J. E., Sen, A. K., & Fitoussi, J. P. (2009). *Report of the Commission on the Measurement of Economic Performance and Social Progress*. Retrieved from http://ec.europa.eu/eurostat/documents/118025/118123/Fitoussi+Commission+report

Ura, K. (2008). *Explanation of GNH Index*. Thimphu: The Centre for Bhutan Studies.

Ura, K., & Karma, G. (ed.). (2004). *Gross national happiness and development, proceedings of the first international seminar on operationalization of gross national happiness*. Thimphu: Centre for Bhutan Studies & GNH.

Wangchuck, D. W. (2012). *Treasures of the Thunder Dragon – A Portrait of Bhutan*. New Delhi: Penguin Books India.

PART V

GROWING OUR FUTURE LEADERS

15

PROTOTYPING IN THE ANTHROPOCENE: A CASE FOR OPTIMISM FROM THE YOUNG SOUTHEAST ASIAN LEADERS INITIATIVE

Christina L. Monroe and Lance C. Boyd

THE ASIA PACIFIC REGION AND THE EAST-WEST CENTER

In the last 60 years, there have been significant economic, social, cultural, and political changes in the Asia Pacific region. This region has experienced industrialization, urbanization, and economic diversification at historically unprecedented rates. As noted by the World Bank (2014), in the last two decades, rapid changes have boosted agricultural output and triggered large movements of people to towns and cities and into work in factories and firms, raising factory-led productivity in most of the region (Packard & Van Nguyen, 2014). The concentration of working people and enterprises has boosted output in fast-growing cities. Countries with low incomes on average a generation ago have been successfully integrated into the global value chain, often through exploiting their labor-cost advantages. Today, therefore, the Asia Pacific region is critical to the US because of the region's rising influence and power, long-standing American allies and new partners, economic growth, and military modernization (East-West Center, 2013).

The East-West Center (EWC) was established by the US Congress in 1960 to promote better relations and understanding among the people and nations of the United States and the Asia Pacific. The EWC brings local and global expertise together to address issues of common concern. The EWC family includes more than 65,000 people from 62 countries who have participated in our applied research, policy, and professional development programs across the Asia Pacific region since 1960. Starting in 2002, the EWC created an in-residence program named the Asia Pacific Leadership Program (APLP) to exclusively address the region's demand for leadership capacity building. Seven years later, the authors, a Senior Manager and Senior Leadership Specialist at the EWC, co-founded the EWC Environmental Leadership Institutes as the first of its kind at the Center. The authors are responsible for the Institute's curriculum, experiential trainings, and coordination of field studies in California and Washington DC, and follow-on mentorship and micro-grants for alumni through an online incubator.

The Sustainable Development Goals (SDGs) established by the United Nations provide shared targets for the EWC's work with diverse communities. The goals enable the EWC to align our work and monitor collective progress across institutions and country boundaries using agreed upon goals. The EWC focuses on multiple SDGs including SDG 5 Gender Equity, SDG 11 Sustainable Cities and Communities, and SDG 14 Life Below Water (United Nations, 2015). However, the EWC Environmental Leadership Institutes and much of our Research Department focuses on SDG 15.

In this chapter, we discuss why and how our leadership training program adopted a prototyping process to build capacity and optimism for ensuring a sustainable future, in line with the SDGs. We specifically focus on SDG 15, Life on Land, that aims to "protect, restore, and promote sustainable use of terrestrial ecosystems, sustainably manage forests, combat desertification, and halt and reverse land degradation and halt biodiversity loss" (United Nations, 2015).

Throughout the chapter, we include lessons learned in the hope of providing guidance for how the field of international leadership education can help bring out the best of our diverse humanity to ensure a sustainable future.

KEY CONCEPTS

The following key concepts inform our discussion on how our leadership training program sought to work for a sustainable future. We adopted a process, namely, prototyping, within the current changing global environment of the Anthropocene epoch, to facilitate the achievement of SDG 15.

Prototyping

Prototyping leverages experiential learning to test and improve ideas at an early stage before large-scale resources are used. While prototyping is common in everyday life, in the workplace "it is a structured way to check that you have an efficient and fitting solution or approach before rolling it out or making a big investment in it" (Nesta, 2014, p. 25). In sum, prototyping is the act of formulating possible solutions to a problem and testing those solutions in small ways before applying them on a bigger scale. Prototyping can help those involved to understand even failure and setbacks as sometimes necessary aspects of an evolving process, forming part of learning, and thus enabling those involved to continue to feel optimistic and empowered through developing and improving their abilities.

The term prototyping gained popularity as part of Lean Startup methodology, created by Eric Ries. When starting a business, Ries suggests, instead of creating an elaborate business plan, raising capital, and launching on a large scale, it was better to undertake something small and cheap first (Ries, 2011). In other words, test prototypes first, then scale up if successful.

Prototyping also gained traction thanks to the design thinking methodology. "Design thinking incorporates constituent or consumer insights in depth and rapid prototyping, all aimed at getting beyond the assumptions that block effective solutions. Design thinking—inherently optimistic, constructive, and experiential—addresses the needs of the people who will consume a product or service and the infrastructure that enables it" (Brown & Wyatt, 2010, p. 32). To design anything, from a laptop to someone's experience of going to the Department of Motor Vehicles, this approach involves testing a prototype before creating the final product or process. Some have claimed that the concept emerged earlier, with Stewart Brand's (2009) Whole Earth Catalog in 1975 and the ensuing movement of people reclaiming rights to use a scientific approach that was no longer seen as the domain of experts in white coats (Guggenheim, 2010). Prototyping celebrates that everyone can be experimenters; we all have our own laboratories.

Anthropocene Epoch

Today, scientists are concluding that human activities rival geophysical forces in driving changes to the Earth system (Steffen, Crutzen, & McNeill, 2007). This has led to the proposal that the Earth has left the Holocene epoch, which extended over the last 10,000 years from when complex human societies developed and has now entered a new geological epoch – the Anthropocene (Crutzen, 2002).

The Anthropocene is characterized by radioactive elements dispersed across the planet through nuclear bomb tests, plastic pollution, soot from power stations, and concrete. The fossil record from the bones left by the global proliferation of the domestic chicken is also a sign marking the Anthropocene for future geologists (Ackerman, 2014). There is now evidence and a term that represents the magnitude of the changes humans are making and experiencing globally at this time (Carrington, 2016).

Sustainable Development Goal 15

The SDGs provide a common platform which our diverse humanity can organize itself around. In our Environmental Leadership Institutes, which we discuss later, we especially focus on SDG 15, Life on Land, which aims to conserve and restore the use of terrestrial ecosystems such as forests, wetlands, drylands, and mountains, halt deforestation to mitigate the impacts of climate change, and reduce the loss of natural habitats and biodiversity (United Nations Development Program, 2018).

Our focus on SDG 15 relates to the need of humans in the Anthropocene to live together with other species and the need for allowing a diversity of ecosystems to thrive. Our work is intended to build capacity among Asia Pacific emerging leaders to achieve the SDG 15 targets. Our work builds their capacity to identify and push for the realization of the SDG targets.

These three key concepts of prototyping, the Anthropocene, and SDG 15 come together in our work to ensure a more sustainable future. We foster prototyping skills in emerging leaders of the Anthropocene to achieve the SDG 15 targets. We believe our work is relevant globally, but we first turn to explain the institutional and regional context of our work in the Asia Pacific at the EWC.

EWC ENVIRONMENTAL LEADERSHIP INSTITUTES

The EWC offers two Environmental Leadership Institutes annually for twenty fellows, aged between 18 and 25 years, in the US for five weeks. Fellows are selected by US embassies in 10 Southeast Asian nations, namely, Brunei, Cambodia, Indonesia, Laos, Malaysia, Myanmar, the Philippines, Singapore, Thailand, and Vietnam. The institutes are under the Young Southeast Asian Leaders Initiative (YSEALI), the flagship program for Southeast Asian leaders of the US Department of State Bureau of Educational and Cultural Affairs. In addition to the 16 exchanges and over 300 fellows hosted in the United States, the EWC also has an active presence with regional programming in Southeast Asia. For example, following the co-creation of successful workshops in Singapore in 2012 and Siem Reap Cambodia in 2016, the EWC hosted the YSEALI Impact XL workshop in partnership with several regional startup accelerators at Inle Lake, Myanmar in May 2018.

   In 2013, the US government launched YSEALI to strengthen leadership development and networking in Southeast Asia, focusing on critical topics identified by youth in the region, including civic engagement, sustainable development, education, and economic growth. YSEALI offers a variety of programs and engagements, including US educational and cultural exchanges, regional exchanges, and seed funding. YSEALI seeks to build the leadership capabilities of the 65% of the population of the region who are under 35 years old, strengthen ties between the United States and Southeast Asia, and nurture an ASEAN (Association of Southeast Asian Nations) community (U.S. Mission to ASEAN, 2013).

   The 10-nation bloc of Southeast Asia includes some of the world's most ecologically diverse areas; all forms of governance ranging from military dictatorships to democracies; and all major world religions. This bloc has also undergone one of the biggest demographic booms the planet has ever experienced. Fifty-four percent of the Indonesian population is under 30 years of age, and more than 50% of Cambodia's population is under 25 years of age (Central Intelligence Agency, 2016, n.d.). In total, there are more people in

Southeast Asia under 35 than the entire population of the United States (U.S. Mission to ASEAN, 2013).

Southeast Asia and the broader Asia Pacific region represent our diverse humanity. How is it possible to bring out the best of the diverse humanity in the region to ensure a sustainable future? We turn now to explain how we use prototyping to build capacity and optimism in emerging leaders from Southeast Asia to help ensure a sustainable future in the Anthropocene.

PROTOTYPE TESTING INSTEAD OF ELABORATE PLANNING

Why not send the fellows home with one good idea and a solid plan? This was the thinking behind our original approach. Before arrival, the fellows would find a partner organization and make a website for their project. During their five weeks in the US, they refined their project plan and presented it to our funders at the US Department of State as their post-program project to be implemented immediately. We had them report back on progress and final results.

Using this model, the fellows were less open-minded to new ideas that were not already aligned with their existing ideas. They were concerned with impressing the funders with the logo and look of the project, rather than with sharing the messy details of implementation. They were only accountable to one partner organization when they returned home, not to a diversity of stakeholders in their countries. They did not have a Plan B, and when Plan A did not work, they were embarrassed or felt they had failed. Without sustained mentorship and moral support, they were unable to derive positive lessons for their next venture.

We were fostering myopia rather than myriad possibilities. We were exposing them to a twentieth century development model and centralized technology and making them translate what they had learned in twenty-first century Southeast Asia. We were also not encouraging flexible thinking or responsive listening to stakeholders' feedback. We were letting them become too attached to their one solution when they needed to embrace the process of problem-solving.

For example, Ali entered our program with a strong academic background in engineering. His research for his university studies focused on biogas. He had great knowledge of the specific details of how to create biogas systems and a strong desire to share the benefits of using biogas as renewable energy. Before the program, we asked Ali and those in his cohort to define a specific project they would further develop during the program. Ali naturally selected his already-advanced project ideas around biogas. At his first presentation, he gave a long lecture on the details of biogas engineering and its benefits. When staff and peers asked questions or gave suggestions, he was dismissive and returned to his pre-program project plan. We realized then that Ali was so committed to his solution that he was blocking the growth of a prototyping mindset. We needed to help Ali to step back, think about the bigger picture of energy generation and use, and consider multiple possible solutions. To be successful in the Anthropocene in the long term, Ali needed to learn a process of creating and recreating solutions alongside a diversity of stakeholders and contexts. Having one good plan might work for Ali on one occasion, but the ability to prototype would help ensure success over time.

In cases like Ali's and others, we were especially concerned about the message being sent that fellows could create a plan by themselves in the US to take back and implement in their communities. We know their community contexts are diverse and quite different than the US; therefore, they would need to consider those differences before creating solutions. We also knew they could encounter resistance from stakeholders who felt they were showing overconfidence in introducing foreign solutions. Community hierarchies and protocols may not support a young person returning from foreign countries who brings ready-made solutions for implementation.

OPTIMISM AND PROTOTYPING IN EWC ENVIRONMENTAL LEADERSHIP INSTITUTES

Our fellows have in-depth knowledge in their disciplines. However, the cross-disciplinary, big-picture view of life on land, as defined in SDG 15, can be overwhelming for them. Our role is to ensure confidence increases at the same rate as problems are explored and to foster an evidence-based, pragmatic optimism.

We start our process of increasing optimism by providing opportunities for critical thinking, which we refer to as unlearning. The process of unlearning starts on the first day of the Institute, through reflection on our species, and considering that, as Steven Pinker (2018, p. 134) writes, "it's time to retire the morality play in which modern humans are a vile race of despoilers and plunderers who will hasten the apocalypse unless they undo the Industrial Revolution, renounce technology, and return to an ascetic harmony with nature."

Unlearning is a central theme during the fourth week of the five-week program when we visited California. We start in Yosemite National Park working with US National Park rangers to explore the history of the area with an emphasis on the indigenous who managed the ecosystem with practices such as setting targeted fires. Fellows unlearn the romantic notion that native people lived in complete harmony with the environment and that "wilderness" does not refer to a pristine sanctuary but instead is a product of civilization (Cronon, 1996).

After visiting Yosemite, we move to San Francisco's Golden Gate National Parks. In Golden Gate, US National Park rangers help us continue to think critically about wilderness by using their urban park and UNESCO Biosphere Reserve. While still in California, we explore emerging alternatives to conventional environmentalism such as the pragmatic approach to environmental protection called Ecomodernism. Ecomodernists are optimistic that humanity can shape a future that promotes protecting beautiful, wild places while ensuring that the seven-going-on-nine billion people in the world can lead secure, free, prosperous, and fulfilling lives. This approach offers an alternative to the "radicalism and fatalism" that conventional wisdom on environmental change offers and instead offers an optimistic view that environmental problems are solvable (Pinker, 2018).

How is a prototyping mindset to be fostered? The Southeast Asian emerging leaders in our EWC Environmental Leadership Institutes begin the process by joining a five-person, mixed-country, interdisciplinary team prior to arrival in the United States. They research one Institute strategy, learn about US organizations currently using the strategy, and develop a training program for their peers to learn the strategy. In the Institute, they share their research, run learning and service journeys to organizations, and mentor their peers to develop their own prototypes to test with stakeholders upon return home.

For example, an Indonesian soil scientist, a Filipina marine biologist, a Laotian English teacher, a Thai sociologist, and a Malaysian environmental engineer are assigned to research how impact accelerators for startups can address environmental issues. Accelerators are typically three-month long programs offering seed funding and mentorship to speed up or accelerate the growth of a new venture. Impact accelerators have adapted the method to support ventures with a social or environmental benefit (Hathaway, 2016). The fellows learn what an accelerator is and read about US accelerators they will work with, such as Elemental Excelerator or Blue Startups. They create a prototype of a startup impact accelerator around, for example, the water-energy-food nexus, to launch in all five countries of the team members. When the team arrives in the US, they lead sessions to teach the other fifteen members of the cohort what an accelerator does. They mentor their peers in developing their own accelerators for their home communities. Team members target cohort members with shared areas of expertise, for example, agriculture, and thus mentor them in how to launch an agriculture accelerator that promotes fish farming, community subscription agriculture (CSA), or biotechnical social enterprises. The cohort members pitch their prototypes to staff working with established accelerators and get feedback to further refine their prototypes for use in their next iteration.

For the authors, the key elements of prototyping are: (1) a mindset of curiosity, (2) openness to feedback, (3) empathy for all stakeholders, and (4) integrity in relation to what the data is showing. Curiosity and openness to feedback ensure that there is no excessive attachment with specific solutions but an ongoing focus on the problem. It allows for personal diversity and the opinions of others to be aired and considered to ensure all options are on the table before proceeding. Empathy for all stakeholders means team members must seek to understand the experience, needs, and desires of others. Not all stakeholders will be able to articulate their needs directly. Thus, team members must be curious and empathetic to allow needs to be revealed. To achieve the SDG 15 targets of caring for life on land, exercising empathy is key. Keeping integrity in relation to what the data are showing means taking an unbiased look at the results of work undertaken. In seeking effective results, there is always a need to clearly measure and benchmark progress.

Prototyping corresponds well with understandings that leadership is contextual and can be exercised from any position with or without formal authority. Our fellows most often operate in hierarchical systems with less access to resources and, given their youth and relative lack of experience, are afforded less credibility. Thus, prototyping that incorporates stakeholders' feedback and creates effective results is a more persuasive means to influence, change, and lead their societies in terms of who they are today.

We use a simulation involving six strangers stranded on an island to reinforce the need for prototyping and foster empathy toward stakeholders. The six strangers range from an injured elderly fisherman to a nuclear scientist badly needed to address an accident at a nuclear reactor. Fellows are asked to decide who will be saved by a pilot who happens to pass the island in a two-seater plane before the approaching hurricane makes air travel impossible.

Arguments ensue over who should be rescued. However, fellows rarely reflect in the heat of the moment and ask, "are we the right people to be making this decision?" or "should anyone else be included in determining who we save?" Once a decision is made or time runs out, actors dressed as the six people enter the room. The group usually becomes very hesitant to say who they have selected once they realize they will have to confront in person those they did not rescue. The characters ask if a decision was made. In disgust, they reply with the question "why didn't you consult us, since we are the ones stranded on the island?" From here one understands the importance of considering stakeholder input in the process of making decisions particularly when they are not present when decisions are being made.

In the simulation debrief, the fellows make the link that the diverse members of their communities who deal with multiple issues, whether deforestation or the loss of biodiversity, are like the characters on the island. The fellows must seek them out, empathize, consult, and collaborate with "those on the island" to find solutions that will work in their home communities.

We let them understand that we are not asking them to make a perfect plan, crafted individually without input from their community while they are in the US. We are instead asking them to create multiple prototypes to share with their communities, and to find out alongside their communities which prototype is likely to work best and which could be implemented together.

At the end of the five weeks, fellows return to their communities with multiple prototypes and a process for getting stakeholder feedback. Over the following few months, they find established partners to host them and collaboratively determine next steps with their team, which usually involves a mix of local and international cohort members. They can then opt to apply for our online EWC Alumni Impact Incubator, which provides mentorship and seed grants to realize their prototype.

We now call the five-week institute training Phase 2 of the program, with Phase 1 involving their work before and Phase 3 their work after. This terminology indicates the lifelong process of prototyping we expect and support. We support the fellows through the EWC and US State Department initiatives such as grant competitions, regional workshops, and the online EWC Alumni Incubator.

PROTOTYPING IN ACTION: SOME EXAMPLES

In this section, we discuss three examples of how fellows used the prototyping process learned in our EWC Environmental Leadership Institutes to return home and generate positive effects in their communities and ecosystems. We share what we learned from each story, and link the effects we uncovered to SDG 15, to address the core question of how the best in our diverse humanity can be brought out for a sustainable future.

ASEAN PEACE: Peace and Environment Accelerator for Community Enterprise

The first success story illustrates the importance of optimism in respect of prototyping for a sustainable future. Ferth, Catherine, and Christian met in our 2015 Institute. They were on different teams but shared a home community in Mindanao in the southern Philippines. There is an armed conflict in Mindanao involving issues of sovereignty and resources that has continued for hundreds of years. Muslim traders from Indonesia and Malaysia settled in Mindanao in the southern Philippines long before the Christian Spaniards came to the country in the sixteenth century. The Spaniards were not successful, as they were in the north, at controlling and converting Mindanao. It was not until the Americans came in the early 1900s that Mindanao was brought under central control but not without ongoing hostility and conflict. Logging and other natural resource extraction have continued to cause conflicts as outsider interests encroach on local populations. The armed conflicts are usually restricted to local areas, but the entire island has been affected by disruptions to education, economic growth, and basic services (Schiavo-Campo & Judd, 2005).

The fellows from Mindanao had experienced first-hand the problems caused by the conflict in their communities. They were especially empathetic to the plight of ambitious youth with talent and drive but with few opportunities. They focused on this issue together and began to generate ideas and prototypes. As part of the Institute, they created prototype designs for zero-waste systems, urban renewal, and wastewater biotreatment. They pitched their prototypes to area experts in the US, received feedback, and incorporated the feedback into their subsequent prototypes. In the final week of the program, we had an intense late-night conversation with them about what they wanted to do with their prototype when they returned to Mindanao. The sovereignty conflict and the ways the conflict had limited the entrepreneurial and inventive spirit of young people in Mindanao weighed heavily on them. They wanted to help their people as well as the ecosystems and other species that share their island. The saw a link between the SDG 15 target of sustainable management of resources and success for the next generation.

In the final days of the 2015 Institute, they crafted another prototype, combining lessons learned from the rapid prototyping of the previous five weeks, and created the ASEAN PEACE Project – Peace and Environment Accelerator for Community Enterprise. The mission of ASEAN PEACE is to provide mentorship, support, and seed funding to young entrepreneurs in Mindanao (ASEAN Peace Project, n.d.). As the name indicates, ASEAN PEACE aims to accelerate community-based enterprises that will contribute to peace and the environment of Mindanao.

Nine months after the Institute, the group launched the first day of ASEAN PEACE programming at Ateneo de Davao University in Mindanao. There, 22 young entrepreneurs spent the week learning about social enterprise development, community development models, and future scenarios. At the end of the week, they pitched their community enterprises to a panel of international and local experts. Projects included an ecotourism sailing venture aimed at reaching homeless children living on the docks and a social enterprise that gave young artists public outlets for their works. The winner, with an agribusiness smart yields app called Cloud Farm, received 2500 US dollars to further his work. Cloud Farm aims to help meet the SDG 15 target of halting deforestation through increasing yields on current agricultural lands, thus eliminating the need to clear additional lands.

Human—Orangutan Conflict Mitigation

The second success story illustrates how optimism and prototyping are key to engaging stakeholders, especially youth who confront major challenges.

Riyan came from Kalimantan on the Island of Borneo for our spring 2017 Institute. The first prototype he proposed was the Pongobater, an incubator concerning Pongo issues. Pongos are orangutans (translated as forest people in Bahasa, the official language of Indonesia) and Kalimantan hosts the world's largest intact community of wild Pongos. He wanted to address the problem of human—orangutan conflict. Throughout the five weeks working with Riyan, it was clear that he had specific people and a setting in mind whenever he spoke about his post-program actions. He was embedded within his work; he had a role as a trainer for International Animal Rescue, and he loved his work with youth and pongos.

He was so thrilled the day we discussed examples of ways humans are contributing to reviving species and ecosystems, specifically, through reforesting in Japan and coral reef creation in Thailand. It seemed to confirm a deep belief he had, otherwise buried by the prevailing message of human destruction, that humans can be positive and productive members of an ecosystem. He seemed to now have the evidence he needed to convince others.

Riyan's team hosted a pitch session for the cohort in which fellows shared their prototypes and got feedback. When it was Riyan's turn to ask questions and give feedback, he always asked the same thing, "how are you going to make it fun?" If they hesitated too long, he offered specific suggestions that clearly came from the first-hand experience. He made sure his peers' serious issues were balanced by fun. He continued to develop his own prototypes and kept "fun" central.

Within weeks of his return home, we saw an excited posting about a "conservation boot camp" Riyan was launching in Kalimantan. We soon received an invitation to Skype with his first cohort and found ourselves fish-faced on a screen yelling punctuated English while Riyan translated into Bahasa. It was a joy to see him leading the cohort, playing the same role that we had played for his cohort, but to an audience completely beyond our reach. We could never directly influence those he can affect, namely, those squirmy rural kids who want to have fun. Riyan was trying to translate back their questions and their ideas. They were prototyping their own ideas for how to mitigate human—orangutan conflicts in their villages. We could not understand what was being said, but we are sure he asked each of them after their pitch, "how will you make it fun?"

Today Riyan is launching an even larger Pongobater with funding from our online Alumni Impact Incubator and support from IAR. With more funding, attention, and his natural optimism, he is able to express his own vision for a good Anthropocene. The effects of his work in advancing SDG 15 are clear. Poaching and trafficking of orangutans decreased in communities where members joined Riyan's conversation boot camp. The communities were also more likely to integrate biodiversity values into their local planning, development decisions, and poverty-reduction strategies.

Human–orangutan conflict is a daunting challenge (Kareiva, Marvier, & Lalasz, 2012) but Riyan did not shy away from it. He instead enlisted the innovating and prototyping mindset of the communities' youngest leaders.

The Chili Padi Academy

The third success story shows the multiplier effect of prototyping strategies and how some fellows generated effects beyond their own communities through their project. Amalina, Jeffrey, and Ines come from three very different communities in Malaysia, Singapore and Indonesia respectively. In their 2015 Institute, we focused on US environmental history and the role of prototyping over time in the US, through investment in innovation, in addition to regulation (Merchant, 2007). In other words, we observed how movements for environmental improvement could metaphorically use not only carrots but also sticks to bring about the desired change. The three fellows wanted to address the need for more cross-border collaboration and understanding in their three countries concerning environmental challenges. A prime example involved deforestation in Indonesia and parts of Malaysia to create palm and rubber plantations (East-West Center, n.d.). The burning of forests to clear the land creates a haze that sometimes blows to great distances and thus creates animosity within other parts of Malaysia and Singapore. The fellows created multiple prototypes, then brought the best of their prototypes together at the end of the five weeks to create the multi-country Chili Padi Academy which won seed funding from the YSEALI Seeds for the Future grant competition.

The Chili Padi Academy, modeled after US startup accelerators studied in our Institute such as Y Combinator, is an environmental leadership accelerator for high school students from Malaysia, Indonesia, and Singapore. At the Chili Padi Academy, high school participants traveled to Singapore to learn leadership techniques, tour behind-the-scenes of organizations such as Singapore's Food Bank, and develop their own prototype initiatives that contribute to meeting SDG 15 targets using creative, youth-led strategies. Two initiatives developed through Chili Padi include Project bECOme which explored methods to reduce plastic waste going into rivers and the Kemaman Used Cooking Oil Collection Center that recycles cooking oil for renewable energy while preventing it from entering the surrounding ecosystems. The high school participants were given five months to test their prototype before a final gathering in Bandung Indonesia.

The Chili Padi Academy team did something rare for a youth-led project: they turned over the reins to the participants. They were not only doing prototyping themselves, but also protected a prototyping space for others to come up with ideas, to experiment, and even to fail. They modeled a prototyping mindset and encouraged their students to think of innovative ideas and develop them. As their mentors, we reflected on this paying forward of protective prototyping spaces. By creating that space for them, we enabled them to return home and create it for others, and so on into the future.

CONCLUSION

In this chapter, we sought to address the central theme of the book on how to bring out the best of our diverse humanity to ensure a sustainable future through sharing our experiences in cultivating optimism and a prototyping mindset among emerging leaders from Southeast Asia. We specifically focused on building capacity to achieve SDG 15 targets.

We began with the institutional and regional context of our work in the Asia Pacific and specifically Southeast Asia. We then provided definitions of the key concepts of prototyping, the Anthropocene and SDG 15. We shared how we use prototyping in our Environmental Leadership Institutes. Lastly, we offered three success stories on how fellows identified a challenge and used prototyping that resulted in positive effects within their communities and led to progress toward SDG 15.

Our purpose in sharing is to encourage others, especially international leadership educators, to see optimism and the sometimes-messy process of prototyping as legitimate approaches for ensuring a sustainable future. We work with a sliver of our diverse humanity, but see the exciting potential our approach has to bring about effects on a wider scale within other communities. Indeed, we see our prototyping method as a key means to achieve the SDGs in the Anthropocene.

REFERENCES

Ackerman, D. (2014). *The human age: The world shaped by us*. New York, NY: W. W. Norton & Company.

ASEAN Peace Project. (n.d.). *Social entrepreneurship*. Retrieved from https://www.aseanpeaceproject.org/app2016. Accessed on May 1, 2018.

Brand, S. (2009). *Whole Earth discipline: Why dense cities, nuclear power, transgenic crops, restored wildlands, and geoengineering are necessary*. New York, NY: Penguin Books.

Brown, T., & Wyatt, J. (2010). Design thinking for social innovation. *Stanford Social Innovation Review, Winter*, 30–35.

Carrington, D. (2016, August 29). The Anthropocene epoch: Scientists declare dawn of human-influenced age. *The Guardian*. Retrieved from https://www.theguardian.com

Central Intelligence Agency. (2016). East & Southeast Asia: Indonesia. In *The World Factbook*. Retrieved from https://www.cia.gov/library/publications/the-world-factbook/geos/print_id.html

Central Intelligence Agency. (n.d.). East & Southeast Asia: Cambodia. In *The World Factbook*. Retrieved from https://www.cia.gov/library/publications/the-world-factbook/geos/print_cb.html

Cronon, W. (1996). *Uncommon ground: Rethinking the human place in nature*. New York, NY: W. W. Norton & Company.

Crutzen, P. J. (2002). Geology of mankind: The anthropocene. *Nature, 415*, 23.

East-West Center. (2013). *Asia matters for America/America matters for Asia [Brochure]*. Washington, DC: East-West Center.

East-West Center. (n.d.). *Economic development and land-use change: Expansion of cash crops in Southeast Asia*. Retrieved from https://www. eastwestcenter.org/research/research-projects/economic-development-and-land-use-change-expansion-cash-crops-in-southeas

Guggenheim, M. (2010). The long history of prototypes. *Limn*, November. Retrieved from https://limn.it/articles/the-long-history-of-prototypes

Hathaway, I. (2016, March 1). What startup accelerators really do. *Harvard Business Review*. Retrieved from https://hbr.org/2016/03/what-startup-accelerators-really-do

Kareiva, P., Marvier, M., & Lalasz, R. (2012). *Conservation in the Anthropocene: Beyond solitude and fragility*. Winter. Retrieved from https://thebreakthrough.org

Merchant, C. (2007). *American environmental history*. New York, NY: Columbia University Press.

Nesta. (2014). *DIY development impact and you: Practical tools to trigger and support social innovation*. Retrieved from www.diytoolkit.org. Accessed on May 25, 2018.

Packard, T. G., & Van Nguyen, T. (2014). *East Asia Pacific at work: Employment, enterprise, and well-being*. Washington, DC: World Bank Publications, xxi. http://doi.org/10.1596/978-1-4648-0004-7

Pinker, S. (2018). *Enlightenment now*. New York, NY: Penguin Books Limited/Viking.

Ries, E. (2011). *The lean startup: How today's entrepreneurs use continuous innovation to create radically successful businesses*. New York, NY: Currency-The Crown Publishing Group.

Schiavo-Campo, S., & Judd, M. (2005). *The Mindanao Conflict in the Philippines: Roots, Costs, and Potential Peace Dividend*. Washington, DC: The World Bank. Retrieved from http://documents.worldbank.org/curated/en/701961468776746799/The-Mindanao-conflict-in-the-Philippines-roots-costs-and-potential-peace-dividend

Steffen, W., Crutzen, P., & McNeill, J. R. (2007). The anthropocene: Are humans now overwhelming the great forces of nature? *Ambio, 36*,

614–621. doi: 10.1579/0044-7447(2007)36[614: TAAHNO]2.0.CO;2; pmid: 18240674.

U.S. Mission to ASEAN. (2013). Young Southeast Asian leaders initiative. Retrieved from https://asean.usmission.gov/yseali/yseali-about. Accessed on May 25, 2018.

United Nations. (2015). *Transforming our world: The 2030 agenda for sustainable development*. New York, NY: United Nations Publications.

United Nations Development Program. (2018). Goal 15: Life on land. Retrieved from http://www.undp.org/content/undp/en/home/sustainable-development-goals/goal-15-life-onland.html. Accessed on May 25, 2018.

World Bank. (2014). *East Asia Pacific at work: Employment, enterprise, and well-being*. Washington, DC: World Bank.

16

EVOLVING LEADERSHIP FOR A SUSTAINABLE FUTURE – CEEDS OF PEACE

Kerrie Urosevich and Maya Soetoro-Ng

INTRODUCTION

Ceeds of Peace (CoP) is dedicated to raising leaders who will create peaceful, just, and sustainable communities. Sustainable communities are those that come together to protect their most vulnerable members, while designing and adapting socioeconomic systems to reflect the unique needs of their people and land.

The accomplishments of such transformative leaders as Leymah Gbowee, Susan B. Anthony, Elizabeth Blackwell, and Shirin Ebadi were not accidental. Rather, all these leaders had to learn and practice peacebuilding skills throughout their lives. What do the engineers of powerful and enduring political and humanitarian changes have in common? We at CoP identified seven essential leadership skills: critical thinking, courage, communication, compassion, conflict resolution, commitment, and collaboration. These skills are called the "ceeds of peace" because they all start with the letter "C" and enable people to grow sustainable, peaceful communities. Such "ceeds" are necessary for establishing healthy foundations for generations to come. CoP brings families, teaching faculty and staff, and community partners together to learn the skills of peacebuilding leadership and pass on those skills to the children in their community.

Peacebuilding efforts are often interventional rather than preventative. For example, resources are given to anti-bullying or anti-violence programs only after they have already had a negative effect on the social environment or have become a public health issue. According to the Center for Public Health Policy (2012), only 3% of healthcare spending goes to public health programs. Violence is predictable and therefore preventable. Given that it, "threatens the lives and physical and mental health of millions of people, overburdens health systems, undermines the development of human capital, and slows economic and social development," we should be focused on a proactive approach to prevent it (Violence Prevention Alliance, 2010).

CoP focuses on preventing the underlying issues that negatively affect communities' health, safety and well-being. The World Health Organization (WHO) published a series of briefings in 2009 that reviewed the evidence of violence prevention programs. The briefings showed how programs that address underlying causes and risk factors can reduce the frequency of violence-related outcomes by up to 50%. (World Health Organization (2010) According to an Institute of Medicine (IOM, 2000) report on behavior change, "It is unreasonable to expect that people will change their behavior easily when so many forces in the social, cultural, and physical environment conspire against such change." Rather than intervening after people are injured and working with one individual at a time, primary prevention means changing the larger environment before problems arise. According to author Rachel Davis, "violence and trauma are linked to the onset of chronic diseases and mental health problems, and caring for chronic diseases represents the costliest and fastest-growing portion of healthcare costs for individuals, businesses, and government. Yet violence is preventable, and prevention is of great value by any criteria." (Davis, 2011, p. 1)

A complex issue such as violence requires a multifaceted, comprehensive solution that moves beyond treating the effects and also addresses the underlying causes of violence at the community and societal levels. Similarly, ethnic or racial conflicts are seldom given attention until after violence erupts. This is partly because people do not recognize that many social ills are intertwined. Solving the issues of ethnic violence or violence against women or deteriorating natural resources while supporting international development demands cross-sector, cross-disciplinary involvement. Critical thinking, collaboration, and problem-solving skills are thus imperative for overcoming the social and economic challenges of the world.

CoP strives to affect cultural change and prevent violence, discrimination, and suffering by supporting the health and resilience of individuals and communities. Specifically, CoP helps local communities and educational institutions raise future peacebuilders by encouraging cultural values such as dialogue, collaboration, mindfulness, and courageous action. CoP emphasizes action because it is never enough to state commitments to change. People must move on their commitments. Leadership for a sustainable future is not a matter of acquiring a particular political mindset; it is about crafting a daily practice of action and service.

Any shift in the culture requires changing educational content and pedagogy. We worked as teacher–educators and facilitators for many years before founding CoP in 2011. We saw that most educational content continues to be presented as meaningless lists of facts to be memorized. We also saw that student "leadership" roles were usually reserved for the students with the highest grades or those that were most extroverted. Furthermore, we noticed that many teachers whom we encountered and asked did not see themselves as leaders, even though they were in a position to champion social, political, and humanitarian change and help their students grow the skills required to be peacebuilders. We realized that it was time for a cultural shift in how leadership is defined and who gets to be perceived as "leaders." They seemed to define leadership as that which is held and displayed in positions of executive power or by individuals at the front of social movements. By contrast, CoP defines "peacebuilding leadership" as practices that can be adopted by anybody to enrich the lives of individuals and communities. CoP works to empower individuals to see themselves as peacebuilding leaders in whatever place and time they reside, no matter whether they lead from out front, behind, or alongside others. Peacebuilding leaders courageously draw upon their unique strengths to stand up and take action when needed. They are nonviolent listeners and communicators who are competent in working across differences and are thus able to change minds, hearts, and policies for the betterment of all. Finally, they appreciate that a commitment to cross-sector collaboration is required to instigate and support the systemic changes necessary for improving human lives and the wellbeing of the planet. Peacebuilding leadership results in systems that prioritize the health of people and the planet; they ultimately sustain a more just and peaceful world.

CoP is specifically aligned with recent local, national, and international efforts focusing on youth leadership for social change. In 2015, the United

Nations Security Council unanimously adopted UNSCR 2250. Called Youth4Peace, this groundbreaking resolution recognizes that "young people play an important and positive role in the maintenance and promotion of international peace and security" ("UNSCR 2250 Introduction", n.d.). The resolution focuses on five key pillars for action: participation, protection, prevention, partnerships, and disengagement and reintegration. The resolution urges UN member states to give youth a greater voice in making decisions at local, national, regional, and international levels and set up mechanisms that enable young people to participate meaningfully in peace processes. CoP provides a working model for teaching peacebuilding leadership among our youth. For example, in 2017, CoP inaugurated *Youth Talk Back* sessions to empower youth to lead themselves through design-thinking processes to identify barriers to peace and strengthen civic engagement skills. The sessions were facilitated by high school students for youth from 12 to 18 years old. Topics of discussion included the importance of voting, gender equality, racial and ethnic tensions, and human rights. Participating students then designed action plans for their schools and communities to address the issues that mattered most to them.

This chapter explores the intersections between peacebuilding, sustainability, and youth leadership. We first define "peacebuilding" as an active process that is intimately linked to the skills necessary for meeting the United Nation's 2030 Sustainable Development Goals (SDGs, United Nations, n.d.). The metrics associated with these goals reflect the aggregate health and equity of societies around the globe; they can also be used to evaluate the health and equity of any given community. We then examine different leadership styles for social change and the importance of investing in raising youth leaders who will promote equity and human rights. The remainder of the chapter summarizes the framework for the CoP workshops and how CoP facilitators empower workshop participants to create action plans that move youth toward becoming peacebuilders able to tackle the most protracted challenges facing humanity.

PEACEBUILDING

Peacebuilding leadership begins by defining "peace" as a dynamic, active process rather than as a passive or neutral state of being or a period of time in which conflict and violence are absent. For this, CoP draws on the work of systems design expert Robert Ricigliano, Director of the Institute of World Affairs at the University of Wisconsin. Ricigliano describes peace as "fundamentally about how people work together (a process measure) to meet the basic needs of a population and how well they are meeting those needs (a substantive measure)" (Ricigliano, 2012, p. 16). CoP, therefore, focuses on sustainable proactive actions for sustained solutions rather than on ad hoc peacemaking or peacekeeping interventions.

To understand this better, it is useful to examine three different kinds of "peace" processes that are often and erroneously used interchangeably: *peacekeeping*, *peacemaking*, and *peacebuilding*.

- *Peacekeeping* is an intervention in specific violent circumstances; it usually refers to using military forces to stabilize an area and prevent outbreaks of additional violence. The deployment of peacekeepers by the United Nations is an example of peacekeeping.

- *Peacemaking* is another interventionist approach but uses diplomatic processes for resolving the conflict. Mediation is one of many peacemaking tools.

- *Peacebuilding* is a systemic, long-term approach for preventing and resolving the conflict. Since it focuses on developing sustainable resolutions, it often generates economic, social, and educational initiatives intended to address structural barriers to peace. Peacebuilding is both strategic and collaborative and involves interpersonal processes intended to transform relationships between individuals and within communities.

These definitions build on Johan Galtung's work on "positive peace" (Galtung, 1975). He posited that peacebuilding processes were structured differently from peacekeeping or peacemaking tools. He also suggested that peacebuilding efforts had to concentrate on the root causes of conflict if it were to make peace sustainable. For example, a high school counselor might use peacemaking methods to help resolve gender-based violent conflicts between young men and women who were in couples. However, to make a sustainable change at the high school, the counselor might need to strategize with administrators and teachers about ways of educating students to understand gender-based violence and recognize healthy versus unhealthy relationships. This would shift the focus from intervention to prevention. Without the use of peacebuilding tools, peacekeeping and peacemaking efforts have no lasting effects.

SUSTAINABLE PEACE, SUSTAINABLE DEVELOPMENT

The UN World Commission on Environment and Development defines sustainable development as "development that meets the needs of the present without compromising the ability of future generations to meet their own needs" (*Our Common Future: Report of the World Commission on Environment & Development*, 1987, p. 2). In 2016, the United Nations set 17 interconnected global SDGs for all nations to aim for by 2030:

(1) No poverty.

(2) Zero hunger.

(3) Good health and well-being.

(4) Quality education.

(5) Gender equality.

(6) Clean water and sanitation.

(7) Affordable and clean energy.

(8) Decent work and economic growth.

(9) Industry, innovation, and infrastructure.

(10) Reduced inequalities.

(11) Sustainable cities and communities.

(12) Responsible consumption and production.

(13) Climate action.

(14) Life below water.

(15) Life on land.

(16) Peace, justice, and strong institutions.

(17) Partnerships for the goals.

Each SDG includes indicators for evaluating the current health and well-being of the people and the planet. Improving any of the indicators within the SDGs should lead to a more prosperous, just, and secure world. For example, progress toward SDG 5 may be evaluated by the numbers of girls attending school and women in the workforce or in government leadership roles, as well as rates of domestic violence against women in society. The same metrics may be used to gauge the efficacy of any systems or programs created to further the global goals.

Some of the measurable or "substantive indicators" of peace, such as "good governance, rule of law and respect for human rights, security, economic vitality, social capital," are related to specific SDGs (i.e., 3, 5, 8, 10, 16). The peacebuilding tools used in CoP's workshops also echo many of the processes needed to achieve the global SDGs. For example, CoPs aim to improve how "society deals with problems or issues on an ongoing basis" relate directly to achieving SDGs 4, 10, 16, and 17. Since conflict is often associated with competition for resources or interests that are shaped by divergent value systems, it is easy to understand that building capacities to work through conflicts collaboratively would assist any country or community in meeting the SDGs.

We at CoP believe that the collective achievement and sustainability of the UN's global goals require younger generations to start learning and practicing peacebuilding leadership skills as early as possible. Youth will then emerge into adulthood prepared to transform the deleterious social and economic conditions that currently plague the human species and the planet.

YOUTH LEADERSHIP FOR SOCIAL CHANGE

Since the solutions to the many challenges facing the world have a relatively long horizon, the youth of every country must learn to lead from an early age, and their elders must give them opportunities to experience the fruits of their labors. We at CoP have discovered that, given the space and time to practice leadership, youth become increasingly courageous and willing to participate in innovative problem-solving processes alongside people who may think very differently from them. Peacebuilding and leadership are tangible, symbiotic, and pragmatic partners. In developing the CoP framework for raising youth leaders, we drew from Kouzes and Posner's (2012) research into leadership development and peacebuilding around the globe. They identified five practices of exemplary leadership:

(1) *Model the way* through words and action. This is particularly important for CoP's pedagogy since children do what they see much more frequently than they do what they're told (Epstein, 2010).

(2) *Inspire a shared vision* to reach consensus on goals and get people excited enough to commit to that vision. CoP helps people create roadmaps to realize a shared future in the first stage of action plan development known as "Envisioning the Harvest" (see below).

(3) *Challenge the process* to change the status quo when necessary. CoP supports this by introducing children and adults to tools that build courage and creativity and foster critical thinking and conflict resolution.

(4) *Enable others to act* as part of viable teams. CoP teaches people strategies that support courage, collaboration, communication, community mobilization, and commitment so they can build teams to carry out action plans.

(5) *Encourage the heart* by recognizing people for good work and celebrating successes. Such encouragement enables participants in CoP workshops to gain more compassion, commitment, and a sense of community, which then helps them build character in the children in their lives.

Although CoP draws primarily on Kouzes and Posner's leadership model, we have also been influenced by other styles, known variously as servant, benevolent, democratic or participatory, cross-cultural, or transformational leadership (Table 1). All these leadership styles share certain vital principles, including ethics, cultural responsiveness, integrity, collaboration, egalitarianism, and community.

These models also suggest that peacebuilding leadership is not primarily the work of governments, business executives, or nonprofit organizations. It is the responsibility of individuals to harness peacebuilding resources, undertake daily acts of peace, and inspire others to do the same. These forms of leadership do not come easily to most people. This is because these styles of leadership require people to take a gradual, step-by-step approach to

Table 1. Influential Leadership Styles.

Leadership Style (Source)	Key Principles or Dimensions	Focus or Scale
Servant (Greenleaf, 1977)	Social responsibility and social entrepreneurship	Improve organizations to enrich individual lives and create a "just and caring world"
Benevolent (Karakas & Sarigollu, 2012)	Ethical sensitivity, spiritual depth, positive engagement, and community responsiveness	Individuals, communities
Democratic/participative (Avolio, Waldman, & Yammarino, 1991; Bass & Avolio, 1993)	Mutual respect, collaboration in planning, goal-setting, and problem-solving processes	Individuals including subordinates, peers, superiors, and other stakeholders
Cross-cultural (House, Javidan, & Dorfman, 2001)	Working across differences; nine cultural dimensions of effective leadership: power distance, uncertainty avoidance, humane orientation, institutional collectivism, in-group collectivism, assertiveness, gender egalitarianism, future orientation, and performance orientation	Individuals and collectives
Transformational (Avolio et al. 1991; Bass & Avolio, 1993)	4 'I's: idealized influence, inspirational motivation, intellectual stimulation, and individualized consideration; creative insight, persistence, energy, intuition, and sensitivity	Integrate needs of individuals throughout organizations

peacebuilding so they can implement change more efficiently later on. Most people are unprepared to adopt such a "go slow to go fast" mentality or do not possess the necessary skill sets because they have not learned them in childhood. Few young people reach adulthood prepared to collaborate with others to solve problems effectively.

CoP aims to rectify these problems by helping children grow leadership and peacebuilding skills from an early age. By building skill sets for action, young leaders realize that peace is not some utopian ideal or slogan, but an ongoing commitment to dialogic and democratic processes. They come to understand that peacebuilding leadership can be undertaken in any profession. They become social entrepreneurs who serve others even as they profit themselves. As they come to recognize the benefit of bettering the circumstances of everyone in their communities, they will be inspired to continue building a more sustainable and resilient future for generations to come.

The conviction that peacebuilding is intentional and starts from within the self is the foundation of the CoP approach. CoP thus provides a research-based framework for raising peacebuilders, outlined next.

CEEDS OF PEACE FRAMEWORK

We started creating the framework for CoP in 2010 by examining the attributes of well-known local, national, and international peacebuilding leaders from the past (e.g., Dorothy Day, Eleanor Roosevelt, Elie Weisel, Wangari Muta Maathai, and Cesar Chavez) and present (e.g., Hina Jalani, John Paul Lederach, Desmond Tutu, Louise Freschette, Jimmy Carter, Oscar Arias Sanchez, Malala Yousafzai, Thich Nhat Hanh, Betty Bigombe, and Gro Harlem Brundtland). While each leader might define peace differently, all transformed theoretical abstractions into community engagement and action. They also drew on the underused peacebuilding resources (human and otherwise) in their communities to implement change.

After identifying the seven most important peacebuilding skills employed by these leaders (i.e., the "ceeds" listed at the beginning of this chapter), we grouped them into three categories according to whether they most directly facilitated peace with oneself, with others, or in communities (**Fig. 1**). Developing skills in each of these categories unlocks the potential for peacebuilding leadership among all people. This became the basic framework for CoP workshops.

CoP workshop facilitators guide adult participants (e.g., teachers, family members, and community leaders) along three peacebuilding leadership paths that correspond to the three categories of "C" skills. Adults learn how to plant critical thinking skills and courage within each child (ceeds with

Fig. 1. Three Categories of 'C' Skills.

self), plant the tools of successful interaction with friends, family members, strangers, and community members (ceeds with others), and plant the principles of civic engagement and servant leadership (ceeds in community). By following these three pathways, adults help children to become leaders. These children might not otherwise have had the courage to speak up or learned how to resolve conflict.

THE 360° APPROACH TO RAISING PEACEBUILDING LEADERS

Implementing sustainable generational and cultural changes is complex work. It takes time and requires patience. CoP therefore takes a 360° approach to raising peacebuilding leaders by providing the "ceeds" (tools) of peacebuilding to a variety of adults who encircle children's lives. Children receive contradictory messages if they are encouraged to develop peacebuilding skills in only one social context. For example, a child who is taught to celebrate diversity at the school, yet hears bigotry at home, may find it difficult to collaborate with and support equality among all community members as an adult. The CoP approach is integrated so that children will receive consistent and mutually supportive messages from adults in all the various spaces (academic, familial, and communal) within which they interact. CoP's main task is to help educators and families think creatively and courageously about their roles and effects on children. It is important to note, however, that CoP does not design curricula for K-12 teachers. Instead, our facilitators share existing methods, programs, and resources with all adults who work with youth. CoP educators build connections between various social worlds so that these caregivers, teachers, and other community members will be able to support one another in raising courageous and kind children.

CoP's flagship program is a three-part workshop series consisting of 24 hours of participation over a six-month period. Teachers receiving professional development credit attend an additional full day workshop each spring. Representative leaders from homes, schools, and the larger community are invited to sit on panels at CoP workshops, where they share their expertise and ideas for change while engaging in dialogue with workshop participants. The 360° workshops thus provide opportunities for greater communication, trust, respect, support, healing, and problem-solving among multiple stakeholders. In addition, CoP offers training on specific topics such as how to have conversations about difficult subjects, level power imbalances, redirect anger toward effective action, work across differences, and practice tools for social change. Since CoP recognizes that modeling peacebuilding skills is even more important than talking about them, the adults who participate in the 360° workshops learn both how to model and teach the "ceeds" of peace to children. By providing such peacebuilding tools to the adults who influence children, these skillsets reach thousands of children.

Examining systemic barriers

While learning to use effective critical thinking skills in their collaborations during the CoP workshops, educators, families, and community leaders are also encouraged to examine the intersections between social, political, and economic structures where peace becomes possible. The 360° approach therefore not only develops peacebuilding skills at the familial and community levels, it encourages people to address problems at the systemic level. All individuals act within ever-changing, socioeconomic systems that benefit or harm people or the planet. Such systems may operate at the small scales of households, places of employment, schools, or communities or they may operate at the large scales of nations, regions, or the planet. CoP asks participants to reflect critically on the systems within which they move and ask themselves whether each of those systems prevent or perpetuate peace. Young and old alike attempt to answer Ricigliano's question, "What factors drive a social system's level of peace?" (Ricigliano, 2012, p. 105).

Many systems have been constructed with the underpinnings of racism, sexism, ageism, elitism, and xenophobia. CoP's peacebuilding leadership skills, coupled with a strong foundation in systems thinking, help young people move away from such underpinnings to become leaders who understand the interdependencies between social, economic, and political systems. To be able to effect change, youth must understand how these systems present economic barriers to many of the members of their communities, how political decisions impact the viability of local businesses and social systems, and how some social systems contribute to crimes against women and girls, for example.

Understanding systems is not enough to change them, however. Professionals in most fields have had the experience of attending conferences, workshops, or camps where they were greatly inspired to make a positive change in the world and themselves, yet they quickly returned to their daily lives without changing anything for very long. In his work around the globe, Ricigliano notes that peace must be seen as an active process if social, economic, and political systems are to be improved: "Defining peacebuilding as an initiative that contributes to building sustainable levels of human development and/or healthy processes of societal change is a key first step toward making peace last" (Ricigliano, 2012, p. 18). CoP is likewise committed to peace as a pragmatic, urgent, and action-oriented process. This means that CoP workshop participants not only learn peacebuilding skills and examine systemic barriers to peace, they also develop action plans that connect these peacebuilding skills to their daily lives and the well-being of their communities.

ACTION PLAN DEVELOPMENT

To put the CoP framework into action, CoP works with communities to create unique plans of action, while taking into account the different resources, priorities, and cultures that exist from place to place. Family members, coaches, teachers, and school staff develop action plans with the help of professional CoP facilitators. The action plans are focused on removing the

Fig 2. Action Plan Process.

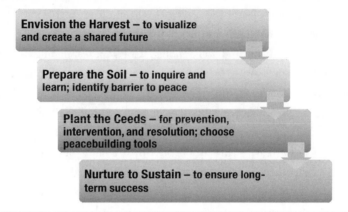

barriers to peace. They are meant to be built from the ground up and tailored to the unique context of each participant.

CoP facilitators work closely with participants to help them develop and implement action plans during and between workshops. Helpful tools are provided for each step of the process outlined in Fig. 2.

Prior to attending CoP workshops, participants are sent reflection exercises to begin the process of developing action plans, starting with visualizing a shared future (envisioning the harvest) and identifying barriers to peace (preparing the soil). During the workshop, they are given action planning templates including guided questions, facilitative support, and examples of action plans to help them begin designing their own action plans. Workshop participants are taught the following basic skill sets: (1) intake and inquiry (gathering facts and histories, identifying interests); (2) barrier identification (identifying barriers to peace such as personal, historical, economic, or systemic issues); (3) creation of shared futures (collaborating to develop a vision of the future in which everyone sees themselves thriving); (4) conflict prevention and resolution (e.g., active listening, using "I" statements, interest identification, mediation, and shuttle diplomacy); and (5) design thinking (collaborating on solutions, rapid innovation, and testing).

Although participants attend the workshop as individuals, they are actively encouraged to create a team of peacebuilders within their communities to help implement their action plans. Following the second day of the workshop, participants begin implementing their plans. They then return the third day some months later for support and to share their successes and challenges with other participants. CoP then offers ongoing, in-depth, technical assistance for participants as they implement the action plans developed in the workshops.

Action plans take many forms and may be implemented at the level of the family, school, sports team, classroom, or community. Some plans involve family—school partnerships, and others involve civic engagement. All plans are expected to have clear outcome goals. A parent might create refrigerator magnets featuring positive parenting strategies or a "Recipes for Peace" booklet or a website that highlights family discussion rituals and tools (such as discussion balls, talking sticks, or a community bowl). Since teachers attending the CoP workshops learn transformative unit planning that is standards-based (Common Core Standards, Hawai'i Content and Performance Standards III, and General Learning Outcomes), interdisciplinary, and multicultural, they might develop integrated curricula or create learning segments that include critical thinking about controversial issues in the community using high standards of peaceful discourse and problem solving. Community members might form a diversified team of men and women, advocacy groups, judges, legislators, and the police department to combat sexual assault in the community.

Each action plan naturally targets one or more of the United Nations' 17 SDGs. Listed below are just a few examples of action plans and organizations that have developed from CoP workshops and programs, along with the specific SDGs each action supports.

- The *Aim to Understand* campaign was created to enable ninth graders to discuss and encounter opposing views and multiple perspectives on such controversial topics as abortion, euthanasia, discrimination, and LGBTQ rights (SDGs 4, 5, 10, 16).

- A *Student Peace Council* (SDG 16) formed at a large K-5 elementary school has led to multiple actions including the *4,000 Acts of Kindness Challenge, Buddy Benches, Peace Gardens, and E Ola Pono (Do Right) Campaign* (SDGs 3, 10, 15).

- Partners in the *West Hawai'i Peace Rally and Ongoing Professional Development* program organize an annual West Hawai'i Peace Rally and

Community Day to strengthen connections and share performances and resources among individuals and organizations in the West Hawai'i community; they also institutionalized ongoing professional development for teachers to target social and emotional developmental skills for all grades (SDGs 3, 4, 17).

- A *Plant and Nurture* program developed by an elementary school counselor on O'ahu brings students together to collaborate on planting and growing their own food in a school garden; the counselor also hosts ohana (family) nights to bring members of the 200 participating families together to learn about the garden and healthy ways for resolving conflict in the home (SDGs 3, 4, 15, 16).

- A *Healthy Relationships Youth Council* (SDG 16) was formed for teenagers and young adults (ages 13–21) to discuss dating violence and healthy versus unhealthy relationships; the council encourages empowerment, setting boundaries, compassion, and personal peace (SDGs 3, 4, 5).

- A *Transition Family Center* was established by school staff primarily to support immigrant families in developing technological, job hunting, and resume writing skills and gain access to social services and housing; since many immigrants are uncomfortable coming onto school campuses, the Center was situated off-campus in a neutral location that facilitated closer relationships to develop among teachers, staff, and families (SDGs 1, 2, 3, 4, 8, 17).

The collective impact of these myriad action plans propels the UN's 2030 Sustainable Development Goals into every school and community.

After implementing these and other action plans, former CoP workshop participants have told us they've seen the following signs of leadership and peacebuilding skills developing among the young people with whom they work:

- Increasing collaboration among students across social groups.

- Decreasing disruptive behaviors.

- Self-directed use of CoP tools by students.

- Reports by children of feeling calmer and more focused.

- Improved emotional regulation by children in the classroom.

- More children standing up for one another and holding each other accountable.

- Routine practice of conflict resolution skills.

Moreover, adults are reporting the multiple and consistent application of CoP concepts and tools in their personal and professional lives. We are proud and hopeful for the future as we see the ripple effects of these action plans spread throughout Hawai'i and beyond.

CONCLUSION: COMMITTING FORWARD

Peace requires more than a willing heart, a bright idea, or a one-time action. Peace requires abundant practice, frequent recommitment, and integration into educational and other systems. In addition, if peace is going to endure, future generations must actively learn the skill sets that sustain and nourish a culture of peace over the long term. Education for sustainability is thus not only a right, but it is also the most critical invest-ment leaders can make toward supporting happy and healthy communi-ties. If children are not prepared to contribute positively and solve problems in their communities, their apathy disempowers them and leads to dangerous behaviors and interactions. CoP is broadly committed to peacebuilding and shifting negative social norms and other barriers to a just and peaceful world through working with school staff, coaches, stu-dents, and families. CoP advocates a global re-allocation of resources away from the military-industrial complex toward education to support such peacebuilding efforts. Learning peacebuilding skills is just as impor-tant as learning to read and write, studying mathematics and the natural and social sciences. Peacebuilding skills are a critical part of what makes a human being successful in their homes, schools, workplaces, and communities.

The CoP were born from the knowledge that every interaction, every decision, every lesson, and every day matter. All the activities, tools, and attitudes promoted by CoP are expected to prevent intellectual rigidity, encourage open-mindedness, and instigate action among the children who will become tomorrow's leaders. We at CoP like to imagine that we are planting the "ceeds" of the future's harvest, and we are utilizing tools like the United Nation's 2030 Sustainable Development Goals and the 360° approach to help nurture the crops. The 360° approach is also essential for ensuring that children will grow into peacebuilders prepared to take care of everybody and build a stronger, safer world for the future. In the meantime, we adults can build canopies to shelter them, taste the fruits of progress, and experience people are working together to meet the needs of our communities.

REFERENCES

Avolio, B. J., Waldman, D. A., & Yammarino, F. J. (1991). Leading in the 1990s: The four I's of transformational leadership. *Journal of European Industrial Training*, *15*(4), 9–16. doi:10.1108/03090599110143366

Bass, B. M., & Avolio, B. J. (1993). Transformational leadership and organizational culture. *Public Administration Quarterly*. Retrieved from http://www.communicationcache.com/uploads/1/0/8/8/10887248/transformational_leadership_and_organizational_culture.pdf. Accessed on June 01, 2018.

Davis, R. A. (2011). The value of prevention. *Social and Economic Costs of Violence: Workshop Summary*. (2011) Forum on Global Violence Prevention; Board on Global Health; Institute of Medicine; National Research Council. Washington, DC: National Academies Press (US); (Oct 25 2011).

Epstein, R. (2010, November). What makes a good parent. *The Scientific American*. Retrieved from www.researchgate.net/publications/47562289. Accessed on June 01, 2018.

Galtung, J. (1975). *A mini theory of peace*. Retrieved from https://www.galtung-institut.de/wp-content/uploads/2014/11/Mini-Theory-of-Peace.pdf

Greenleaf, R. K. (1977). *Servant leadership: "A journey into the nature of legitimate power and greatness"*. New York, NY: Paulist Press.

House, R., Javidan, M., & Dorfman, P. (2001). ProjectGLOBE. *Applied Psychology: An International Review*, *50*(4), 489–505. doi:10.1111/1464-0597.00070

IOM. (2000). Institute of Medicine Committee on capitalizing on social science and behavioral research to improve the public's health. In B. D. Smedley & S. L. Syme (Eds.), *Promoting health: Intervention strategies from social and behavioral research* (p. 2). Washington, DC: National Academy Press.

Johnson, T. D. (2012). Prevention and public health fund paying off in communities: Success threatened by cuts to fund. *The Nation's Health*, *42*(6), 1–31.

Karakas, F., & Sarigollu, E. (2012). Benevolent leadership: Conceptualization and con-struct development. *Journal of Business Ethics*, *108*(4), 537–553. Retrieved from https://link.springer.com/article/10.1007/s10551-011-1109-1. Accessed on June 01, 2018.

Kouzes, J. M., & Posner, B. Z. (2012). *The leadership challenge: How to make extraordinary things happen in organizations*. San Francisco, CA: Jossey-Bass.

Our Common Future: Report of the World Commission on Environment and Development. (Rep.). (1987). Retrieved from http://www.un-documents.net/our-common-future.pdf

Ricigliano, R. (2012). *Making peace last: A toolbox for sustainable peacebuilding*. Boulder, CO: Paradigm.

Center for Public Health Policy (2012).*The Prevention and Public Health Fund: A Critical Investment in Our Nation's Physical and Fiscal Health"*. The American Public Health Association. Retrieved from http://www.apha.org/NR/rdonlyres/8FA13774-AA47-43F2-838B-1B0757D111C6/0/APHA_Prev-FundBrief_June2012.pdf

United Nations. (n.d.). Sustainable Development Goals. Retrieved from https://www.un.org/sustainabledevelopment/sustainable-development-goals/. Accessed on October 9, 2018.

UNSCR 2250 Introduction. (n.d.). Retrieved from https://www.youth4peace.info/UNSCR2250/Introduction. Accessed on June 01, 2018.

Violence Prevention Alliance. (2010). *Violence Prevention Alliance: Conceptual framework* (p. 1). Geneva: World Health Organization. Retrieved from http://www.who.int/violenceprevention/en/index.html

World Health Organization. (2010). *Violence prevention. The evidence. Overview*. Series of briefings on violence prevention: the evidence. Geneva: Author. Retrieved from http://whqlibdoc.who.int/publications/2009/ 9789241598507_eng.pdf)

17

LET'S GET SUSTAINABLE: A FIVE-DAY MBA RESIDENCY ADVENTURE

Grace Hurford and Philippa Chapman

PURPOSE

This chapter addresses the growing need to focus on how teaching and learning at MBA level can be reoriented toward leading for sustainability and how such interventions can be measured. We share the design and delivery that we have found to be useful in challenging attitudes and developing skills. We also outline the impact of a five day rural experiential learning residency on mainstreaming sustainability into working and personal lives. The international online MBA program under discussion was developed as a means to meet Millennium Development Goal 8: *To develop a Global Partnership for Development.* Since the advent of the Sustainable Development Goals (SDGs) in 2015, the goals we now seek to deliver on are SDG 4: *Ensure inclusive and equitable quality education and promote lifelong learning opportunities for all* and SDG 17: *Strengthen the means of implementation and revitalize the global partnership for sustainable development.* But what has surprised and delighted us over the years is how many other SDGs have been met as a result of this innovative residency program. Perhaps most importantly, this chapter seeks to capture some of the joy and fulfillment that arises from nurturing and supporting students to lead for sustainability. We see our students beginning to realize what is possible in, and for, our world – bridging the divide between urgency and agency in their own communities with enthusiasm and skill. Through their quotes and case studies we gain an understanding of how, as a result of the program, they are bringing their humanity into play in the pursuit of a sustainable future. Therefore, this chapter is their story as well as ours, and we hope as you read this account that their voices come through in their diverse and authentic community settings.

THE GROWING NEED FOR CHANGE

There is a growing body of evidence that business is attempting to move away from a sole profit orientation toward a more socially responsible model, to respond to the threat of global warming (Benn, Dunphy, & Griffiths, 2006). As many academic, public service/NGO, and business people alike recognize that our generation is the first, and possibly last, with the ability to meaningfully address such pressing global challenges, there is now a sense of urgency in many communities to take the lead in meaningful action. Despite this awareness of the need for change, there are limited data on the corporate action (Deitche, 2010; Kiron, Kruschwitz, Haanaes, & von StrengVelken, 2012). Business leaders need to be educated to understand the possibility of operating more sustainably (Benn, Dunphy, & Griffiths, 2014; Elkington & Zeitz, 2014; Schein, 2015) and the development of specialist MBAs is part of this policy response. There are sparse empirical findings for effective pedagogic methods (Hesselbarth & Schaltegger, 2014), which create real challenges for designers of these courses. Overall, there seems to be a lack of evaluation that goes beyond the anecdotal (Shriberg & MacDonald, 2013). Therefore, when we discuss how leadership for sustainability should be taught, our evidence is drawn from immediate post-residential data collected from over 300 international MBA students, (2014 to 2017: summary in Fig. 1), and a subset of 100 students after graduation (between 2011 and 2016), to systematically evaluate where and how students have been able to put theory into practice.

BACKGROUND TO THE PROGRAM

The University of Cumbria, UK, developed its (predominantly online) MBA in Leadership and Sustainability in 2011−12, in collaboration with the

Fig. 1. Module Evaluation Feedback 2014–17; WordCloud Summary.

Robert Kennedy College which is based in Zurich. It was intended to be flexible and accessible, yet challenging. It was designed for students who would not otherwise be able to study, either because of their location, the pattern of working life, and/or seniority within their organization, thereby delivering on SDG4 (although the advent of the program pre-dated the SDGs). Students themselves are not drawn from one particular sector: they represent global companies, third-sector aid agencies, armed forces, and family businesses, and they work in/on deserts, glaciers, submarines, refugee camps, battlefields, and oil rigs, as well as in cities and towns worldwide (examples of country of origin are given in Table 1).

There is a five-day residency, which is the only face-to-face contact within the program. Groups of around 36 students at a time, from approximately 20–30 countries worldwide, come to Ambleside in the heart of the Lake District National Park, UK (a World Heritage Site) to participate in a week-long program of experiential activities including seminars, outdoor work, and group-work. Delivery is applied, participative, interactive, involves the whole person, and makes use of the natural environment linking to nature and helping learners to understand their connections with life around them (Nolet, 2009). A close parallel pedagogically would be the Burns Model of Sustainability Pedagogy, which "integrates ecological design, systemic and interdisciplinary learning, multiple perspectives, an active and engaged learning process, and attention to place-based learning" (Burns, 2013, p. 166).

Table 1. Examples of Country of Origin of Post-graduation Survey Respondents.

Canada	Cambodia	Singapore	France
Switzerland	Russia	Kenya	Turkey
USA	UAE	Japan	Cameroon
Zimbabwe	Afghanistan	Malaysia	Nigeria
South Africa	Belgium	Haiti	Ivory Coast
UK	Libya	South Sudan	New Zealand
Sweden	Australia	Qatar	Jamaica
DRC	Kuwait	Finland	China
Italy	Angola	Pakistan	Tanzania
Niger	Ethiopia	Greece	Saudi Arabia
Mali	Serbia	Lebanon	India
Mauritius	Germany	Zambia	Egypt
Mozambique	Ghana	Malawi	France

The team comprises teachers, researchers, and activists, united in their determination to put these values into practice, while the location enables students to employ experiential learning and use critical thinking, indoors and outside, with the Lake District as a forum for sustainable business inquiry (SDG 17). From small beginnings, the program has now grown into 11 specialist MBAs with just over 2000 students in total in 2018.

THE DELIVERY TEAM

The residencies are very much a team effort, delivered by a committed and diverse teaching, facilitation, and administration team of people who work closely together. The importance of involving individuals who are passionate, caring, and empathetic of students' needs cannot be over-stated. Effective team planning and collaboration are critically important and students' thoughts from module evaluations bear out a sense of group progress as well as strong team work: "Residency felt like a story/flow (almost like a journey)" and "Expertise, professionalism and enthusiasm of staff were contagious." The module is judged to be "delivered patiently and concisely" with "thorough research and preparation," while the pastoral care and collaborative approach are highlighted as well: "excellent team work of staff" and "high care and attention" (to students).

SEMINARS VERSUS LECTURES

The emphasis is on seminars rather than lectures. Tutors commence a session by sharing some data and asking a series of questions. They often then move to the back of the classroom and subgroups of students come to the front to present their thoughts and reflections. In this way, tutors' roles evolve very quickly from information disseminators into facilitators of knowledge and discussion. By the end of each week, students take over the whole of the last morning, presenting group project work on leading for sustainability within Cumbria and beyond. Role blurring is positively received but more importantly demonstrates a participative culture. The core culture of the residency is, therefore, to empower individuals, organizations, and communities with practical tools and actionable insights to manifest the vision of a future where all life can thrive. As student module feedback demonstrates, students feel "empowered" *in* "a participative environment" and encouraged "to voice [...] different perspectives" and "hear other people's stories." They note that "everyone had equal opportunities to make their contributions" and the "interactive nature" as well as "continuous involvement of the students" leads to "a very impressive feel of inclusiveness."

EXPERIENTIAL LEARNING ACTIVITIES

Using material from iconic local philosophers and writers and linking practical activities/games with business, students are able to probe deeper questions of ethics and social responsibility and challenge management orthodoxies. Student module feedback underlines the strengths of this approach: "the experiential learning approach enhances thoughtfulness and participation..." "Experiential learning is new to me and very intuitive [...] the experiential exercises set the stage."

The significant emphasis on experiential learning is worth closer study, and five examples of experiential learning activities and their impacts from the residency are summarized below:

Playing the Trading Game (Enhanced Prisoner's Dilemma)

This game, which demonstrates in a fun and interactive way why "rational" individuals might not cooperate even if it appears that it is in their best interests to do so, was originally framed by Merrill Flood and Melvin Dresher in 1950 (Felkins, 1995). It is designed to create a disorienting dilemma, (Mezirow, 2000) with company stakeholder groups asked to make decisions about whether to play a "W" card or an "S" card against each other, having been furnished with minimal details save for starting "credits" and credits to be won or lost dependent on the various combinations of the two. The post-mortem in small groups enables students to explore notions of self versus whole, leading to a "self-examination of feelings of guilt or shame," (Mezirow, 2000, p. 22). The wider discussion in the room then moves us to a "recognition that one's discontent and the process of transformation are shared and that others have negotiated a similar change" (Mezirow, 2000, p. 22). Finally, as we move away from the scores and content of the game, toward the parallels with caring for our planet, we are all able to "explore options for new roles, relationships and actions" (Mezirow, 2000, p. 22). Powerful and typical student comments encapsulate the experience of competition, followed by shame and then resolution:

> *It was really a feeling of shame for me, the momentary joy of winning disappeared seeing that some players along the value chain were already thrown off balance because we refused to consider their interest and collaborate with them.*

Students consider this "an eye-opening moment" which makes them "more self-aware." Critically, students state that these activities "cemented the learning" giving them "new perspectives" and "provided holistic understanding." This level of insight resonates with a key goal: to inspire belief in what's possible in evolving our collective leadership to ensure a sustainable future for all.

Taking Part in an Ethical Role Play

An initial group of five or six students is presented with an ethical challenge: whether they, as an NGO, should bribe an official or not in order to get planning permission for a children's health center (disorienting dilemma,

Mezirow, 2000). The range of responses, as well as the role play from the corrupt official, always produces much laughter and some discomfort. While this scenario had been acted out on a stage by a few students in previous courses, the dilemma is now played out through a series of meetings, so each student is at some point engaged in a developing role play. Again the response and aftermath creates a self-examination of feelings of guilt or shame? (Mezirow, 2000, p. 22) followed by a discussion on consequentialist versus deontological approaches to ethics which lead us to "acquisition of knowledge and skills – provisional trying of new roles" (Mezirow, 2000, p. 22) and finally, through subgroups spotting and building on strategies for combating corruption (such as use of the media, reorganizing the flow of resources to a more grass roots project led by trusted local people), "a building of competence and self-confidence in new roles and relationships" (Mezirow, 2000, p. 22). Students commented that this enabled them to: "learn more about myself," that it was a "great revelation," and that it "opened my eyes" to the endemic nature of corruption and the need to address this at all levels of society. This sense of "revelation" speaks to our intentions within the module: to awaken the world to the potential of this pregnant moment in global history – as well as providing the tools to act.

Balancing a Bamboo Pole and Climbing Through a Loop

Morning exercises such as these are used to foster teamwork and to encourage students to think about new ways of achieving success when there are time constraints. Balancing a bamboo pole as a group is much harder than doing it alone, and getting a group of people through a two-meter climbing loop encourages people to think laterally, to question assumptions about rules, and also to listen. Students comment that these are "practical exercises that sometimes appeared unconventional but were highly effective" and that both games stimulate reflections on "trust, working together, shared goals and responsibility." There is also a significant effect on "group dynamics, problem solving, mutual respect and harnessing diversity." The emphasis on diversity, trust, and collaboration that emerges from these activities meets a key module aim: to be comprehensive and inclusive in gathering best practices and solutions.

The Coffee Exercise

Students are somewhat surprised to be issued with a selection of ground coffee bags on their first afternoon and asked to analyze how sustainable these are, across a range of criteria. The analysis enables us to reveal important findings of labeling, packaging, carbon footprints, as well as health, social, and cultural issues. But the most enduring memory for the students is sensory, as they handle and smell the product, whilst the product explaining to their peers the rationale behind their rankings.

The Lakeland Walk

This is an important part of the Ambleside residency — it gives us all an opportunity to reconnect with nature but also to reflect on our practice through the lens of local poet and philosopher William Wordsworth (1850). Thinking about key moments and critical times, identifying and valuing other peoples' input in our lives, and generating our own visions for the future all occur while walking in Wordsworth's footsteps. Thus, walking over the brow of a hill, seeing the darkness of a cave, or feeling the texture of a tree all become part of this transformative process. The power of place and landscape sometimes stir difficult memories. Students from war-torn and famine areas often tell us that this is the first time they have been able to deal with these difficult memories, in a safe, beautiful and supportive setting. A quote that sums up this experience was emailed by a student in the autumn of 2017, and is reproduced in full because of its power as well as agency:

> [...] As I was able to travel down memory lane and reconnected
> with my spots of time, it was a healing experience with tears as
> I closed my eyes to reflect on those incredible moments that infuse
> strength in me. Vision and focus were re-energized and it was as
> though I came alive again as to what I should be doing. Finally,
> I saw how others could be dream helpers for me and how I could
> contribute to help others sustain and achieve their visions also.

This response demonstrates the way in which students are re-grouping through this module and beginning to use partnerships to help leverage sustainable change in their own communities.

Tutors who join these walks find renewal in these reflections as well as students. As we shape our thoughts about leading for sustainability and how this common purpose links the residency together, we note that reflection on practice is critical to developing and nurturing this sense of purpose (Craig & Snook, 2014). Students generally report the importance of the rural location and being "in a natural environment (which) cemented the learning" as well as the impact of being "in beautiful surrounding nature (which) helped in concentrating and reflecting." There is a strong sense of synthesis as well as refreshment: "Digging deeper in nature […] invigorated by the nature." All the experiential learning is consolidated by embedding a reflection into the post-residency assignment, enabling students to connect theory and practice very powerfully on their return home.

ASSESSMENT

As tutors, we are particularly keen to provide a residency that works for each student, and learning that is helpful for students when they return home. Therefore, all students tailor their own success criteria on the first day of each residency, and a summary of these indicates their priorities – broadly a hunger for knowledge and agency in the field of leading for sustainability (see Fig. 2). The success criteria are re-visited throughout the

Fig. 2. A Summary of 70 Students' Own Success Criteria (2015–16).

week and integrated into a post-residency module evaluation questionnaire (MEQ) at the end of the fifth and last day. Students score themselves out of ten on how they have met their own success criteria. The scores are highly variable, but this process enables students to develop skills of self-evaluation and priority setting as well as a chance to measure progress throughout the week. It is also an opportunity for staff to understand what motivates students beyond achieving their MBA.

Within the module there are three assignments. The pre-module assessment is about the student's own leadership or ethical experiences and sets the tone for the whole residency. Students formatively assess each other's work on the first evening and give feedback to each other in small groups the next day. This enables them to engage quickly with the assessment criteria but also to learn from each other. The richness of their stories and this feedback process is often reported to be one of the most valuable aspects of the week – they feel "confident [...] enlightened [...] satisfied." The use of live and local business case studies during the week culminates in assessed group project presentations, and the emphasis on translating models and ideas into real-world practice continues in a post-residency assignment. An example of a real-world post-residency assignment that is also designed to avoid plagiarism is shown below in **Table 2**.

Students are encouraged to keep a reflective learning journal of the week which informs the post-residency assignment. All of this contributes toward a very practical and applied approach, as evidenced again from student feedback: "theory and practice got connected" and "I'm full of ideas to implement within our organization," and we see real enthusiasm to start the task: "I can't wait to implement!" – again demonstrating how this residency module has inspired belief in the possibility of healing and securing our planet.

Table 2. Example of Post-residency Assignment.

Following on from your pre course-work consider:

"How should I lead for sustainability and what key objectives should I aim to meet in my own organization or community when I return from this module? What approaches to leadership will enable me to address issues of purpose and sustainability?"

Draw from theory and your personal experience to develop your argument. Ensure that you critically reflect on *experiential learning* gained within the Residency.

MEDIUM TO LONG-TERM IMPACT

Design and delivery are all very well, but we also need to consider what happens after students go home. In this section we have gathered together some important data demonstrating that students have become energized about a future they now know is possible and that they can help to create, often from positions of influence in business and governments, enabling meaningful engagement as a global force. These data provide consistent and compelling evidence that the residency fulfills an important goal in that it provides a launch pad for the mobilization of diverse networks, around a shared vision for a sustainable future.

We asked a sample of 100 students to describe their sustainability engagement before and after the residency, and to classify this under two headings – personal and workplace/beyond. Responses indicate that the number of people reporting sustainability activity in personal life as "change agent" more than doubled from 38 before the residential module to 78 after. Three examples of specific personal life initiatives are cited are in Table 3.

Table 3. Personal.

Quote 1:

Before: "Not consciously"

After: "Deliberate reduction of carbon numbers, low consumption car use, reduced mileage, lower home energy consumption, recycling plastics, informed shopping with eye on green products, etc."

Quote 2:

Before: "No"

After: "Yes, about to launch a blog on sustainability issues sensitization. About to switch career to sustainability and CSR advisor and trainer."

Quote 3:

Before: "No"

After: "(1) Now senior fellow for Sustainable Communities at the Ark Earth Foundation (affiliated with the World Bank, UN, and OGP) (2) Expert adviser at Green Development Initiative."

The number of people reporting sustainability activity in their workplace and beyond, also more than doubled after the module, from 35 to 75. Four quotes are shown in Table 4.

Table 4. Workplace and Beyond.

Quote 1

Before: "Hadn't worked in the sector before (health)."

After: "Very important, my views got me my job."

Quote 2

Before: "No because I believed that would be overreaching."

After: "Now I believe that nothing is overreaching. Now I try to share my experience with my peers in other missions (locations.)"

Quote 3

Before: "Just limited on understanding what my country is implementing as sustainability policies."

After: "Now could positively contribute in writing guidance and be a policies maker in seeing my Nation affecting sustainability as a unique way to transform people and the way they behave."

Quote 4

Before: "Was an activist leaving others to lead."

After: "More 'leader' active in social and political issues and giving social/political leadership."

The findings in this chapter provide empirical data suggesting that a five-day residential program can mainstream sustainability activity into working and personal lives (and beyond). Perhaps the most compelling evidence, however, comes from students' own stories. This is where the data begin to suggest the true power of the residency module in tackling a much wider range of SDGs than we had ever dreamed of. There are numerous examples of initiatives that our students are now leading, and a small selection of five (together with the relevant SDGs) is summarized:

Cape Town, South Africa: Set Up My Own Energy Efficient Business -Example of SDG 6 (Clean Water and Sanitation) and SDG 12 (Responsible Consumption and Production).

"Since completing my MBA, I have left the Pharmaceutical Industry as CEO and have now started an Energy Efficiency Business [...] to provide the service of converting businesses/buildings into "Green" organizations. This course changed my life and fulfilled my passion for the environment. Today we are reducing energy consumption of businesses by up to 65%, converting hazardous cleaning chemicals to more environmentally friendly compounds, reuse and capture of rainwater, reduction of water consumption through various devices, ensure the company reduces waste and help with responsible disposal thereof and we create significant awareness programs for staff members and especially with senior management. We are now in the process of putting together a sales and technical team to focus on households."

Nairobi, Kenya: Franchise Director Coca Cola: Leading in Eco-Friendly Housing - Example of SDG 6 (Clean Water and Sanitation) and SDG 7 (Affordable and Clean Energy).

"Since completing my MBA I have a strong emphasis on water and energy usage, minimization of carbon footprint through fleet and cold drinks equipment, and sustainable community initiatives to empower the communities in which we operate. My personal hobby is residential development. I design my houses to use solar energy for water heating and capturing of rain water. My most interesting insight and take-out was the concept of leadership of place. As a result, many of my fellow developers are following my lead to design and build eco-friendly housing developments."

Zimbabwe, Food/ Agriculture Sector: Combating Soil Degradation – Example of SDG 9 (Industry, Innovation & Infrastructure), SDG 12 (Responsible Consumption and Production) and SDG 13 (Climate Action).

"Personally, I am now conscious of sustainability and at my village I hold awareness programs to my folk. I have also started a conservation program to prevent soil degradation. I now make sure that we are not only compliant with the Environmental Management Agency regulations but that we improve further in how we manage our waste. As Chairman of the Stockfeed Manufacturers Association I make sure we discuss sustainability issues at all our meetings. These have a direct bearing to droughts, pollution etc. The discussions we have at the above meetings are passed up to national level."

Johannesburg, S Africa: Asset Management: Set Group Target for Carbon Reductions and Create Initiatives to Engage All Our Stakeholders – Example of SDG 9 (Industry, Innovation & Infrastructure), SDG 12 (Responsible Consumption and Production) and SDG 13 (Climate Action).

"Helping to monitor, manage and reduce our direct and indirect environmental impacts [...] As part of improving the way we manage our direct environmental impacts we have developed a Group Climate Change Strategy. This aims to improve the completeness and accuracy of our emissions data, set a Group target for carbon reductions and create initiatives to engage all our stakeholders. Our biggest direct environmental impact is through the buildings we own or lease. We work hard to improve their environmental performance by refitting existing units/building or leasing more environmentally friendly new ones. At Group level we have policies that encourage engagement with our communities and employee volunteering. We support and invest in a range of areas, but the three focus areas that are common across the Group are financial education, enterprise and skills development, and community development. This means using our approach to responsible business when pricing ESG risk and opportunity in our investment decisions, and then using this information to ensure we act as a responsible steward of our customers' assets."

Belgrade, Serbia: UNAMID United Nations: Engineer Lowering Carbon Footprint on Construction Machinery – Example of SDG 9 (Industry, Innovation & Infrastructure), SDG 12 (Responsible Consumption and Production) and SDG 13 (Climate Action).

"We are building and running living and working accommodations for civilian and military personnel in the areas with poor or no infrastructure. Everything we do has an impact on environment, hence, it's important to understand the environment we are operating in and minimize our footprint and, actually, help improve the environment. I plan better to minimize carbon footprint, i.e. insist of reducing idling of construction machines. I insist on lowering carbon footprint in or operation, i.e. insist in keeping construction machines at work site overnight, instead of driving them back and forth. (At national level I did not get involve before- because I believed that would be overreaching.) *Now I believe that nothing is overreaching.* Now I try to share my experience with my peers in other missions (locations.) When I came back I insisted on educating people in my environment by sharing my experience and understanding of how we interconnect with our surroundings."

DISCUSSION, IMPLICATIONS, AND APPLICATIONS

The above responses indicate the potential power of a five-day residential module to create changed behavior among alumni. This can be done through dissemination of new research findings (*leadership of place*), by empowering people (*now nothing is overreaching*), through self-reflection and career changes, (*my views got me my job*) by considering the business benefits as well as the social justice case (*sustainability policy as a viable differentiator*), and by taking the widest view of sustainability (focus on helping the *nation's productivity, alleviating poverty and national growth*). The residency has enabled activists to become more effective in leading change, (*giving social/political leadership*) and managers to aspire to a policy-making role at sectoral and nation-state levels (*positively contributing in writing guidance and being a policy maker*).

The implications of the research are that even short (five days) MBA residencies in rural settings, facilitating a re-connection with nature, and using a range of experiential learning methods, can contribute to bringing out the best of our diverse humanity to achieve sustainable development at an international level in short as well as longer term. Within this chapter, we have provided evidence of positive action on 7 of the 17 SDGs (4, 6, 7, 9, 12, 13, and 17). Our research has shown a doubling of sustainability activity in both personal and work environments amongst our alumni sample. Therefore, with over 2000 students worldwide currently, and over 60% of these in senior, decision-making roles, it is not difficult to imagine the ripple effect of this kind of geographical reach and scale.

The change is made possible when teams work collaboratively, with adequate facilitation and administrative support, and make time to regularly review pedagogy as well as practice. We hope our findings will be useful to people involved in planning and delivering educational leadership and sustainability programs as well as practicing managers who want to train and support their staff to change attitudes and behaviors in their own communities and workplaces. We also hope our story will inspire others to take risks and to try new pedagogic approaches in experiential learning: not just empowering and enthusing students to lead for sustainable change but to enhance meaning, fulfillment, and joy for staff in their working lives as well.

REFERENCES

Benn, S., Dunphy, D., & Griffiths, A. (2006). Enabling change for corporate sustainability: An integrated perspective. *Australasian Journal of Environmental Management, 13*(3), 156–166.

Benn, S., Dunphy, D., & Griffiths, A. (2014). *Organizational change for corporate sustainability*. (3rd Ed.). Abingdon: Routledge.

Burns, H. (2013). Meaningful sustainability learning: A study of sustainability pedagogy in two university courses. *International Journal of Teaching and Learning in Higher Education, 25*(2), 166–175.

Craig, N., & Snook, S. A. (2014). From purpose to impact: Figure out your passion and put it to work. *Harvard Business Review, 92*(5), 105–111.

Deitche, S. M. (2010). *Green collar jobs: Environmental careers for the 21st century*. Santa Barbara, CA: Praeger.

Elkington, J., & Zeitz, J. (2014). *The break-through challenge: 10 ways to connect today's profits with tomorrow's bottom line*. San Francisco, CA: Jossey-Bass.

Felkins, L. (1995). The Voter's Paradox. An introduction to the theory of social dilemmas. *The Ethical Spectacle, I*(9), 2–3.

Hesselbarth, C., & Schaltegger, S. (2014). Educating change agents for sustainability – learnings from the first sustainability management master of business administration. *Journal of Cleaner Production, 62*, 24–36.

Kiron, D., Kruschwitz, N., Haanaes, K., & von StrengVelken, I. (2012). Sustainability nears a tipping point. *MIT Sloan Management Review, 53*(2), 69–74.

Mezirow, J. Ed. (2000). *Learning as transformation: Critical perspectives on a theory in progress*. San Francisco, CA: Jossey-Bass.

Nolet, V. (2009). Preparing sustainability-literate teachers. *Teachers College Record, 111*(2), 409–442.

Schein, S. (2015). *A new psychology for sustainability leadership: The hidden power of ecological worldviews*. Sheffield: Greenleaf Publishing Limited.

Shriberg, M., & MacDonald, L. (2013). Sustainability leadership programs: Emerging goals, methods & best practices. *Journal of Sustainability Education*, 5.

Wordsworth, W. (1850). The prelude or, growth of a 'Poet's Mind'; an autobiographical poem. *Internet Archive* (1 ed.), London: Edward Moxon, Dover Street. Retrieved from https://archive.org/stream/prelude00unkngoog#page/n9/mode/2up

ABOUT THE AUTHORS

Abigail Abrash Walton serves as Faculty in Antioch University New England's Department of Environmental Studies. Previously, she served as Program Director for the Robert F. Kennedy Memorial Center for Human Rights, and as Visiting Fellow at Harvard Law School's Human Rights Program.

Ejaj Ahmad is the Founder and President of Bangladesh Youth Leadership Center (BYLC). The recipient of an Ashoka Fellowship and an Eisenhower Fellowship, he holds a Master's in Public Policy from Harvard University and a Master of Arts with honors in Economics from St. Andrews University.

Lance C. Boyd is a Senior Experiential Leadership Education Specialist training leaders from across the Indo-Asia Pacific region. Lance co-founded the East-West Center's first Environmental Leadership Institute and Online Impact Incubator. Notable initiatives developed in his classes include the ASEAN Peace Accelerator, Middle East Environment Leadership Program, and ASEAN Food Rescue.

Michael R. Carey is an Associate Professor of Organizational Leadership in the School of Leadership Studies at Gonzaga University in Spokane, Washington. He has taught leadership studies at the graduate level for 30 years. Carey earned his BA from Loyola Marymount University and both his MA and PhD from Gonzaga University.

Philippa Chapman is Innovation Advisor and previously Manager of Institute for Leadership and Sustainability (IFLAS) at University of Cumbria. Work has included business support, training, mentoring, project consultancy, and international development across private, public and voluntary sectors. She has assisted hundreds of businesses to grow and embrace sustainability.

Jennifer M. Chirico, PhD, is the Founder and CEO of Sustainable Pacific Consulting, a Certified B Corp that specializes in sustainability and responsible business. She is an Adjunct Professor at Hawaii Pacific University in the Global Leadership and Sustainable Development master's program. She holds a PhD in Environmental Policy.

Barry A. Colbert, PhD, is Associate Professor at the Lazaridis School of Business & Economics at Wilfrid Laurier University, and Director of The Cooperators Centre for Business & Sustainability. His work has appeared in the *Academy of Management Review, Business and Society* and the *Sage Handbook of Complexity and Management*.

Karen Cvitkovich is passionate about diversity of perspective being one of the greatest assets to social change. With over 20 years of global experience, she assists organizations in the areas of global leadership and teams. The co-author of two books and certified coach, Karen holds a MS in Organizational Development.

David H. García has focused his career on increasing transformative educational opportunities in Latin America. With a BA in Government from Harvard and a master's in Education from the University of Notre Dame, he currently leads educational initiatives at Cirklo in Mexico City, where he resides with his partner and many plants.

Grace Hurford, Senior Lecturer, leads the MBA residential modules based in Ambleside, UK and has also contributed to a number of postgraduate health programs locally and nationally. Her doctoral research was in mental health policy and planning and she is a Senior Fellow of the Higher Education Academy.

Elżbieta Jabłońska, a passionate educator and speaker, is also a successful entrepreneur, executive coach, and consultant with two decades of experience across diverse cultures. Her doctoral dissertation focuses on Leadership based on Gross National Happiness.

Wanda Krause is Acting Head of the MA in Global Leadership and Assistant Professor of Leadership Studies at Royal Roads University, Canada. She runs a coaching business at wandakrause.com, and her passion is global leadership in building civil society.

Elizabeth C. Kurucz, PhD, is Associate Professor of Organizational Behaviour at the University of Guelph. Her research has appeared in the *Journal of Business Ethics*, the *Journal of Cleaner Production*, the *Oxford*

Handbook of Corporate Social Responsibility, and she is lead author of *Reconstructing Value: Leadership Skills for a Sustainable World*.

Christina Monroe is Senior Manager of the Leadership Program at East-West Center. She designs, delivers, and manages a suite of international leadership programs for university students to mid-career professionals from over 50 countries. Recent programs include an accelerator workshop in Myanmar for young ASEAN impact entrepreneurs and U.S. State Department-funded institute for natural resource managers.

Ebere Morgan, PhD, is a Leadership Consultant, communicator, scholar, and educator. He advances thought leadership in multiple professional disciplines. He holds a doctorate in Leadership and Strategic Change and serves as Professor at Seneca College, Canada. He is President at Deztiny Strategics Inc and is passionate about all things Leadership.

Jessica Nicholson, PhD candidate in Management/Organizational Leadership at the University of Guelph, researches and writes on the contributions of care ethics and relational leadership to well-being, caring organizations, positive psychology and sustainability. Her work has been published in the *Journal of Business Ethics* and presented at several international conferences.

Mehrad Nazari, PhD, MBA, is a speaker on workplace transformation and author of the multi-award-winning book *Enlightened Negotiation: 8 Universal Laws to Connect, Create, and Prosper*. In addition to having served as a Professor of Business Negotiation, he is a recognized luminary in the field of human potential through mindfulness, yoga, and meditation.

Anette M. Nystrøm works for Sustainable Pacific Consulting where she helps businesses move toward greater resiliency. She is a Norwegian graduate student in the MA Global Leadership and Sustainable Development program at Hawaii Pacific University.

Mariana Quiroga is a Cross-Disciplinary Strategist, experienced Designer, and an Embodied Movement Facilitator. With a communication background, government experience, and an MBA in Design Strategy, she leads the experience strategy department at Cirklo. Mariana is passionate about working with entrepreneurs and creatives helping them embody their purpose and design the future they dream of.

Hugh O'Doherty teaches Leadership at Harvard's John F. Kennedy School of Government. In Ireland, he was Program Director in the Glencree Center for Peace and Reconciliation. He has an EdD from the Harvard Graduate School of Education and has consulted in Bosnia, Croatia, Cyprus, Nepal, and Bahrain, among other locales.

Adriana Salazar leads Cirklo's Culture and Intelligence initiatives. With experience in psychology and visual arts, Adriana identifies and connects with the team's needs to design and facilitate a more purposeful and transparent work environment, and develop co-creation tools toward the alignment of values and strategy for business growth and organizational health.

Maya Soetoro-Ng serves as an Adviser to the Obama Foundation, working closely with their international team to develop programming in the Asia Pacific region. Prior to her work with the Obama Foundation, she was the Director of the Matsunaga Institute for Peace and Conflict Resolution at the University of Hawaii at Mānoa.

Dung Q. Tran is an Assistant Professor of Leadership and Organizational Development in the School of Business, Arts, and Media at Cabrini University. Prior to relocating to Philadelphia, Pennsylvania, Tran taught courses in Organizational Leadership, Communication, and Theology at multiple Catholic universities in Seattle, Washington, and Los Angeles, California.

Kerrie Urosevich, PhD, has spent 25 years rooted in local and international peacebuilding, public policy, and violence prevention efforts. She is co-founder of Ceeds of Peace, the Lead Network Designer for Collaborative Leaders Network, and Affiliate Faculty at the Matsunaga Institute for Peace at the University of Hawaii.

Elizabeth A. Walsh, PhD, is a Visiting Assistant Professor in Urban and Regional Planning at the University of Colorado at Denver. Through action-oriented, place-based, transdisciplinary, and community-engaged research, she has collaborated with diverse partners (primarily in Boston, Austin, and Buffalo) to advance ecologically sustainable and socially just communities through regenerative development.

INDEX